MODERN PIONEERING

care to insure the longest possible life. The sprayer that lasts five years is twice as expensive as the machine giving ten years of efficient service if the original cost is the same.

After being used in an orchard the outfit must be thoroly flushed to clean out all of the chemicals. The solutions used in spraying are very injurious to the sprayer and the hose, and the life of an outfit is reduced by carelessly allowing it to become gummed up with dirt. The hose used with a power sprayer is an important factor and the best is none too good. A broken or leaky hose is a great nuisance on a good day for spraying when time means money. Have the hose long enough to enable the man on the ground to stay far enough behind to avoid being drenched with the misty spray thrown out by the man spraying from the tower. The long hose enables the ground man to do thoro work and this is impossible when he is hastily jerked along behind the wagon with the chance of being unable to carefully finish the tree on which he is working.

The nozzles should always be carefully cleaned and wiped with an oil rag after using. Usually the simpler the construction of the nozzle the more efficient will it work.

The farmer who is spraying a large orchard will find that it pays to obtain proper clothing for his own protection. A hat with a broad rubber brim will assist in keeping the solution away from hair and eyes. It sometimes pays to wear goggles to protect the eyes as lime-sulphur solution is very strong and the operator once thoroly blinded with the mixture never forgets the experience. Rubber gloves are sometimes used to protect the hands from the effects of the spray solution. Old leather gloves can be rubbed with engine oil and they will keep out the spraying mixture for two or three days and possibly longer.

When spraying with lime-sulphur is on the program many housewives take the regular silverware from the table as enough of the sulphur will stick to the clothes of the spray men to turn the silver dark after being used for only one meal. This only shows how necessary it is to protect the spray operator from as much of the solution as possible.

Small orchards cannot be expected to return sufficient profit to warrant the purchase of a power sprayer unless it can be done in cooperation with neighbors. The barrel sprayers are useful and they are not expensive. Small tank sprayers can also be mounted on wheelbarrows and wheeled around the orchard. It requires two men to use even the barrel sprayer as one man cannot direct the rod and pump at the same time and expect to do efficient work.

The farmer owning a good outfit for spraying must expect to manage the work himself unless his hired men have had some experience with spraying. The best of equipment is useless if managed by a man who carelessly sprinkles the trees without regard to the size of the area missed by the solution. Careless spraying is not profitable. It is just as expensive as good work but does not bring good returns. A farmer must teach his employees how to manage the engine to obtain the best

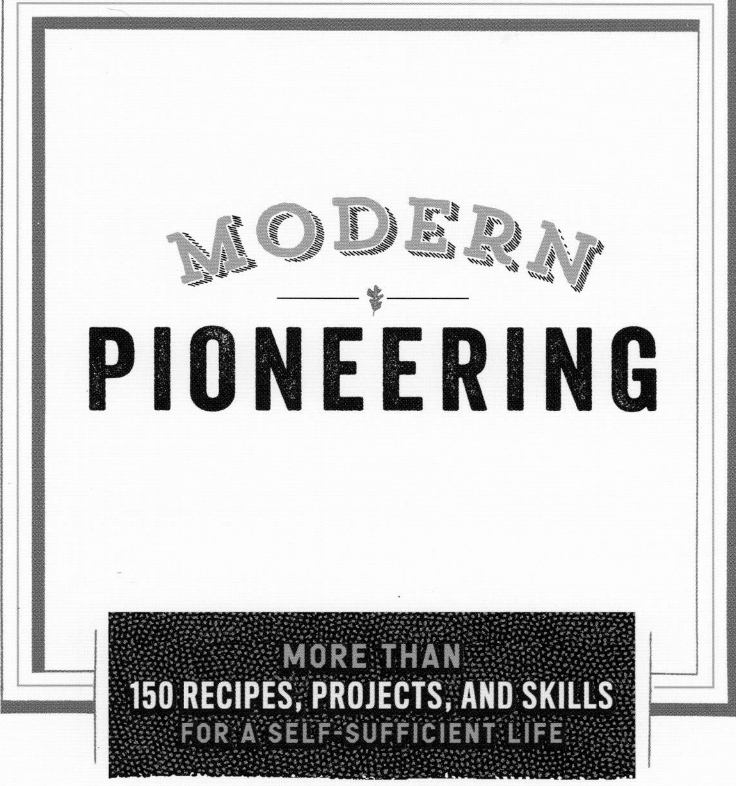

MODERN PIONEERING

MORE THAN
150 RECIPES, PROJECTS, AND SKILLS
FOR A SELF-SUFFICIENT LIFE

GEORGIA PELLEGRINI

CLARKSON POTTER/PUBLISHERS
NEW YORK

Published in the United States by Clarkson Potter/Publishers, an imprint of the Crown Publishing Group, a division of Random House LLC, a Penguin Random House Company, New York.
www.crownpublishing.com
www.clarksonpotter.com

Clarkson Potter is a trademark and Potter with colophon is a registered trademark of Random House, Inc.

Library of Congress Cataloging-in-Publication Data
Pellegrini, Georgia.
Modern pioneering : more than 150 recipes, projects, and skills for a self-sufficient life / Georgia Pellegrini; illustrations by T. Kristian Russell.—1st ed.
p. cm.
1. Vegetable gardening. 2. Gardening. 3. Cooking (Vegetables) 4. Self-reliant living. I. Title.
SB321.P46 2014
635—dc23 2013025178

ISBN 978-0-385-34564-4
eISBN 978-0-385-34565-1

Printed in Hong Kong

BOOK DESIGN BY DANIELLE DESCHENES
ILLUSTRATIONS BY T. KRISTIAN RUSSELL
COVER DESIGN BY DANIELLE DESCHENES
COVER PHOTOGRAPHS BY GEORGIA PELLEGRINI

10 9 8 7 6 5 4 3 2 1

FIRST EDITION

For my grandmother Frances Pellegrini and my great-aunt Ann Gray, the most fearless girls I know.

CONTENTS

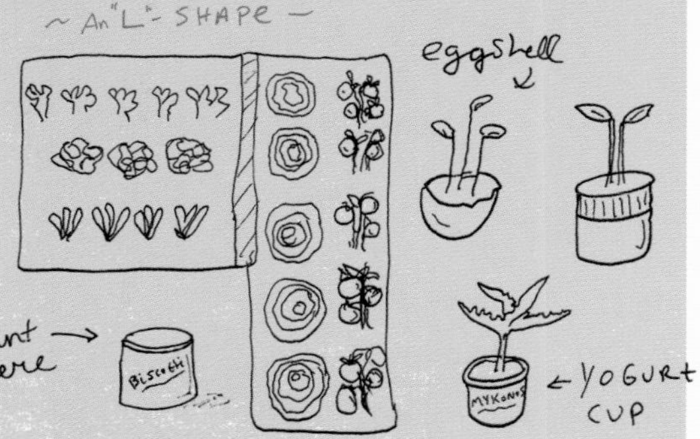

~ An "L"- SHAPE ~
eggshell
plant here
Biscotti
MYKONOS
← YOGURT CUP

Ball
MASON

THE WILD

THE REST

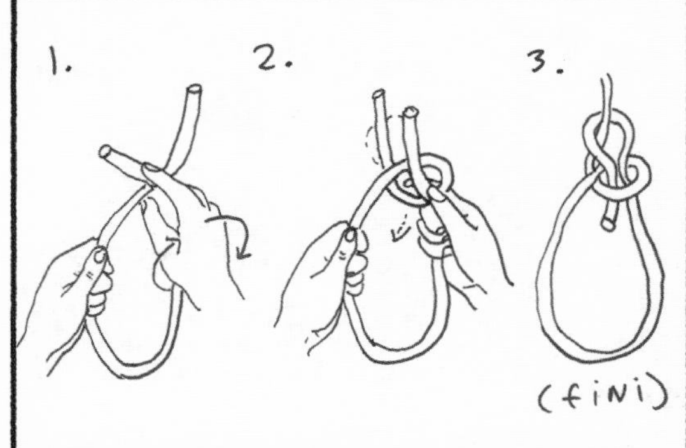

INTRODUCTION

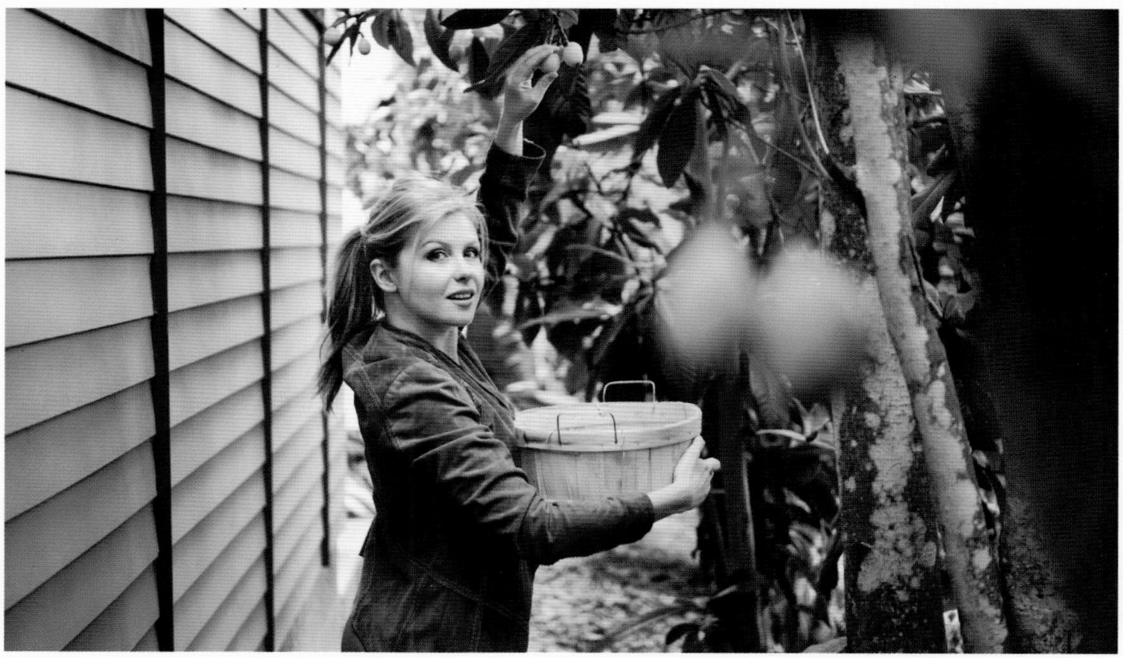

BECAUSE OF GREAT-AUNT GRAY, I HAVE ALWAYS LIKED TO GET DIRT UNDER MY FINGERNAILS. BECAUSE OF GRANDMA PELLEGRINI, THOSE FINGERNAILS HAVE ALWAYS BEEN WELL-MANICURED. THEY ARE THE TWO WOMEN WHO OPENED MY EYES TO WHAT IT MEANS TO BE A FEARLESS GIRL, THE LAST OF A GENERATION THAT KNEW HOW TO KILL A CHICKEN IN THE BACKYARD FOR DINNER, THAT WASTED NOTHING, THAT MADE THE BEST OF WHAT THEY HAD AND NEVER POINTED OUT WHAT THEY DIDN'T. THANKS TO THEM, I LEARNED TO COOK WITH ECONOMY, WITH RESPECT FOR SIMPLE INGREDIENTS.

For them it wasn't about survival, it was a way of life. I can still picture Great-Aunt Gray standing in her gardens, hunched over with shovel and trowel, her white hair puffing out from below the brim of her baseball hat, her floral skirt falling just above her oversize muddy sneakers. We were both raised in Sparkill, a tiny hamlet in New York's Hudson Valley, on the same land that my great-grandfather bought and cultivated in the early twentieth century and affectionately named Tulipwood. She and I would take long walks through the gardens and woods, and she would point out every tree and shrub that her father, my great-grandfather, had planted. Years after she passed, the metallic labels she used to identify her plants still twinkle in the sun as a reminder of her determination to preserve old varieties.

As a young girl at Tulipwood, I dug up fat worms by the side of a creek and fished for trout for my breakfast; I foraged, inspecting mushroom guidebooks with scholarly interest. I painted, using only wild berries and crushed grass as my ink, and hung from vines until they fell, then made vine wreaths that I studded with dandelions and rose hips (see page 285). I made jams and pickled green tomatoes and climbed apple trees to get the very finest fruit. I learned the names of plants with Great-Aunt Gray as my guide—and helped her protect her budding flowers from an overabundance of marauding midnight deer.

For much of my childhood, Great-Aunt Gray's sister, my grandma Pellegrini, lived with her in the house they grew up in. She preferred to grow plants, particularly herbs, as close to the kitchen as possible, even in the kitchen, so they were within arm's reach to use in her cooking. Grandma Pellegrini taught me about unusual herbs and all of their healing attributes. As I picked white eggplants in the hot August afternoons, I learned to stop and smell the rosemary and to look for purslane, a weed that she taught me has an extraordinary amount of omega-3 (see page 216). I also learned to wear a little homemade lip gloss while doing it (see page 74).

Grandma Pellegrini was famous for her rustic cornbread, and Great-Aunt Gray for her homemade ice cream, which they prepared with the bare minimum of sugar in order to accentuate the other flavors. They probably would have eliminated sugar from their recipes altogether if they could have gotten away with it, such was their disdain for added sweetener. There was comfort and strength to be found in Grandma Pellegrini's pans of steaming meatloaf and the fluffiness of her 7-Herb Frittata (see page 83), all made with an artist's temperament; reassurance to be found in the deliberate churn of Great-Aunt Gray's ice cream maker, which set the day's tempo.

In the years since then, I have spent countless hours exploring the outdoors and I have lived in small urban spaces without the luxury of lush land around me. No matter where I am, I always have the desire to feel the dirt slip between my fingers, to stir ruby-colored jam in a pot and watch it grow thick. And I have come to realize that Grandma Pellegrini and Great-Aunt Gray's generation got more than a few things right. Now, more than ever, there is a collective yearning that courses through cities and suburbs across the country, a need to be disconnected from the virtual and reconnected to the rhythms of nature. Many of us are seeking to experience things more viscerally, the way our grandmothers did, either at the stove or outdoors, often hunched over, cooking, curing, weeding, burning, or digging, even parking chicken coops in our driveways instead of cars. In an age of the information highway, social networks, entertainment junkies, and the blurry line between reality and virtual reality—all sedentary pastimes—we are looking for ways to access what is real and lasting and tangible, to access the DIY values and can-do, improvisational spirit of our grandparents' generation, to extinguish the manic flicker of the computer screen and learn how to use our hands again.

City dwellers are suddenly foraging with gusto, and food is no longer just a vehicle to satisfy our stomachs, or even our sense of morality; where it comes from is not enough anymore. It now also has to ignite our imagination, take us to another place that is more grounded, where we can feel, for example, what it is like to scatter a fistful of rose petals onto a hazelnut cake (see page 101) or on a panna cotta that has been soaking in a bath of rosemary syrup (see page 75), and anticipate the taste of the preserved lemons aging on our shelf (see page 154). For many of us, a palmful of handpicked raspberries now brings more delight than designer food at designer restaurants.

Modern Pioneering savors this moment in time, a period of rediscovery, when we are looking at food and the farm through fresh eyes, making the do-it-yourself mentality work for a very modern age. This book shows you that no matter where you live, you can learn how to step off the grid in your own way, one that is bright, colorful, stylish, edgy, and alluring.

This is your guide for how to do more with less, to delight in your little patch of garden behind your home, to enjoy life in the process. Since I left Great-Aunt Gray's gardens at Tulipwood, I've added labels to my own plants, I've foraged and hunted food for my own meals, I've raised chickens and honeybees. But recently after moving to an urban city, I discovered, in the back of my new home, a loquat tree—full of luscious fruit that was entirely unfamiliar. This humble discovery was every bit as transforming as those other experiences, and a reminder that the lost world we seek can be within arm's reach.

We need to fill our manicured hands with berries that we have picked ourselves. Only then do we feel truly full.

Georgia Pellegrini

THE GARDEN

CHAPTER
№ 1

EFFICIENT GARDENING

YOU CAN SATISFY YOUR DESIRE to get back to the land in an economical and efficient way, even if the land is only a small garden, a patio planter, a fire escape, or your windowsill. If you are just dipping your toe into the water, there are plenty of lists to get you going, including the easiest fruits and vegetables to grow, where to grow them, and the most basic tools to start with.

Within these pages, you will also find choices for efficient garden shapes if you have a bit of soil available to you, or if you don't, instructions for how to build a raised bed for your driveway, or a narrow planter for your back alley. The basic home tool kit you'll put together will aid you in these projects. Or simply make seed bombs and foray into guerrilla gardening when you don't have any space of your own. The recipes allow you to delight in what you have produced, to mark the seasons by the scents of the herbs growing on your windowsill and cooking in your kitchen, making you more self-sufficient in the process.

WHAT TO GROW

THE KEY TO CHOOSING YOUR PLANTS is to make a gardening plan that inspires you and to keep to that plan when you march off to the gardening store. Every plant can be alluring when you are hungry to grow. Before you buy, consider the following questions to make the most of your space, time, and dollars.

What Are Your Favorite Smells and Flavors?

What colors would you like to see when you wake up every morning? What smells would you have fill your kitchen? What flavors do you want to taste in your tea or your omelet for breakfast?

These are the most important questions you can ask yourself when thinking about what food to grow, whether it be on your windowsill or in the patch of grass along the sidewalk. Do thoughts of lettuces named Golden Frills and Ruby Streaks thrill you? Me too! And just because they say gardeners are supposed to grow tomatoes doesn't mean you should, unless you salivate at thoughts of homemade ketchup, tomato marmalade, and panzanella salad—in large quantities. There is no need to toil away at a garden or even a window box unless it is producing something that you want to eat. So pick your favorites, the same way you would at a restaurant. Your micro plot of land, your fire escape, or your windowsill are going to be your menu.

What Do You Spend the Most Money On?

If you are thinking about the economics of growing your own food, ask yourself what you eat in a given week. Are you a lover of tomato sauce? Or is fried okra more your thing? Are you buying a lot of lettuce at the grocery store because you are a chopped salad fiend? Try planting what will save you money.

What's Missing from Your Grocery Store?

Speaking of your grocery store, what do you wish yours had more of? Does it have candy striped beets, purple potatoes, white eggplant, or other unusual flavors and colors? Or a wonderful assortment of hot peppers for all of your homemade hot sauce needs? If the answer is no, try growing several varieties to diversify the flavors available to you in your cooking.

What Are the Demands of Your Space and Your Life?

Think about your particular environment. How much sun does your chosen gardening spot actually get? Also consider your time. Is the plant high-maintenance? How much will it yield? Find the answers before you decide. If you're a busy lawyer, do you really want to fuss over a single artichoke and give it valuable space?

THE EFFICIENT GARDENER'S

BASIC TOOLS

The beauty of efficient gardening is that you don't need many tools. The best tool you can have, in fact, is a community of gardening friends to share information and ideas with. Online forums, local gardening clubs, and community gardens are a wonderful resource.

You'll also want to invest in a few high-quality tools, which are hard to come by as gardening stores seem to carry more and more tools with plastic handles and poor construction. The older and more sturdy tools are made of steel and can often be purchased used.

As for the tools that you need for efficient gardening, skip the wheelbarrow and even the standard shovel and stick to a few of these basics to get the job done.

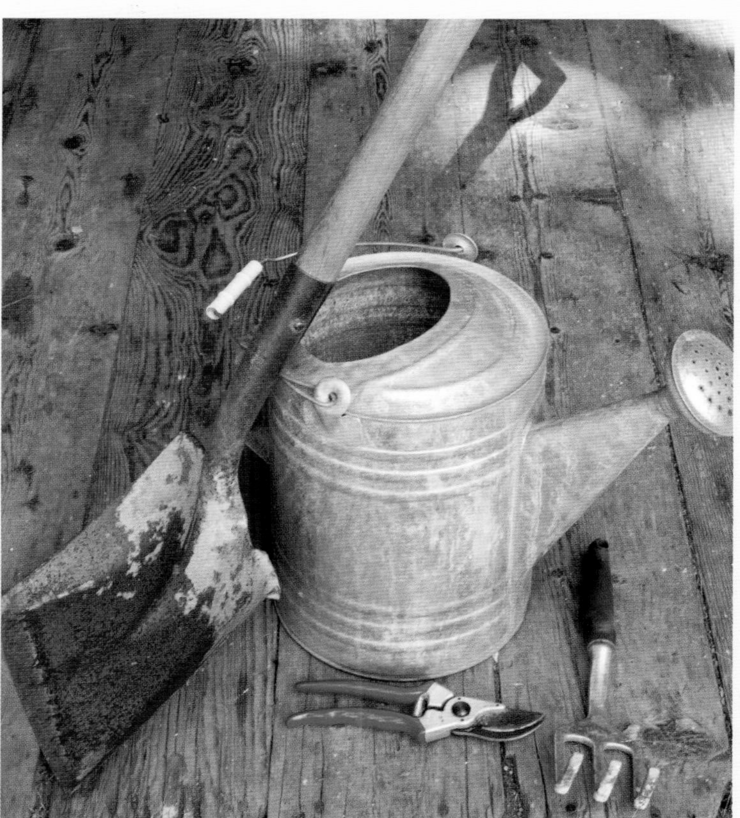

FOR OUTDOOR GARDENING

SPADE for preparing planting holes for transplants and for scooping soil into containers.

HAND CULTIVAR OR HOE for loosening soil and preparing the ground for planting. These can be three-pronged forks, pared-down versions of the familiar long-handled hoe, or designs that combine the best of both.

ROSE SHOVEL, a smaller shovel that is just as good as a big one and much easier to use.

HOSE with a variable setting on the nozzle or **WATERING CAN** with tiny holes at the spout. Self-coiling spiral hoses are a great small-space option.

PRUNING SHEARS for cutting back branches and harvesting.

FOR INDOOR GARDENING

HAND TROWEL for preparing small planting holes for transplants and for scooping soil into containers.

HAND FORK for aerating and mixing soil.

SCISSORS OR PRUNING SHEARS for snipping back herbs and stems.

WATERING CAN

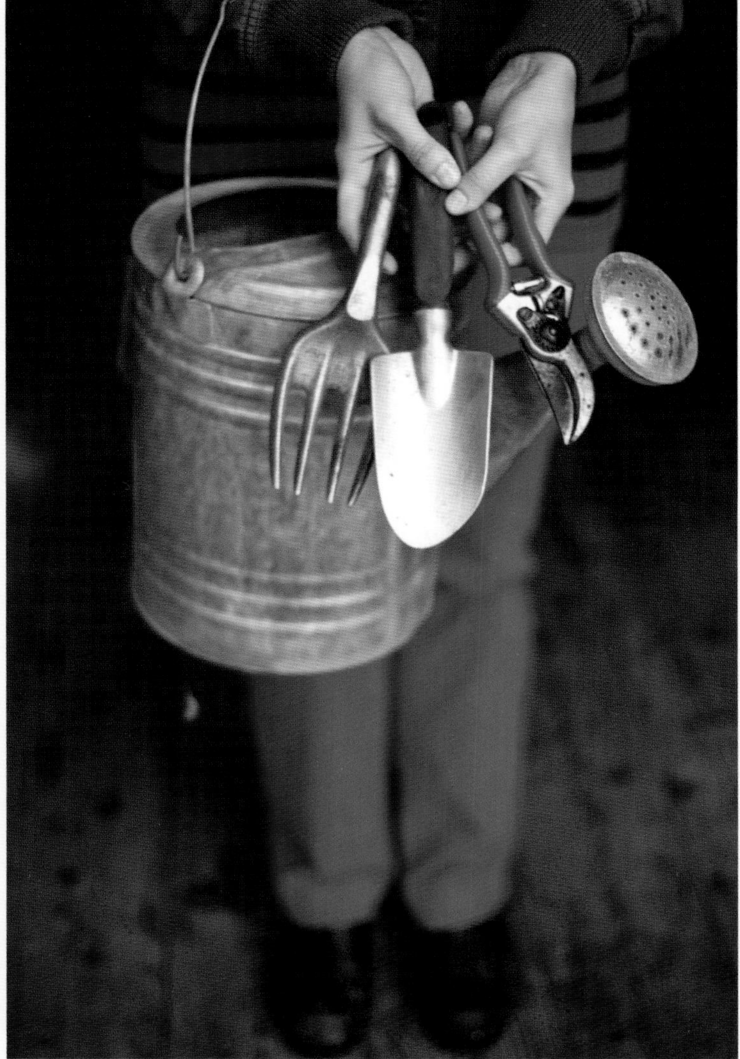

Keep your tools sharp and the wood and metal well-oiled with boiled linseed oil, which you can get at most home-improvement stores. Then store them in a dry place to protect them from the elements, preferably close by so that they're always at your fingertips. In fact, if you keep them looking nice you can hang them on the wall for decoration.

If one of your tools begins to show minor rust, use a wire wheel to remove it. For significant rust on a special tool, consider investing in having it professionally bead-blasted, which is the process of smoothing a surface with glass beads.

THe Easiest fruits & Vegetables to grow.

- Beans
- Beets
- Carrots
- Cucumbers (gherkin?)
- Herbs*
- Kale
- lettuce
- peas ← out of POD
- peppers
- potatoes
- Pumpkin
- Radishes
- Spinach
- Squash* & Zucchini
- Strawberries
- sweet corn
- Swiss chard
- Tomatoes

* fines (French)

florets →

THe Best Vegetables to Grow for Protein (And How to eat them)

- Adzuki beans (sprouted raw)
- Beans (black, garbanzo)
- Broccoli (cooked)
- Brussels sprouts (cooked or raw)
- Collards (cooked without stems)
- Edamame (steamed)
- Fava beans (raw)
- Kale (steamed, no stems or midribs)
- Lentils (cooked)
- Peas (green, cooked)
- Pumpkin (seeds)
- Spinach (raw)

Plants that do well in cooler weather

- Arugula
- Beets* (* just beat it)
- Broad beans
- Broccoli
- Broccoli rabe
- Brussels sprouts
- Cabbage
- Carrots
- Cauliflower
- Celery
- Chard
- Chinese cabbage
- Chives
- Collards
- Fennel
- Kale
- Kohlrabi
- Leeks
- Lettuce
- Onions
- Parsley
- Parsnips
- Peas
- Potatoes (early or late)
- Radicchio
- Radishes
- Rutabaga
- Spinach
- Turnips

KOHLS
(Big box store)
(unrelated)

Plants that do well in warmer weather

- Artichokes
- Bush beans
- Corn
- Cucumber
- Eggplants
- Melons
- Okra
- Onions (bulb)
- Peanuts
- Peppers (sweet)
- Pole beans
- Pumpkins
- Rhubarb
- Squash
- Sweet potatoes
- Swiss chard
- Tomatoes
- Watermelon
- Zucchini

BUSH ← BUSH BEANS

HOMEMADE SEED STARTING CONTAINERS: THE MANY POSSIBILITIES

There are many materials already in your home that you can "upcycle" as a container for planting your own garden seeds.

Eggshells ARE GOOD for compost, But they ARE ALso great FOR starting seedlings. THey ARe Biodegradable so wHen the seedLINGS ARe Ready to Be PLANTED iN THe GROUND, ALL YOU HAVe to do is BREAK THE SHeLL AND PLANT THE whole tHing in the soil!

HOW TO TURN EGGSHELLS INTO FLOWER VASES

Here is another whimsical way to upcycle your eggshells after breakfast. Save your eggshells from time to time and you will always have a vase on hand!

1. When you crack the eggs try to tap the shells higher up on the egg so you are left with a deep cup.
2. Rinse the shells and let them dry in the sun on a windowsill.
3. Choose your flowers and cut them short, those with smaller buds like violets, buttercups, and paperwhites work best.
4. Set your eggs in egg cups or trim an egg carton down so you just have a secure base of cups to hold the eggshells.
5. Fill each eggshell about three-quarters of the way up with water and add your flowers.

STEPS TO GROWING

SEEDLINGS

To unlock a seed from its dormancy, it needs four things: water, light, oxygen, and the right temperature.

Warm-weather crops (see page 17) like tomatoes, melons, eggplant, and peppers need to be started indoors so they have enough time to bear fruit before the cold weather sets in. Other plants, notably root crops like carrots and parsnips, should only be sown directly in the ground since they don't like to be disturbed once they germinate. If you have started seeds in plastic flats, they will need to be transplanted twice: first, when leaves appear, into larger containers so that they have room for their roots to grow, and second, into the ground.

Here are the steps to successfully germinating seeds:

1. If starting the seeds indoors, fill the containers with soil mix. The best combination for seeds includes not just straight potting mix, but equal parts potting mix, humus, and vermiculite. Tamp it down gently, leaving ½ inch or so of space at the top.

2. Moisten the soil before you sow. It should be sponge-damp but not soaking wet. This applies to both outdoor and indoor planting. Maintain consistent moisture. For plants that you germinate in pots, it is ideal to water them from below by setting a tray under the pots and filling it with water. The soil will soak up the water through the bottom of the pots. If you can't do that, a delicate sprinkling with a watering can will do.

3. Check the seed packet for information on how deep and far apart to sow the seeds. As a rule of thumb, the bigger the seed, the deeper it needs to be planted, at a depth of about twice its diameter. Lettuce seeds, for example, should just be barely scratched into the surface of the soil, whereas bean seeds need to be covered with an inch of soil.

4. Label your containers or rows so you can keep track of what they are.

5. Place the seed containers in a warm, bright area. Most seeds germinate best in temperatures from 60°F to 75°F. Put them on top of the fridge or in a sunny window. If you cover them with a clear dome or plastic bag they may not need to be watered again until they germinate. The surface of the soil should feel damp, not wet, so if you do water, do it gently. A kitchen sink sprayer is a good option.

6. After seeds have emerged, give them a lot of light, otherwise they grow leggy, meaning tall, thin, and weak. Seeds can get plenty of heat but without light they will become floppy. This can sometimes happen when seeds are started too soon in the spring season. Fluorescent tube grow lights come in handy here. But if your seeds do become leggy you can fix most seedlings when you transplant them by burying them almost up to the seed leaves. Be sure not to overwater if you do this.

7. Once the seeds germinate and form their first true leaves, transfer them into individual pots that are slightly larger, about the size of a yogurt cup. This will allow for proper root development before they are transferred into the ground.

HARDENING OFF

Seedlings are ready to be transplanted into the ground when they have three or four true leaves, which are different from the first two leaves that form upon germination to produce and store food. Once these true leaves have formed, indoor seedlings will need a transition phase where they can get used to the outdoors in small doses.

Hardening them off means you simply place the containers outdoors for increasingly longer periods of time:

Look up the date of the last expected frost in your area and don't attempt to harden off or transplant if temperatures are expected to fall below 45°F. Cool-weather plants like lettuce and kale will tolerate some cold, but warm-weather plants like tomatoes and melon will be much more sensitive.

Start by setting the seed containers in the shade for 2 to 3 hours a day.

After a few days, transition slowly to the sun for 2 to 3 hours a day and bring them indoors at night.

After a week or so, leave them out overnight.

TRANSPLANTING

Once seedlings have been hardened off they are ready for their permanent home in the outdoors:

Dig the planting hole slightly deeper and about twice as wide as the plant pot.

If you haven't added compost or fertilizer to the soil yet, do it now.

Gently remove the dirt and seedling from its container and place it in its hole, making sure its soil is level with the surrounding soil.

Do not bury the stem, except in the case of tomatoes, which enjoy being planted deeply.

Water the transplant and let it grow!

THINNING INGROUND PLANTS

Thinning your seedlings can seem wasteful, but it is necessary if you want any of them to succeed. As the seeds germinate, you will pull some of them out of the soil to make room for others to grow fully, ensuring there are enough nutrients for fewer healthy, mature plants to flourish. Do this in stages so that if an herbivore comes along, your fledgling garden isn't wiped out. Your seed package will tell you how many inches of space to thin the seedlings to. If it says 8 inches apart, begin by thinning so that they are 2 inches apart, a week later thin so they are 4 inches apart, and so on until they are 8 inches apart.

USE EXCESS
SEEDLINGS
FOR SALAD

Save the seedlings that you pull from the ground and eat them for dinner. They are delicious in a salad and people pay top dollar at farmers' markets for this delicacy. The best option in this case is to cut the seedlings at the base with a pair of scissors rather than pull them, so that you have dirt-free micro greens ready for the table. The remaining root will disintegrate on its own underneath the soil.

PLANT ROOT VEGETABLES NEAR BUSY STREETS

If your environment is especially urban, consider how close you are planting to busy streets and car exhaust. Building a raised-bed planter is one way to work around poor soil. But if air pollution or busy streets are a concern, then opt for root vegetables to avoid most of the grime.

GETTING CREATIVE WITH GARDEN SHAPES + SPOTS

Space-efficient gardening can produce five times more produce than traditional row-style gardening. In addition, by concentrating your soil preparation in a small area, your garden efficiently accesses the nutrients in the soil. There is also less space for you to weed and water, which means the small plot is well cared for and can flourish. All of these shapes are equally effective and give you options depending on your circumstances:

AN L-SHAPE: This shape works well at the corner of a parking lot or house. You can extend the sides of the L to suit your space.

TERRACING: This shape is perfect for a steep slope and can be shaped to follow the natural contours of the space. You can hold the soil in place by laying boards, logs, or stones along the edge. Each terrace should be at least 2 feet deep.

THE ROUND GARDEN: In addition to being efficient, this shape can look artful if you grow the right things. Any combination of tall and low-growing plants can be used, so long as the tall plants are set in the center and the smaller on the outskirts. This will ensure that they all get adequate sun. Make sure you create a path to access the inner plants so that you can weed.

A PARKING STRIP: If you are tight on space, the strip of grass between the sidewalk and the street is one of my favorite places to plant a few hearty vegetables. Who needs grass there anyway? Swiss chard does particularly well. Just check your local community rules to make sure they will allow this.

A BACK ALLEY: It is amazing how charming an alley can look with a few boxes of rainbow Swiss chard, purple Peruvian potatoes, yellow corn, and a quince tree. You can even add a worm bin. When people ask what the worm bin is, tell them you are urban tumbling—haven't they heard of the latest craze?

GARDEN SHAPES & SIZES

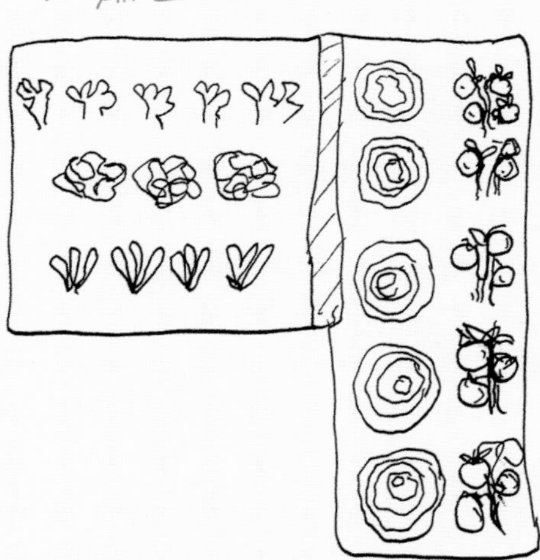

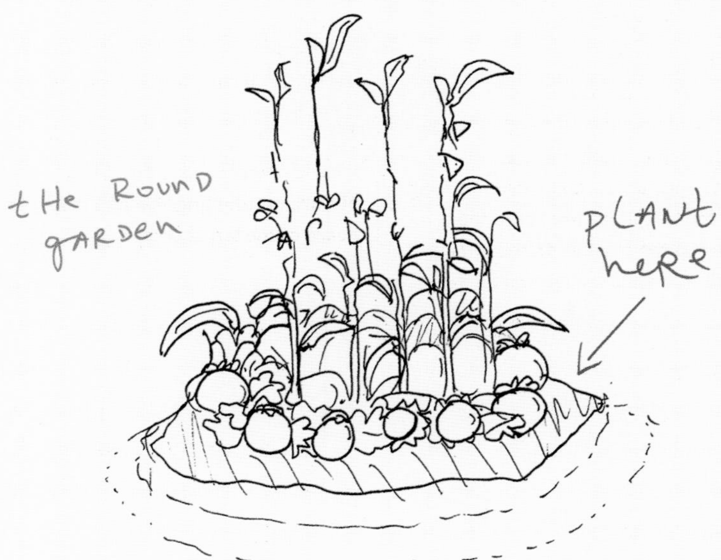

POTION
№ 1

REALLY DIRTY HAND CLEANER

To get really stubborn dirt off your hands, mix ¼ cup sugar with 1 tablespoon dish soap and rub the paste vigorously on your hands. Rinse and dry your hands, then follow with a mixture of ¼ cup sugar and 1 tablespoon olive oil. Rinse and dry again and the dead skin cells on your hands should have sloughed off, leaving your hands much more tidy.

HOW TO BE A

GUERRILLA GARDENER

If you are feeling particularly fearless, cities are filled with unused and neglected spaces in which to plant a vegetable or three. Abandoned lots, unused planter boxes, walking paths—the possibilities are endless. Keep in mind that you may get reprimanded or your produce might get mowed down by a landscaping crew or stolen by passersby, but if you are up for a little uncertainty, or just want to make a statement about the possibilities that we typically overlook, it can be thrilling to see what you can produce.

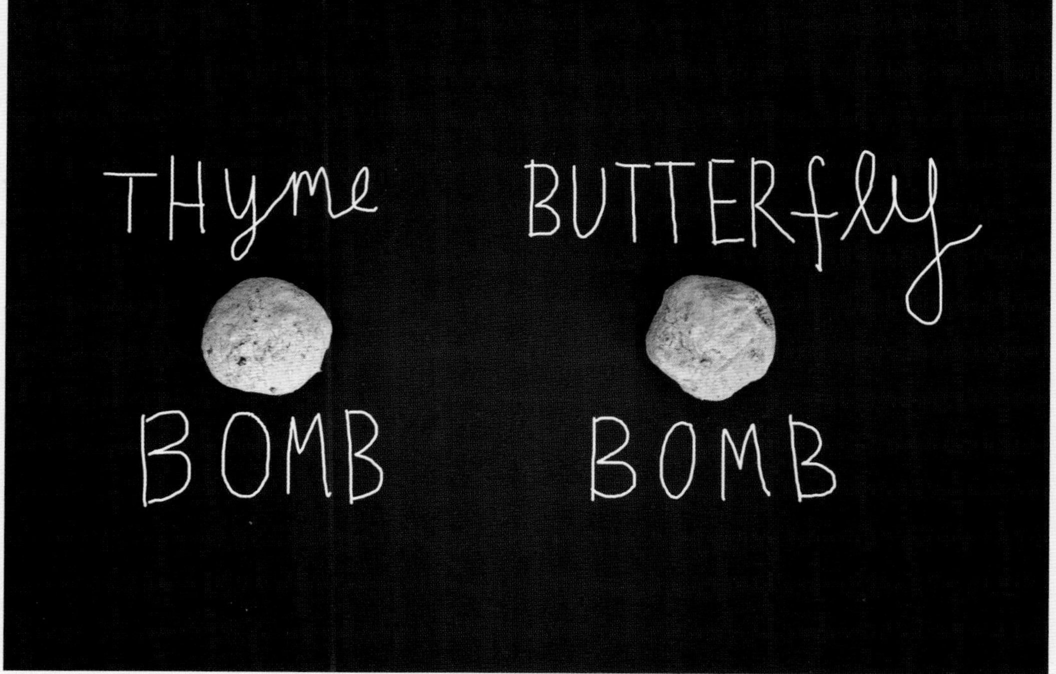

HOW TO BUILD A SEED BOMB

MAKES 10 TO 12 BALLS

Seed bombs are one way to go guerrilla with the landscape around you. They consist of balls made from organic matter that have all of the ingredients a plant needs to grow, wherever you drop it. It is a way of improving land that needs a little love, maybe a patch of grass along the sidewalk or the lot of a boring-looking office building. Carry the seed bombs around in a plastic bag in your purse and drop a bomb wherever you think it is needed. Or perhaps do a little drive-by bombing from your car on a Friday evening. It makes for a unique date night.

Choose self-seeding options like herbs, arugula, lettuces, and kale, so that they flourish after the bomb has been dropped. Butterfly bushes are fun because they self-seed and don't need to be well-cared-for. And they will attract butterflies like crazy wherever they flourish. We could all use more butterflies. Also choose beneficial plants that improve the soil by attracting good insects such as anise hyssop, fennel, clover, and calendula. Wildflowers are another beautiful option though they can be invasive, so do a little research first. Then, bomb away!

PREP TIME: 30 minutes
INACTIVE TIME: 48 to 72 hours
TOTAL TIME: 48 hours, 30 minutes

- 2½ cups dry powdered clay (purchase this from an art supply store or online in any color)
- 1½ cups organic compost
- ½ teaspoon seeds
- Latex gloves, to avoid getting dry, chalky hands (optional)

1. Using your hands, thoroughly mix the dry clay, compost, and seeds in a bowl. You can wear latex gloves, if desired.
2. Slowly add water, working the mixture with your hands after each small addition until the mixture holds together without crumbling. It is very easy to add too much water, so go slowly. If the mixture becomes too wet, work in more compost to bring it back to a balanced consistency that can be formed into a sturdy ball.
3. Pinch off small chunks of the mixture, rolling each chunk into a ball approximately 2 inches in diameter. If the surface seems to crack, wet your palms slightly to help seal the surface.
4. Set the balls on pieces of cardboard and let them dry 2 to 3 days.
5. Drop them wherever you want new plants to grow and let Mother Nature do her work.

COMMON

HOUSEPLANT HURDLES

AND HOW TO OVERCOME THEM

PROBLEM: **The leaves and stem of your plant are starting to wilt, and are turning brown and crisp, or new leaves are smaller and much darker than normal.**

SOLUTION: This is a sign of extreme dryness, so act swiftly by watering the plant thoroughly, then soaking the pot in a bowl of water for 15 minutes. Spray the leaves with a sink hose or mister to slow down the rate of transpiration.

PROBLEM: **The leaves are wilting but your soil is wet. There is green slime on your soil, or the leaves are yellow and the flower buds are falling off.**

SOLUTION: This is a sign that your plant has been overwatered and is drowning from not enough oxygen. Put the plant into a warm room and do not water it for at least 7 to 10 days. Then check the root ends of the plant to see if there are any white roots. If there are, the plant is still alive and should be watered sparingly.

PROBLEM: **The leaves have brown edges and are wilting.**

SOLUTION: The sun may be too harsh on the plant and scorching the leaves. Feel the pot and see if it is hot. If it is, then the roots are too hot also and the plant should be moved to a less sunny spot.

PROBLEM: **The green leaves are turning light yellow, the leaves are twisting and contorting, or new growth doesn't look as green and full.**

SOLUTION: The plant isn't getting enough light. Prune it back and slowly adjust it to bright conditions, maybe by moving aside curtains or any obstructions to light. If possible, set it outside for the summer.

PROBLEM: **Your plant is growing slowly with only small, poorly colored leaves.**

SOLUTION: Your plant needs nitrogen in the form of plant food, which is essential for growth, especially during the spring and summer. Feed it every two weeks with a weak liquid fertilizer for indoor plants, or for outdoor plants add nitrogen in the form of organic materials like compost or composted manure. If the potted plant hasn't had its soil changed in two years, then you should change the soil as well.

PROBLEM: **Your plant looks lanky and unhealthy, with brown spots on the leaves and weak growth. There is also a buildup of white residue around the pot.**

SOLUTION: This is a sign that you are overfeeding your plant. First, remove any visible fertilizer, then leach the plant by flooding the pot with water for 30 minutes so that the fertilizer moves away from the soil . After this, feed the plant only sparingly and just water it until it looks healthy again. Then reintroduce feeding, fertilizing no more than every two weeks.

COMMON

OUTDOOR PLANTING HURDLES

AND HOW TO OVERCOME THEM

PROBLEM: **Your site has too much sun.**

SOLUTION: Choose heat-loving or drought-tolerant plants, and use them as a barrier for more sensitive plants.

PROBLEM: **Your site doesn't have enough sun.**

SOLUTION: Set mirrors or the shiny side of aluminum foil on the side of your plant that gets the least sun to bounce light back onto it. Choose plants that prefer shade—and start a mushroom garden while you are at it.

PROBLEM: **You live in a very cold climate with few warm months.**

SOLUTION: Start seedlings indoors in some nifty home-made growing containers (see page 30) well before the last frost. Choose varieties that have a short growing cycle and that do well with colder weather. Choose your growing place carefully, and make sure it has as much light as possible.

PROBLEM: **Your soil doesn't seem to be rich and healthy.**

SOLUTION: That is what raised beds and containers are for: You can choose what soil you put in them. And in the meantime, you can work to improve your soil with compost, manure, and nutrients. You can also try to lower the pH of your soil by adding sulfur, or raise the soil's alkalinity by adding lime. See page 28 for instructions on how to make a raised bed.

PROBLEM: **The nearest water source is far away.**

SOLUTION: Position a barrel nearby to catch rainwater. Also, choose drought-resistant plants, and a combination of plants that all require about the same amount of water. You can also layer newspapers and straw on top of the soil to help keep it from drying out.

PROBLEM: **Your soil doesn't seem to have very good drainage. It is dense and heavy.**

SOLUTION: Go for the raised beds and containers for your planting (see page 28). Also, begin to incorporate sand into your soil; and if you plant in the ground, opt for plants that like a lot of moisture.

PROBLEM: **It is windy in your area.**

SOLUTION: Group your plants together to create a united front. Use a wall of hardy plants to screen the more tender ones. A trellis will also work. Choose wind-resistant plants, like those with flexible stems, which can bend and sway without breaking.

PROBLEM: **You are very tight on growing space.**

SOLUTION: Practice succession planting, grow climbers on a trellis or vertically in containers, find a community garden space, or—my personal favorite—help an elderly person manage his or her garden in exchange for sharing the fruits of your labor.

PROBLEM: **Your plants' stems are drooping and bending and seem too long.**

SOLUTION: Leggy plants, or plants with very long stems, might need more light—put the plant in more direct sun. If it is a plant like tomatoes, which have long stems to begin with, try moving it to a bigger pot.

PROBLEM: **Your plant growth seems stunted, and it isn't producing any fruit or flowers.**

SOLUTION: Your plants might be too crowded, which is restricting root growth. Try spreading them out more (if you are tight on space, see the tip above!).

RAISED BEDS

Raised beds are especially useful when the garden soil is not ideal. You can even add a raised bed where there was no soil to begin with, on a patio or driveway where the beds can be contained with wooden boards or rocks. Planting vegetables and fruits this way can be advantageous as well as attractive because you can control the nutrients of the soil when it is contained, and weed, walk around, and access from all sides. It is also easy to practice crop rotation and succession planting in these well-contained garden beds. Because the space is smaller the soil warms up more quickly, which allows you to get a head start on planting. And because you are not walking on these beds, the soil doesn't become compacted but stays nice and airy with good drainage.

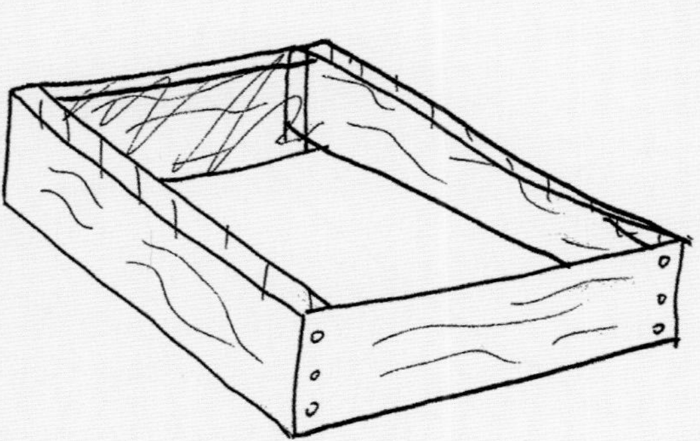

how to Build a Raised Bed

This project results in a very simple frame that you can adjust to your desired dimensions. You will want to use pressure-treated wood so that it will age without rotting. Cedar is a nice option, though it can be pricey. Adding planter fabric to the base isn't absolutely necessary, but it will be helpful in preventing runoff, especially if you place your planter in a driveway or uneven surface.

As shown in the equipment list opposite, there are a couple of routes you can take to build your frame depending on how much equipment you have. A power drill is not necessary, but it will allow you to make a pilot hole to ensure that you don't split the wood when hammering in nails or fastening screws. The equipment opposite makes a 2 × 4-foot raised bed, but you can simply cut the wood to a size that works for you and follow the same instructions to assemble it.

HAVE THE WOOD PRECUT

The best thing you can do for yourself is to ask the place where you buy your wood to cut it to size for you. Most of them will, and you'll save time and cut down on the number of tools you need.

One 12-foot-long 2 × 8-inch piece of pressure-treated wood, cut into two 4-foot lengths and two 2-foot lengths

12 galvanized tenpenny nails or 12 decking screws (see correlating tools at right)

Planter fabric

Organic soil

TOOLS IF THE WOOD IS NOT PRECUT:

Tape measure

Pencil, to mark the measurements

Carpenter's square, to ensure a perpendicular cut line

Wood saw

TOOLS IF YOU ARE USING A HAMMER AND NAILS:

Hammer

Power drill (optional; if you want to ensure you don't split the wood)

5⁄32-inch twist drill bit (optional; if you want to ensure you don't split the wood)

TOOLS IF YOU ARE USING SCREWS:

Power drill

5⁄32-inch twist drill bit

Driver bit to match screws

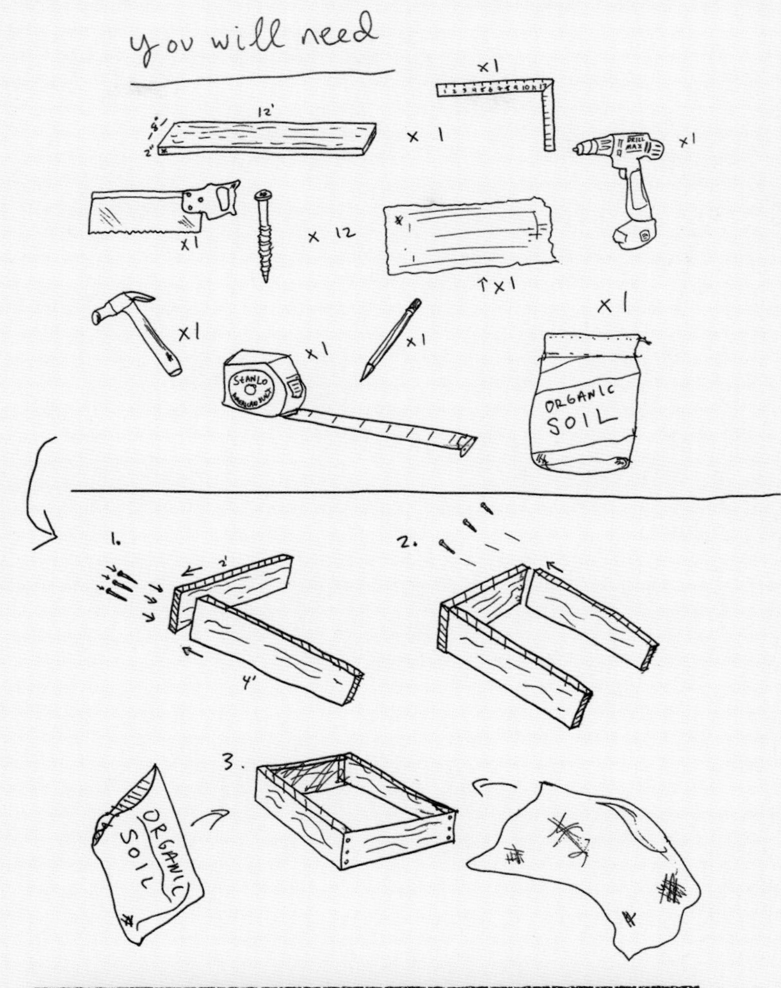

1 Bring a 4-foot piece and a 2-foot piece of wood together so they make a right angle. Allow the end of the 2-foot piece to meet, overlapping the end of the 4-foot piece. Hammer in three nails, or alternatively drill in three screws.

2 Add the next 4-foot piece so that it is being overlapped by the 2-foot piece and hammer in three more nails. Finish your rectangle by hammering in the 2-foot piece at the other end.

3 Line the bed with planter fabric and add high-quality organic soil.

CONTAINER
GARDENS

Growing in containers is an efficient way to get plenty of produce when you don't have land to plant in. Even if you do have space, containers may be easier to control and protect. Miniature varieties of most vegetables, which require less space and time to mature, are available.

Advantages of container gardening:

- If you are renting your home, you can take your garden with you.
- You can select your soil more carefully.
- Containers can be moved around if the weather becomes threatening, especially around the beginning or end of the growing season.
- You can control water and pests more easily.

There are a whole host of possible planting containers available for this (see at right), but you can expect the following differences from planting in the ground:

- You will want to be careful to use the right type of soil—soil that has good drainage and is lightweight (see page 42).
- Because of the intensive growing environment and care that container plants get, they can be spaced closer together than if they were in an outdoor garden, and the plants will need to be watered more frequently, almost every day. Stick your index finger straight down into the soil and if it doesn't feel moist, water away.
- A measured amount of fertilizer will also need to be added about every 2 to 3 weeks. Follow instructions and be careful not to fertilize too much.

FABULOUS AND UNLIKELY GROWING CONTAINERS

It is hard to make a horde of plastic containers look stylish, so here are some other ideas to try:

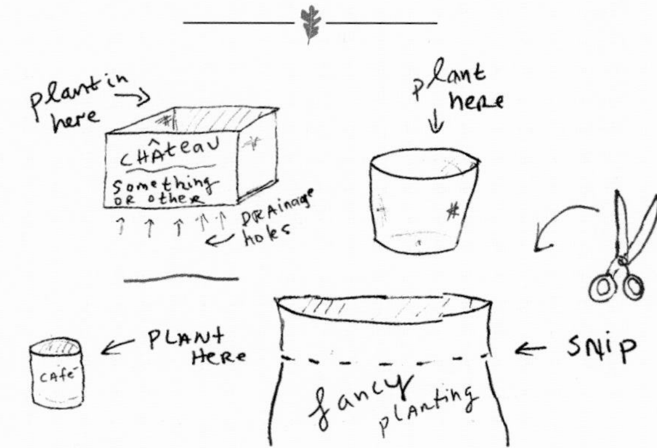

A BAG OF PLANTING MIX can become an instant planter with a few snips of the scissors. Even a plastic garbage bag with the proper soil will work. It may not look pretty, but it is certainly economical. Be sure to poke drainage holes in the bottom and make sure the bag isn't see-through since roots don't like light. Tomatoes, zucchini, potatoes, chard, and peas are some examples of vegetables that grow well this way.

A DRAWER FROM AN OLD DRESSER can easily become a planter box or a frame for a raised bed. You will need to drill drainage holes at the bottom as well as line it with planter fabric. These containers are great because they are often deep enough, 12 inches, to grow root vegetables. Since this wood is often pretreated, you will want to finish it with a fast-drying oil that doesn't need to soak in over time. Danish oil is a good option; it is made of part tung or linseed oil and part varnish. The more layers of oil you add, the longer the wood will last.

A LADDER OR AN OLD BOOKCASE LAID FLAT on the ground can serve as an attractive compartmentalized frame for herbs and low-growing vegetables like radishes, spinach, and lettuce.

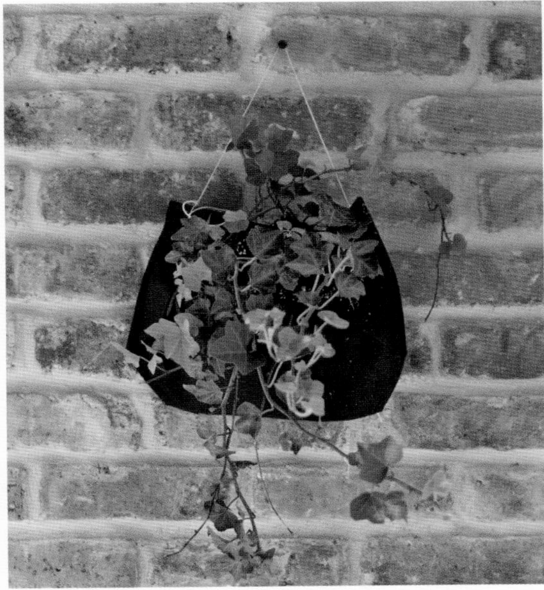

A FABRIC POCKET made of felt and lined with plastic can be fastened to the wall and planted with hanging nasturtium or other edibles. There are some you can buy already made, but you could also use a hanging shoe pocket with a tray underneath to catch any water.

A METAL LAMPSHADE TURNED UPSIDE DOWN is an instant decorative plant holder.

WINE CRATES can be found at high-end wine stores and antique markets and are great for growing salad greens. You will need to add drainage holes to the bottom and finish the wood with weatherproofing oil. This wood is untreated typically, so it will soak up cheaper finishing oils like linseed, but it will take much longer to dry. If you are pressed for time, Danish oil is a better way to go. Whatever you choose, resist pure varnish, it will seal the wood but if any water gets into cracks, the wood will rot from the inside. To ensure these boxes will last, you may also want to add braces to the corners to prevent the wood from warping.

FOOD TINS are an attractive and funky way to upcycle materials and put them to good planting use. Cookie tins, large olive oil and tomato containers, coffee tins, and whatever else you stumble upon in the Dumpster can make for a stunning display. Use nails to poke holes in the bottom as well as the sides for proper drainage.

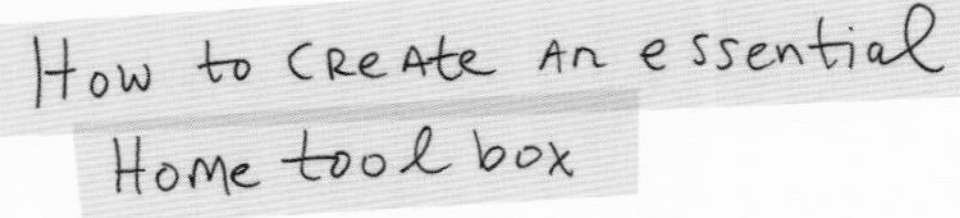

No matter how handy you are, everyone needs a few tools for a little self-sufficiency around the apartment or house. Get a basic tool bag and fill it with these must-haves. You will begin to collect extras as you take on various home decor and craft projects.

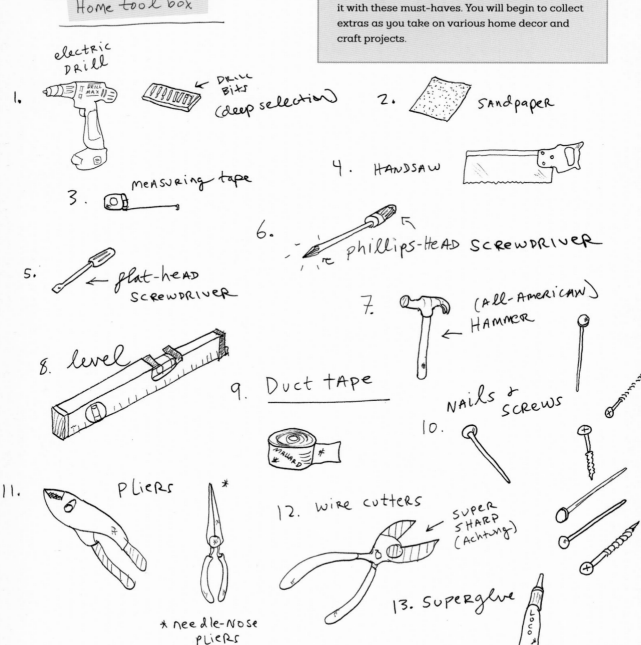

1. electric drill
   Drill bits (deep selection)
2. Sandpaper
3. Measuring tape
4. Handsaw
5. flat-head screwdriver
6. phillips-head screwdriver
7. (All-American) hammer
8. level
9. Duct tape
10. Nails & screws
11. Pliers*
12. wire cutters
    Super sharp (Achtung)
13. Superglue

* needle-nose pliers

HOW TO USE VASELINE TO DISTRESS WOOD

THIS IS A QUICK AND EASY WAY TO GET THE VINTAGE, ANTIQUE WOOD LOOK WITHOUT SPENDING MONEY ON THE REAL THING. USE IT TO REFINISH A PLAIN PLANTING CONTAINER, OR GIVE AN OLD PLANTING SHELF A MAKEOVER. THE VASELINE PREVENTS THE PAINT FROM FULLY COVERING THE WOOD AND CAN BE WIPED AWAY ONCE THE PAINT DRIES, GIVING IT A VINTAGE LOOK.

Rag
Vaseline
Newspaper, brown paper bags, or drop cloth
Spray paint

1. Dip the edge of the rag into the Vaseline and make streaks along the grain of the wood in random locations on one side.
2. Lay the newspaper, bags, or drop cloth on the ground and then lay the wood on top.
3. Apply the spray paint following the directions on the can. Let dry for about an hour.
4. Using the rag, remove the Vaseline thoroughly. Voilà, you have a vintage-looking surface.

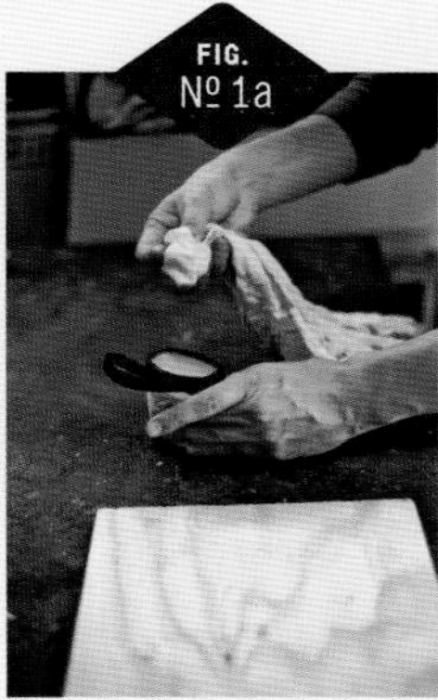
FIG. № 1a

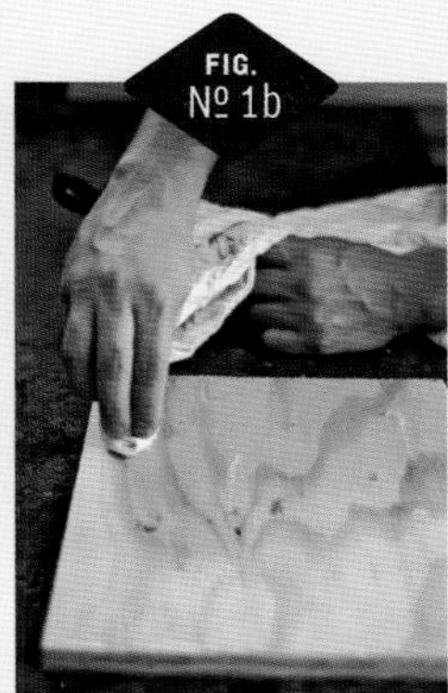
FIG. № 1b

FIG. № 3

FIG. № 4a

FIG. № 4b

HOW TO BUILD A PLANTER

FOR NARROW SPACES

I LIKE THIS PLANTER BECAUSE IT LOOKS CLEAN AND MODERN WHEREVER YOU PUT IT, FROM A PARKING LOT TO A BACK ALLEY TO A SMALL DECK. MAKE A SKETCH OF YOUR PLANTER AND THE DIMENSIONS FIRST SO YOU HAVE A CLEAR PICTURE OF WHERE IT WILL FIT.

When you are ready to assemble it, use a heavy hammer to give you more power when you bang in the nails. A dinky hammer won't take you far and you will have a tired arm. Or if you are into power tools, you can use a drill bit to make a pilot hole before you hammer in your nails. Alternatively, use screws if that is more your thing.

You can make this planter to fit your space and customize the size accordingly using these same steps.

TO BUILD THE PLANTER:

Handsaw if you don't have your wood already cut for you by the store where you purchase it

Hammer or nail gun

Box of galvanized 2½-inch nails or decking screws

Sixteen 8-foot-long 1 × 4-inch pieces of lumber, each cut at the end so that you have 16 pieces that are 83 inches long and 16 pieces that are 13 inches long (Note: They are technically only 3½ inches wide even though they are called 4 inches)

One 7-foot long 2 × 11-inch piece of board, cut to 81 inches (which will leave you with one 3-inch piece of scrap)

One 10-foot-long 2 × 4-inch piece of lumber, cut so that you have a total of 4 pieces that are all 27 inches long (which will leave you with one 12-inch piece of scrap)

Level

Measuring tape

Pencil

Plastic garbage bags or drop cloth for painting the wood

Danish oil, linseed oil, tung oil, or eco-stain for the wood (optional)

Paintbrush (optional)

TO GARDEN IN THE PLANTER:

1 roll of planter fabric

Rocks

6 to 8 bags of planting soil

1. Create a frame for the base by hammering together two 83-inch pine pieces with two 13-inch pine pieces so that you have a narrow rectangle.

2. Drop the 2 × 11 × 81-inch piece of lumber inside the frame. Hammer the frame into the base piece on all corners.

3. Hammer each of the four 2 × 4 × 27-inch pieces of lumber, one at a time, to each corner so that they stand upright.

4. With a level, measuring tape, and pencil, mark the posts where you will add additional slats. Start at ½ inch above the frame pine board and mark ½ inch, 3½ inches, ½ inch, 3½ inches, etc., until you reach the top of the posts. This will tell you where to nail the pine slats and ensure that they are even. You will be left with a slat that is ½ inch above the posts, which looks nice.

5. Begin nailing in the slats on all sides, making sure the pine boards go in the spaces that have been marked for them. It is best to have a second person hold up the one end while you hammer the other. Or a good clamp will work as well. Keep going until you have hammered in all the slats. It may take awhile if you are hammering by hand rather than with a nail gun, or without the help of pilot holes. Take some iced tea breaks and know that you are getting some good arm muscle.

6. Once it is fully hammered together, lay some plastic garbage bags or a drop cloth around the base. Stain the wood with Danish or linseed oil, or a combo stain and polyurethane, if desired.

7. Once dry, line it with planter fabric, drop rocks at the base for drainage, and fill with dirt. Plant away!

ORGANIC EGGS
FRENCH TOAST
PASTA
BLOODY MARYS

WHAT TO GROW AND

WHERE TO GROW IT...

If you live in an urban area or a dwelling without any land, you have more space than you might think, no matter your whereabouts. Is your rooftop flat and easily accessible? Does the fence along your building have a little bit of dirt to plant some pole beans? Does your fire escape have space for a planter box or a few round containers? How about your windowsill or driveway?

There are plenty of options no matter your circumstances. Climbing plants do beautifully on balconies and rooftops; short plants like lettuce, radish, and carrots do well on a windowsill. Here are some ideas to get you going.

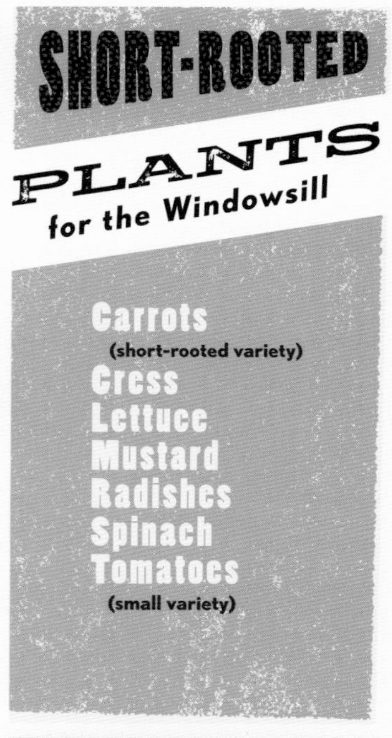

SHORT-ROOTED PLANTS for the Windowsill

- Carrots (short-rooted variety)
- Cress
- Lettuce
- Mustard
- Radishes
- Spinach
- Tomatoes (small variety)

BALANCE SUNLIGHT WITH A MIRROR

Place a mirror opposite a window to help bounce light back onto the dark side of growing plants. This will ensure the plants grow evenly, rather than leaning toward the sun.

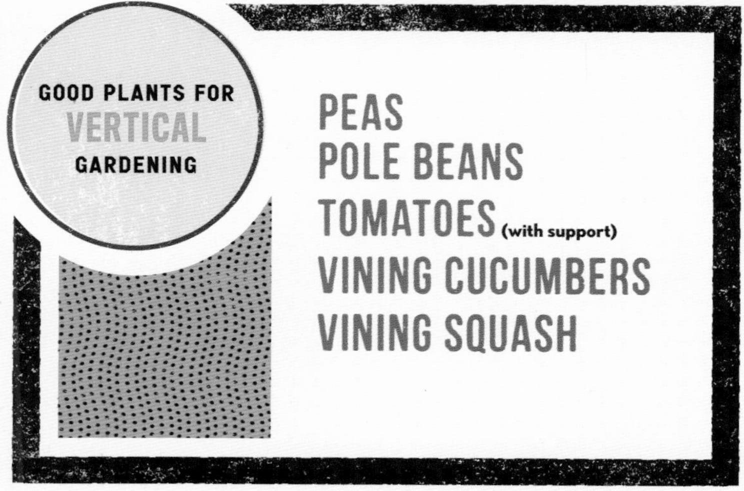

GOOD PLANTS FOR VERTICAL GARDENING

- PEAS
- POLE BEANS
- TOMATOES (with support)
- VINING CUCUMBERS
- VINING SQUASH

ON THE BALCONY, ROOFTOP, PATIO, OR PLANTER BOX

Beets

Broccoli

Brussels Sprouts

Bush Beans

Cabbage

Carrots
(short-rooted variety)

Cucumbers

Eggplant

Green Beans

Green Onions

Kale

Lettuce

Mustard Greens

Onions

Peppers

Potatoes

Radishes

Spinach

Squash
(bush variety)

Swiss Chard

Tomatoes
(small to medium variety)

Turnips and Other Root Veggies

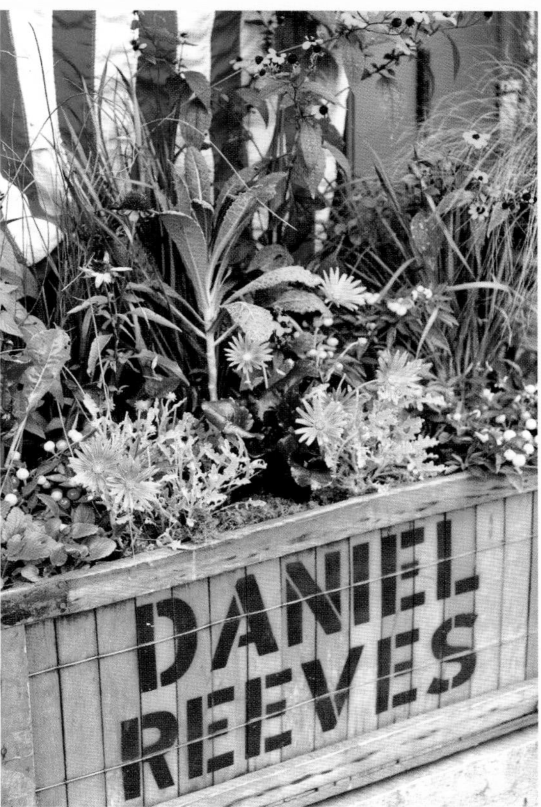

HOW TO ATTRACT BUTTERFLIES, HONEYBEES, AND HUMMINGBIRDS TO YOUR WINDOWSILL

A beautiful window box will not only transform your view, it can transform an entire street. If you have ever stopped to admire a lush window box bursting with vibrant color you know what I mean. From the inside, a room with a view like that can change your outlook. And it is made even better when all of the butterflies, honeybees, and hummingbirds pay a visit, too.

To attract them, combine ½ teaspoon honey and ½ teaspoon sugar in a shallow, red-colored saucer of 4 teaspoons warm water. Hummingbirds like the color red, for the others it doesn't matter. Place a cotton ball in the center and set the saucer on the outside of your windowsill. Butterflies, honeybees, or hummingbirds will land on the cotton and use it as an island from which to feed on the nectar. Plant vibrant colors in your window box with short flower tubes for the butterflies, and long tubular flowers like honeysuckle for the hummingbirds, and nectar- and pollen-rich plants like basil, rosemary, and lavender for the honeybees.

8 TIPS

FOR OUTDOOR CONTAINER OR ROOF GARDENING

1 Use soil that is specifically intended for container gardening. It will be lighter and have better drainage to help prevent the soil from drying out quickly from wind and sun. A good container soil will have a balance of organic compost, something to aerate the soil like sawdust, sand, or humus, and a fertilizer.

2 For growing vegetables use boxes that are at least 8 inches deep. Herbs and flowers can be in shallower containers.

3 Boxes should be as wide as the space will allow in addition to 8 inches deep, and should have ½-inch drainage holes at the bottom every 5 to 6 inches. Cypress and redwood are good durable woods; you can also use oak. Just make sure none of the wood you use is treated with chemical preservatives, which will leach into the soil. The insides of wooden boxes do best when you paint them with a wood preserving material like asphaltum, which is a natural tar-like substance that creates a waterproof coating and can be purchased at home-improvement stores. You can also purchase paraffin, spray it on the wood, and burn it off with a blowtorch. This locks it in the cell walls of the wood to prevent leaching. The outsides can be painted as desired.

4 If you need a lighter load for your windowsill, use a lightweight container like resin, fiberglass, or plastic as well as a light soil designed for container gardening.

5 If you would like, you can add a layer of straw, leaves, and other light matter to improve drainage at the bottom of the pot. Rocks and shells aren't necessary. The top layer should have good-quality manure, loam, and mulch to finish.

6 Container gardening soaks up a lot of water, and the smaller the containers are, the more often they will need water. If you buy a pot size bigger than you need, this will give you a bit more breathing room in how often you have to water. Also, the plant will only grow as large as the container it is in. So give it room to grow by buying a pot larger than it initially requires.

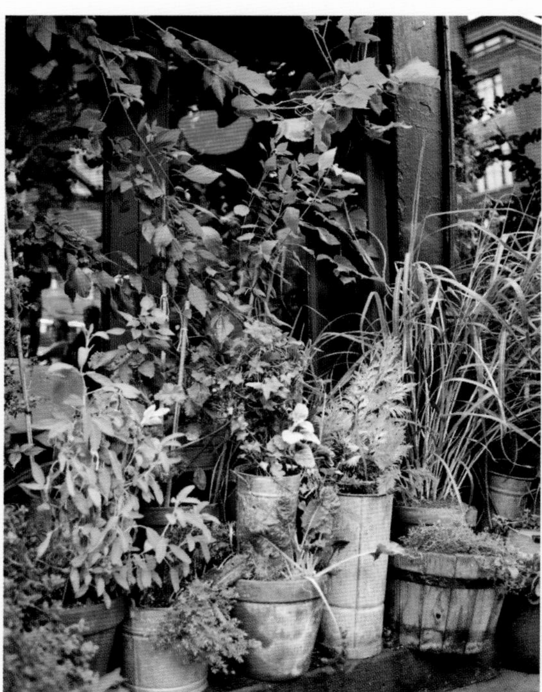

7 Always use a container with a drainage hole, and avoid the saucers that go under pots since they will capture the water and rot the roots if not emptied. If you are worried about stains without the saucer, buy planters with legs, or a rolling platform, then set a small saucer underneath the dolly legs to catch the water.

8 When reusing growing containers, clean them well before planting for a new season. Diseases and pests can linger in pots from previous years, which will prohibit a healthy crop, especially when you are starting from seed. Soak the containers overnight in 9 parts water to 1 part bleach, then let them sit out to dry before planting.

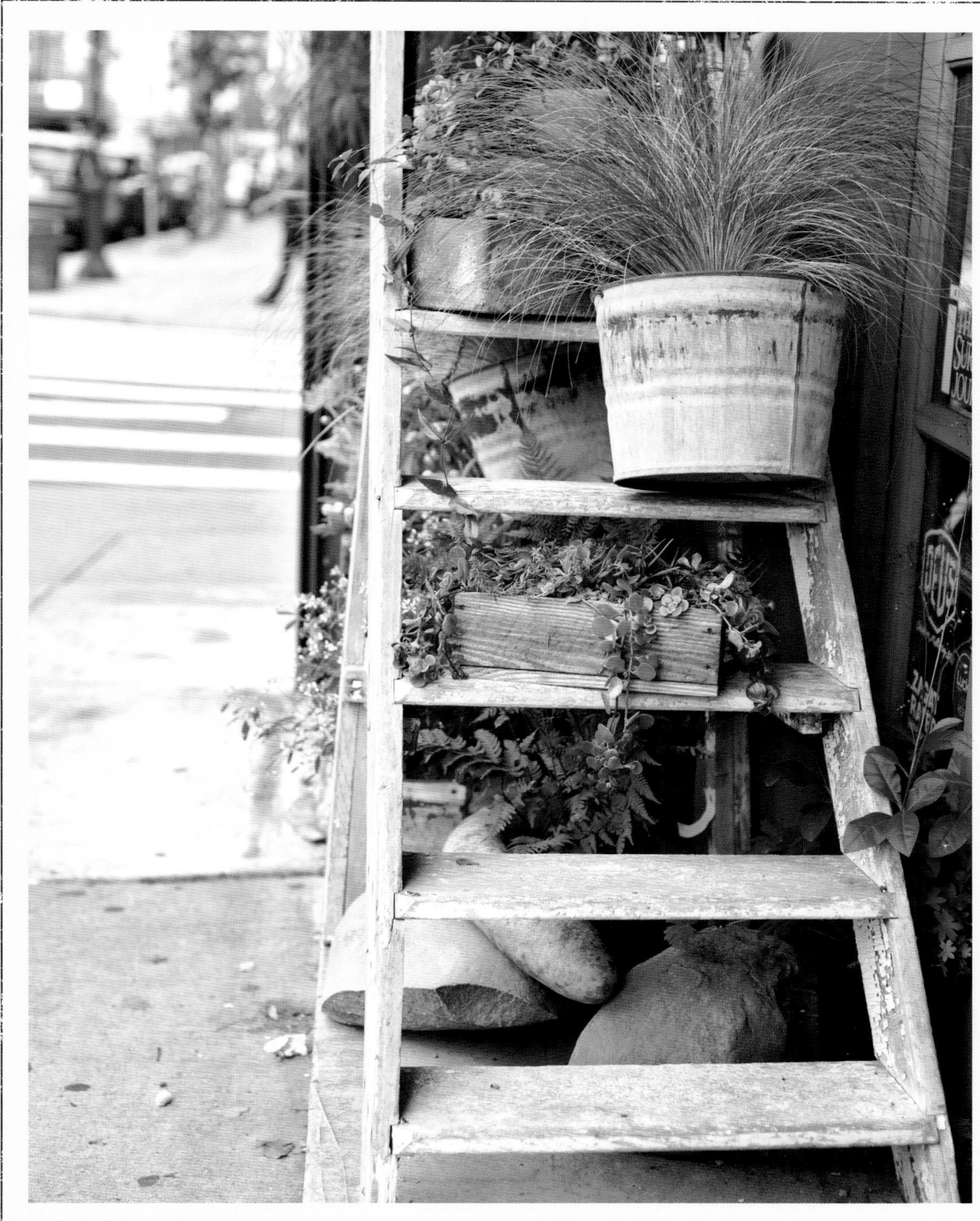

MIX YOUR OWN

SOIL

Traditional garden soil doesn't give container plants enough aeration and water, but you can easily adapt it to work for containers. The main thing you will need is an ingredient to separate the soil particles that will create air channels throughout the soil, allowing it to breathe and preventing root rot. Many people use peat moss, but because of the environmental issues associated with harvesting it, it is better to use an alternative like rotted sawdust or humus, which can be purchased at garden-supply stores. Some will also recommend vermiculite or perlite, but these, too, are controversial and probably not local to your area, so avoid them if possible.

HOMEMADE ALL-PURPOSE CONTAINER SOIL MIX

4 parts multipurpose potting soil

1 part rotted sawdust or humus

2 parts composted fine bark

1 handful (per pot) of slow-release fertilizer such as powdered sea kelp or fish manure

ON "SLOW-RELEASE" FERTILIZER

If the all-purpose potting soil that you purchase contains slow-release fertilizer, you won't need to add any before 8 weeks pass. After that you will have to add fertilizer yourself.

GROWING INDOORS

UNDER LIGHTS

Don't underrate how cool indoor gardening is. Not only does it soften the boundary between nature and your everyday life, but it also can help purify the air you breathe inside your home. When gardening indoors you have to work a little harder for the light; for example, turn your pots regularly so they get even light exposure and don't lean toward the sun. In the height of summer, you may need to pull the plants a few feet from the window to limit the harsh sun, especially near south-facing windows.

If you are opting for vegetables, they will need lots of light to flourish, and if you are without any outdoor options or are only getting northern sunlight, then there are artificial lighting options galore. Fluorescent tubes that produce a lot of red and blue rays from the UV spectrum are a great substitute for sunlight and are often designed especially for indoor gardening. Incandescent lamps are commonly used because of their high levels of warm red light. Four 4-foot fluorescent tubes placed 6 to 12 inches above the plants will provide enough light to cover a 3 × 4-foot area.

PLANTS TO GROW UNDER LIGHTS

Beets

Carrots

Celery

Cabbage

Cucumbers

Endive

Onions

Radishes

Watercress

HOW TO BE A FRUIT BOWL GARDENER

Did you know that you can germinate your avocado pit after you eat it? The same goes for your mangoes, papayas, pomegranates, ginger, goji berries, apricots, peaches, lemons, limes, oranges, and even chickpeas. Tropical plants need a lot of moisture and warm temperatures of 70°F to 85°F, which is easy to achieve indoors. Make sure the pit comes from very, very ripe fruit (rotten is even better!), and once you have put it in potting soil and watered it, tent it with a plastic bag to increase the humidity.

Once the seeds have germinated, which can take several months, remove the plastic and water the plant regularly. If the seeds are inside the pit, like with the mango, rinse the pit and dry it out overnight, then slice open the pit, remove the beans, and plant them. Don't get too hopeful about getting an avocado from your avocado plant; most of these plants won't bear fruit. But they are nice-looking and will work to help purify the air indoors.

THE ART OF

WATERING

When

The best time of day to water is early in the morning before you go to work, about 7:00 am, when the plant will use the water most effectively. Late in the afternoon is almost as good, when the sun is low and less water will be lost to heat evaporation. If the evenings are going to be hot, avoid watering late in the day as this can lead to fungal infections, since heat promotes bacteria.

How Much

For container plants, the soil should be moist but not soaking. Water until it rises to the rim of the pot, then stop. Let the excess drain into the saucer and after fifteen minutes, if the water hasn't been reabsorbed, toss it away. If it is a very heavy pot, a turkey baster comes in handy here to remove the excess water.

How Often

For outdoor plants in particular, a very deep soaking twice a week is better than a sprinkling several times per week. This is because the water needs to saturate up to 12 inches deep into the soil in order to reach the roots and not evaporate in the process. If the water doesn't penetrate deeply enough, it will encourage the roots of the plant to grow up and sideways, putting them at risk for drying out in the sun. By contrast, overwatering will leach nutrients into the soil and make the plants more susceptible to fungus and disease.

By Soil Type

The type of soil you have will also give you a sense of how much and how often to water. For example, clay soil is harder to saturate and will need to be watered for longer periods in order to penetrate to the roots but less frequently because it will hold water longer. Sandy soil requires more frequent watering since water drains quickly from it.

FIGHT
APHIDS
WITH WATER

If you keep finding leaves that are curling, yellow, or are covered in a sticky substance, check the underside of the leaves for tiny insects. Aphids dwell there and will chew on leaves, excreting a sticky substance that can cause fungus and bacteria on plants. A blast of water from a hose aimed directly onto the leaves of plants will often be enough to remove them. There are also natural organic spray solutions available that can be made at home, everything from soapy water with a pinch of cayenne to alcohol spray.

HOW TO TURN A PLASTIC BOTTLE INTO AN

IRRIGATED PLANTER

START

Take a large plastic bottle with a screw cap and make 1 to 3 very tiny holes in the cap. Fill up the bottle with water, screw on the cap, and turn it upside down. Insert the neck of the bottle into the soil. This will act as a drip irrigation, which is particularly handy when you are going out of town.

FINISH

CROP

ROTATION

Even though it is tempting to repeat your garden pattern, it is best to give vegetables of the same family a new spot in the garden or containers each year. This will ensure that any lingering pests and diseases won't be in the soil and that the new plant will have a strong start in the garden.

THESE ARE THE VEGETABLE FAMILIES TO KEEP IN MIND AS YOU PLAN YOUR ROTATION

Amaranths Family: Beet, chard, spinach, quinoa

Cabbage (BRASSICAS) Family: Broccoli, Brussels sprouts, cabbage, cauliflower, Chinese cabbage, kohlrabi, mustard greens, radish, rutabaga, turnip

Cucumber (CUCURBITS) Family: Cucumber, gourd, muskmelon, pumpkin, squash, watermelon, zucchini

Grasses: Corn, millet, rice, barley, wheat, rye

Legumes Family: Peas, lentils, soybeans, broad beans

Nightshades Family: Potatoes, eggplant, tomatoes, hot and sweet peppers, okra

Onion (ALLIUMS) Family: Chive, garlic, leek, onion, shallot

Sunflower Family: Endive, Jerusalem artichokes, lettuce, sunflowers, salsify

Umbelliferous Family: Carrot, celery, parsnip, parsley, fennel, celeriac, coriander, cilantro

HOW TO

WEED

BY NOT WEEDING

This is my favorite way to deal with weeds when the season begins—no uprooting required! It saves you time and also increases worm activity in your soil so that if you do eventually want to work the soil, it is soft and pliable. You will need a lot of cardboard, which you can often get for free at bike shops, grocery stores, and random Dumpsters near you. Alternatively, you can use thick layers of newspapers. This method also works for planting bulbs in the fall that you want to come up weed-free in the spring, since the cardboard will have disintegrated in time. Before you start, don't forget to eat at least a few handfuls of your delicious edible weeds before covering them! Purslane, dandelion greens, and wild garlic are some of my favorites (see pages 216, 217, and 220 for recipes).

Early in the season, lay the cardboard over the weedy area that you want to garden, then cover the cardboard with a 6-inch layer of mulch, compost, straw, grass clippings, and the like.

Now wait for the worms to do the work for you. Without light the weeds will die; in the meantime, the cardboard will begin to deteriorate. You will be able to plant right into the new bed. Check every few weeks to see if the cardboard has rotted and the soil is pliable.

HOW TO

SAVE SEEDS

FOR THE FUTURE, ESPECIALLY HEIRLOOMS

There are two components to seed saving—harvesting the seeds and storing them. But the process really begins with choosing which plants to grow. Many seed growers sell hybrids because they are bred to have certain qualities—like long shelf life and disease resistance. These varieties don't grow true to form when the seeds are saved and replanted. So if you are saving seeds, only do it with nonhybrids since they are self-pollinating and will grow again true to type.

1. To save seeds like peas or beans, simply let them dry on the vine and shell them. For fleshy fruits—like a tomato—let the fruit become overripe on the vine. Scrape out the seeds, and let them soak in a jar of water until they begin to ferment and the light white seeds and pulp float to the top. Pour off and discard what has floated to the top, then transfer the heavy, dark, fertile seeds at the bottom of the jar to single layers of paper towel on a flat surface. Let them dry (for a day or two), and then separate them as best as you can.

2. To store the seeds, place them in an envelope and seal it. Label it clearly with the date they were saved and the specific variety of plant. Store them in a cool, dry, dark place. If they get wet, the seeds will be activated, depleting them of the nutrients needed for them to grow later. Adding silica packets to the envelope will ensure they stay dry.

3. Share your heirloom seeds with other growers to help keep them in circulation. Seed-swapping events take place all over the country and are facilitated by botanical and community gardens (see Find It, page 296).

OTHER CONSIDERATIONS

1 Save the seeds from fruits that look most true to their form. Plant them again the following year to see if they stay true to type. If you plant your first seeds early enough, you can gain a season by planting a second crop from the freshly picked seeds in the same season.

2 Don't plant all of your seeds of a particular variety at one time. Instead, save a few in case some don't germinate or poor weather causes crop failure. This way you will never lose a variety completely.

3 If you do grow heirlooms, keep an eye out for mutations. That is how family varieties start; one variety of vegetable or fruit mutates from a particular variety and when replanted, it stays true to its new form. Give it a name and call it your own.

4 If you want to grow hybrid seeds, plant them as far away as you can from your heirlooms to avoid crossing, or plant them at different times so the flowers don't pollinate one another. This is especially true where there are a lot of bumblebees, which are aggressive about pollinating certain flowers, like the bean blossom.

THE SHELF LIFE OF COMMON SEEDS

Beans: 3 years
Beets: 3 to 4 years
Cabbage: 3 to 5 years
Carrots: 1 to 3 years
Cauliflower: 4 to 5 years
Corn, sweet: 2 years
Cucumbers: 5 years
Eggplant: 4 years
Kale: 3 years
Lettuce: 4 to 5 years
Melons: 4 years
Onions: 1 year
Peas: 1 to 3 years
Peppers: 2 years
Pumpkin: 4 years
Radishes: 3 to 5 years
Spinach: 3 to 5 years
Squash: 4 years
Swiss Chard: 4 years
Tomatoes: 3 to 4 years
Turnips: 5 years
Watermelons: 5 years

THE EASIEST SEEDS TO SAVE

BEANS

CILANTRO (that has been allowed to bolt and go to seed)

DILL (that has been allowed to bolt and go to seed)

LETTUCE (that has been allowed to bolt and go to seed)

PEAS

PEPPERS

TOMATOES

HOW TO STORE SEEDS

Use a photo album to store seed packets. It is nice and neat and easy to sort through. Just make sure the seeds are stored in a cool, dry place. Alternatively, store them in the refrigerator or freezer.

THE BEST SEEDS TO BUY

WHEN BUYING SEEDS, LOOK FOR PACKETS MARKED "OP" (OPEN-POLLINATED), WHICH MEANS THEY WERE POLLINATED BY INSECTS, BIRDS, THE WIND, OR OTHER NATURAL MECHANISMS AND WILL THUS STAY TRUE TO TYPE WHEN REPLANTED. THESE MAY BE HARD TO FIND AT YOUR LOCAL GARDEN STORE, BUT THEY CAN BE FOUND ONLINE (SEE FIND IT, PAGE 296).

HERBS

FRESH HERBS ABSOLUTELY TRANSFORM ANY DISH. Even a humdrum frozen meal can be made into something worthwhile with a scattering of fresh herbs on top. And there is something about picking your morning brew for tea fresh from the windowsill that sets a good tempo for the day. They will also add vibrancy to very plain, repetitive foods, and are thus useful to dry and store to have on hand, especially in the colder months when there is less diversity in your garden.

HOW TO CUT HERBS

When herb plants are about 8 inches tall you should start pruning them and using the clippings in your recipes. The more you do this, the healthier your herbs will grow. By pruning back a plant, you send it into emergency defense mode and it will begin shooting off extra leaves in all directions, making the plant bushy and full rather than tall and spindly. For this reason, it is much better to cut the stems than pluck the leaves when harvesting. It will force water and nutrients to the remaining leaves and stem instead of wasting the plant's energy on the stem where the leaves have already been plucked.

Always cut your herbs in the morning. As the sun gets hotter the natural oils retreat into the stem and away from the leaves, so cutting them early will ensure that what you harvest is the most potent. If your herbs are outdoors, stop pruning 3 to 4 weeks before the first frost so that the plants can harden off and survive the winter.

1. When you are ready to prune and harvest herbs, rinse them first with a garden hose or watering can to remove any excess dirt.

2. For leafy herbs like basil, mint, and lemon verbena, cut the main stem, close above the second set of leaves from the base. For herbs with more woody branches like thyme and rosemary, cut back the oldest branches so that more tender growth will sprout. Keeping them on the stem rather than just picking the leaves will help preserve their fragrant oils.

3. If you decide to rinse them after they have been cut, do it gently, and dry them in a salad spinner or on a layer of paper towel.

START A COFFEE TIN

HERB GARDEN

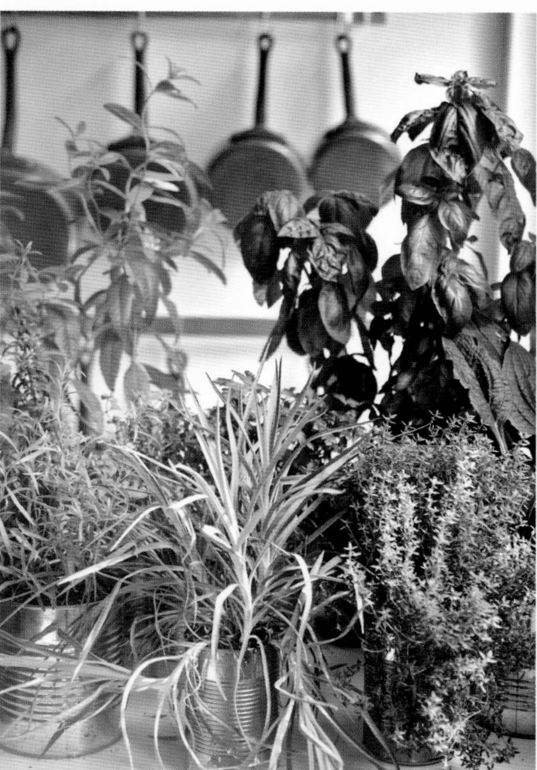

TENT HERBS

IN THE WINTER

To keep herbs inside over the winter, they will need a lot of moisture. Set the pots on a tray of pebbles, tent the plant stems under a plastic bag, and spray the leaves with water to help increase the humidity on the windowsill. The tray will catch the water you add over time, and the pebbles will keep the plants from sitting in it.

The closer your herbs are to your kitchen, the more you will use them, which is why this method of container herbs is most practical. Upcycled coffee tins are an attractive and portable way to grow herbs. In these tins you prolong their life so that you can enjoy them in the summer on your steps or fire escape, and bring them indoors easily for the winter. You can move the tins wherever the sun is and wherever they look most stylish. And it doesn't just have to be coffee tins; for larger plants use large tomato cans, large olive oil cans, and anything else you can dream up.

1. If you are planting your herbs from seed, level off your soil and sprinkle the seeds on top.
2. Pat them down and sprinkle with water, but don't cover them with soil. They will take longer than most plants to germinate, up to 3 weeks. Or you can give yourself a nice head start by using small plants from the nursery.
3. Poke holes in the tin can with a hammer and nail at the bottom and on the sides, then add extra soil to the can, transferring the plant from the plastic container to the can and watering thoroughly.
4. The best plants you can grow are ones that are compact and bushy because they have the most concentrated oils. You won't need to fertilize them other than once in the beginning of the season.
5. They are best harvested right as their flowers start blooming, which is when they are most potent. As the season chugs along, prune them and shape them to your liking, snipping off the flowers to encourage outward growth, and using the clippings for your meals.

HOW TO

PRESERVE

YOUR OWN HERBS

There are several ways to preserve your herbs for the cold months when there is less flavor variety available in your garden. The preserved herbs will be in their best state if kept in a cool, dark place for up to three months, and should be discarded once you can preserve the next year's harvest.

Hanging

The most decorative way to preserve herbs is in bundles, hanging upside down from a rack or windowsill. The longer drying time may cause a slight loss in potency, but it is worth it. You can do bouquets of the same variety, or mix and match herb combinations. You will want to dry them in a cooler place than you would vegetables because they are more delicate. You can protect them from the elements by drying them in a paper bag upside down in an airy place. Once the herbs are dry enough to crumble easily in your hand, remove the leaves from the stalks and store the leaves in small, tightly sealed containers. The less air in the container, the better the shelf life of the herbs will be.

Heat

For seed herbs like fennel seed, let the plants mature until the seeds separate from the dry flower clusters easily. They will have lost their green color by then but not so much so that they drop on their own. Cut the heads off and spread them on a brown paper bag in the sun, stirring them around occasionally. Do this for several days, but take them in at night. Once they are thoroughly dry, store them in sealed mason jars in a cool, dark place for up to a year.

A dehydrator set to 95°F will work well to dry herbs, as will laying them on a tray in the open air. You could also use an oven at its lowest temperature with the door ajar, or simply leave the pilot light on. The time it takes will vary depending on the moisture content of your herbs, so check them every hour. And if you want to be really efficient about it, you can even do it in the microwave, 30 seconds at a time. The goal is warm but not too hot. Keep in mind that some of the more delicate herbs like basil and thyme will lose their potency if they are heated in an oven or microwave, so it's best to hang or freeze them.

Freezing

Herbs with tender leaves, like basil and lemon verbena, freeze and maintain their color better than others. They retain more of their fresh flavor when frozen, versus the more potent flavor when dried. Rinse the herbs and lay them to dry for several hours until they wilt. Then transfer them into containers or packages that will freeze well and store in the freezer. They are now ready to cook with, or turn into compound butters (see page 54) or flavored oils.

KEEP PRESERVED HERBS GREEN

To help them maintain their color, blanch the herbs prior to freezing them: Bring a large pot of water to a rolling boil and prepare a bowl of ice water on the side. Hold the herbs by their stems and dip them into the boiling water for 10 seconds, being careful not to burn yourself, then drop them into the ice bath. Pat them dry on paper towels and then transfer them to freezer bags with stems on or off.

Basil is particularly prone to turning black, so the best solution is to puree the leaves in a blender with a few dashes of olive oil and then freeze it as a paste. You can then thaw it and turn it into pesto with the addition of garlic, grated Parmesan, walnuts, and more olive oil, or you can use the paste for stirring into vegetables, spreading onto roasted meats, and so on.

SAVORY
THyme
TARRAGON
OREGANO
SAGe

HERB BOUQUET COMBINATIONS FOR COOKING

CLASSIC BOUQUET FOR STOCKS AND SOUPS:
parsley stems (not leaves), black peppercorns, thyme, bay leaf

FOR COOKING BEEF AND OTHER RED MEATS:
bay leaf, thyme, marjoram, savory, and 1 sprig of rosemary

FOR COOKING FISH AND OTHER DELICATE SEAFOOD:
bay leaf, thyme, fennel, celery leaves

FOR COOKING THE BEST ROASTED CHICKEN AND OTHER BIRDS:
bay leaf, thyme, tarragon, lemon peel

FOR COOKING PORK:
bay leaf, thyme, sage, fennel, marjoram, rosemary

FOR TOMATO SAUCES:
bay leaf, thyme, basil, oregano

THE BEST HERBS TO GROW AND DRY FOR TEA

ANGELICA	BASIL
BERGAMOT	BORAGE
CALENDULA	CATNIP
CHAMOMILE	FENNEL
HYSSOP	LAVENDER
LEMON BALM	
LEMON GEM AND ORANGE GEM MARIGOLDS	
LEMON VERBENA	
MONARDA	PEPPERMINT
PINEAPPLE SAGE	
ROSEMARY	SAGE
SCENTED GERANIUMS	
SPEARMINT	STEVIA
THYME	VIOLETS
WOODRUFF	

THE BEST HERBS TO GROW FOR SAVORY COOKING

Basil	Garlic
Bay Leaf	Lemon Balm
Caraway	Lovage
Chervil	Marjoram
Chives	Mint
Coriander	Oregano
Dill	Parsley
Fennel	Rosemary

THE BEST HERBS TO GROW FOR MEDICINE

Chamomile (for tense muscles)
Echinacea (for colds and flu)
Feverfew (for headaches)
Horehound (for coughs)
Hyssop (for sore throats)
Lemon Balm (for stomachaches)
Peppermint (aids indigestion)
Rosemary (for sore throats)
Sage (for sore throats)
Thyme (for detoxifying and immunity boosting)
Yarrow (for inflammation)

THE BEST HERBS TO GROW FOR DESSERTS

Anise

Basil

Chamomile

Lavender

Lemon Balm

Lemon Verbena

Mint

Rosemary

Scented Geraniums

Stevia

Thyme

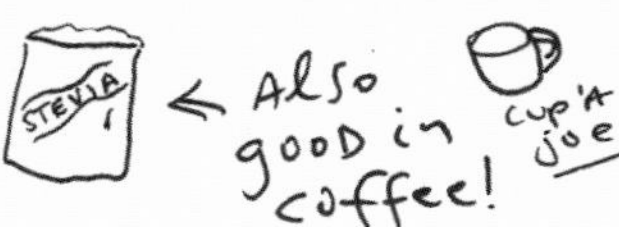

EDIBLE FLOWERS

A handful of edible flowers sprinkled over a summer salad is a sensory experience. So don't neglect to plant flowers in your garden—just make sure they are edible ones! Here are some beauties to consider:

BACHELOR'S BUTTON/ CORNFLOWER	DAYLILY	NASTURTIUM
BORAGE	DIANTHUS	ROSE PETALS
CALENDULA	ELDERFLOWER	SQUASH BLOSSOMS
CHIVE BLOSSOMS	GARLIC FLOWERS	SUNFLOWER
CLOVE PINKS	LAVENDER	VIOLAS
DANDELION	LILAC	VIOLET
	MARIGOLD	

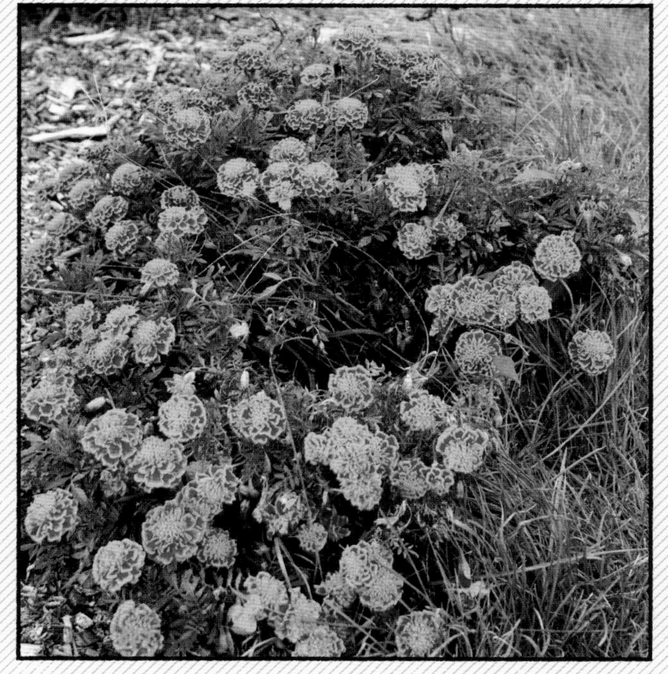

RECIPES

THESE RECIPES USE THE FRUITS, VEGETABLES, HERBS, AND FLOWERS suggested in this chapter, all of which can be grown well in small domestic spaces. They are simple, accessible ways to enjoy your harvest, allowing the pure fruits of your labor to shine and making you a more self-sufficient eater in the process.

VEGETABLE AND FRUIT RECIPES

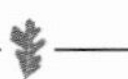

CARROT BUTTER

MAKES 1 CUP

This is a flavored butter that relies on the juice of carrots rather than the typical herbs and onions you see in many compound butters. I like to keep this on hand in the refrigerator or freezer and use it to flavor steamed vegetables or spread on morning toast with a sprinkling of cinnamon or coarse salt flakes. If you don't have a juicer, carrot juice is available at many grocery and health food stores these days, in the refrigerated section or even freshly pressed at juice bars.

PREP TIME: 5 minutes
COOK TIME: 15 minutes
TOTAL TIME: 20 minutes

- 1½ cups pure freshly pressed carrot juice
- ½ teaspoon ground cumin
- ½ teaspoon ground coriander
- ¼ teaspoon paprika
- 16 tablespoons (2 sticks) cold unsalted butter, cut into tablespoons
- Salt and freshly ground black pepper to taste

1. In a small nonreactive saucepan, simmer the carrot juice over a low heat until it is reduced to a fourth and covers the bottom of the pan by about a quarter inch, about 10 minutes.
2. Turn off the heat and whisk in the cumin, coriander, and paprika.
3. Over low heat, whisk in the cubes of cold butter two at a time, letting each cube melt halfway before adding the next two. Taste and add salt and pepper as needed.
4. Transfer the liquid to a half-pint mason jar, cover with a lid, and immediately put it in the refrigerator for 2 weeks or in the freezer for up to 6 months.

BUTTERED RADISHES

SERVES 6

Radishes are one of the simplest and most rewarding vegetables to grow for a beginning gardener. Simple spicy radish with a dollop of high-quality soft butter and a sprinkling of salt is an equally satisfying and simple way to enjoy them. Make this recipe in advance for a gathering with a bunch of multicolored heirloom radishes. Spice them up with your favorite herbs and seasonings like saffron, curry, and fennel seeds.

PREP TIME: 5 minutes
COOK TIME: 20 seconds
INACTIVE TIME: 30 minutes
TOTAL TIME: 35 minutes, 20 seconds

4 tablespoons (½ stick) cold unsalted butter
1 bunch (12 to 15 pieces) radishes, washed and stems trimmed down to 2 inches
Coarse sea salt to taste
Saffron threads or ground saffron (optional)

1. Place the butter in a small ramekin or glass bowl and microwave on high for 10 seconds. Check it by stirring with a spoon to see if it is the consistency that you want: opaque and creamy, thin but not clear, like melted chocolate. If it is not there, repeat for 10 seconds more, and then check again. Repeat until the butter is barely melted and stirring it with a spoon melts any last lumps. (If you take it too far, walk away and let it cool.)
2. Dip each radish into the butter, give it a shake, and dip it again. Lay it on a plate and repeat with the remaining radishes.
3. Sprinkle the radishes with the salt and saffron, if desired, and refrigerate for 30 minutes. The butter will harden and the seasonings will stay stuck to the surface of the radish.
4. Serve as party appetizers or an afternoon snack.

STUFFED
SQUASH BLOSSOMS

SERVES 4 AS AN APPETIZER

Toward the end of the season, when you have had your fill of garden squash, pick the blossoms that form on the vines before they bear fruit. They are less likely to mature into full fruit anyway as the weather gets colder, and the flowers themselves have a delicate squash flavor, so they are wonderful tossed in salads or deep fried and stuffed with delicious things. And if you aren't growing squash in your garden, farmers' markets and even some grocery stores have plenty of blossoms toward the end of summer and into fall.

PREP TIME: 15 minutes
COOK TIME: 5 minutes
TOTAL TIME: 20 minutes

- ½ cup grated Parmesan or Pecorino Romano
- Zest of 1 lemon
- ¼ cup finely diced shallots
- ¼ cup finely chopped fresh basil
- ½ cup ricotta cheese
- ½ cup panko bread crumbs
- 8 large squash blossoms
- 3 tablespoons unsalted butter or grape-seed oil
- ¼ teaspoon salt, plus more for sprinkling on the finished blossoms

1. In a small bowl, combine the cheese, lemon zest, shallots, basil, ricotta, and bread crumbs and mix well with a spoon. The mixture will be crumbly but should pull together well when pressed. If it is too dry, add more ricotta.
2. Gently open the squash blossoms with your fingers. Using a teaspoon or your fingers, fill the insides with the mixture until it is plump (about 2 tablespoons depending on the size of the blossom), and press the tips of the petals together with your fingers to seal.

3. Add the butter to a skillet over medium heat. When the butter is hot, brown the squash blossoms on all sides, 4 to 5 minutes total.
4. Transfer to a dish, sprinkle with a touch of salt, and serve.

TIPSY
WATERMELON SALAD

SERVES 4

Watermelon varieties are available in dwarf sizes and don't require the land you might think you would need to grow them. The fruit can be served with savory ingredients as much as sweet ones. Here is a little savory medley with a boozy dressing for a decidedly grownup salad. Basil can be substituted for arugula, which is equally delicious though not as spicy.

PREP TIME: 10 minutes
COOK TIME: None
TOTAL TIME: 10 minutes

2 tablespoons whiskey
Juice of 1 lime
2 tablespoons extra virgin olive oil
1 pinch cayenne pepper
1 small watermelon, well chilled, rind removed, and cut into ¾-inch thick rectangles, about 4 cups
Maldon salt flakes or coarse sea salt to taste
Freshly ground black pepper to taste
1 small fennel bulb, very thinly shaved
2 cups baby arugula leaves

1. In a small bowl, add the whiskey, lime juice, olive oil, and cayenne pepper and whisk to combine.

2. Lay a thick rectangle of watermelon on a plate and sprinkle with salt and pepper. Top with shaved fennel and arugula. Drizzle several tablespoons of the whiskey dressing over the top of it all, finish off with another sprinkle of salt and more pepper, and serve.

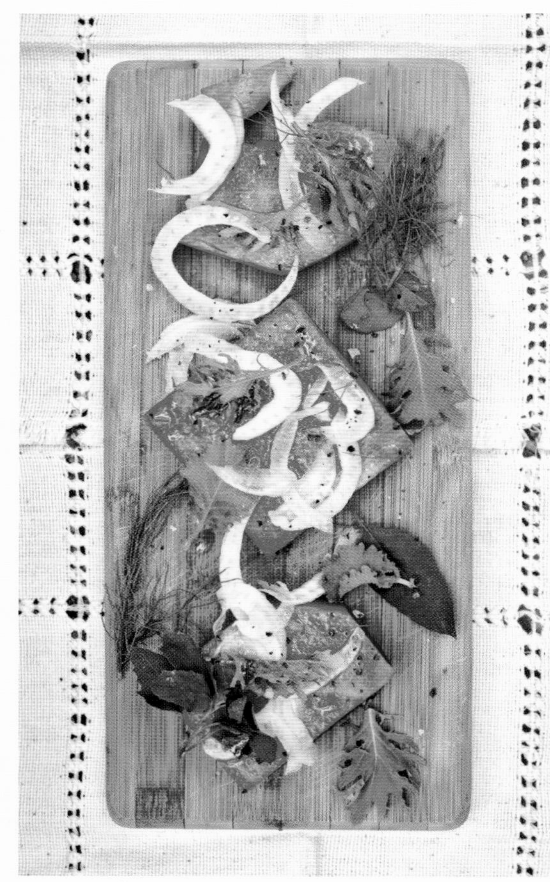

HOW TO

MAKE A WATERMELON KEG

MAKES 8 TO 12 CUPS, DEPENDING ON THE SIZE OF THE WATERMELON

Grandma Pellegrini and Great-Aunt Gray used to love to have garden parties, and I like to think that this would have been my creative contribution. A watermelon keg is a festive way to serve beverages on a hot summer day. You can then fill the keg with whatever liquid you would like. Simply add water or a clear alcohol, which will then absorb the watermelon. Since the size of a watermelon will vary, keep in mind that there should be a 1:1 ratio between the amount of flesh and the amount of alcohol or water, and save any remaining watermelon for a Tipsy Watermelon Salad (opposite). You will need a spigot to make a proper keg, which can be purchased at home-brewing stores or on the Internet.

PREP TIME: 10 minutes
COOK TIME: None
TOTAL TIME: 10 minutes

1 medium oval watermelon
4 to 6 cups of water or alcohol

1. Cut off ½ inch from the bottom end of the watermelon so that it sits on a flat surface. Cut about 2 inches from the top end, cutting through the rind completely in order to get at the flesh.
2. Using a large spoon, scoop out the watermelon flesh from the top of the watermelon and transfer it to a bowl, making sure to leave about 3 inches of flesh at the bottom of the watermelon for the spigot to nestle into.
3. Determine where to place the spigot on the surface of the watermelon, then press it firmly into the rind to make an indentation. Using a pointed paring knife, create a small opening, making sure to cut inside the line of the circular indentation.
4. Press the spigot gently into the hole. Scrape away the flesh on the inside of the watermelon to reveal the end of the spigot.
5. In a blender, combine 4 to 6 cups of watermelon flesh with 4 to 6 cups of water or alcohol. Fill the watermelon with the liquid and serve over ice.

SPICY RED PEPPER HUMMUS

MAKES 3 CUPS

The color of this hummus is a fabulous bold orange and the red peppers add an underlying sweetness. Keep some of the seeds from your jalapeños in the mix for a nice kick. The more you take out, the less spicy it will be, and unlike many peppers, jalapeños become much milder as you cook them. If you want to kick the heat up a notch, try other peppers like the flavorful habanero. As the hummus sits over the next day, the flavor will improve.

PREP TIME: 10 minutes
COOK TIME: 15 minutes
TOTAL TIME: 25 minutes

- ½ cup plus 4 tablespoons extra virgin olive oil
- 2 red bell peppers, seeded and chopped
- 4 jalapeños peppers, seeds reserved and chopped
- ¼ cup chopped shallots
- 8 cloves garlic, chopped
- Salt and freshly ground black pepper to taste
- 2½ cups canned chickpeas, rinsed and drained
- 1 tablespoon fresh lemon juice

1. Add 4 tablespoons of the olive oil to heat a heavy-bottomed 10-inch skillet over medium-high heat, and add the red peppers, jalapeños, shallots, and garlic and sweat until soft, about 10 minutes.
2. Season with salt and pepper to taste to help release the juices and stir with a wooden spoon. Add the chickpeas and cook, stirring often, until the mixture is softened further and the juices have reduced slightly, about 5 minutes.
3. Turn off the heat and let cool slightly. Transfer the mixture to a food processor or blender and blend, adding the remaining ½ cup of olive oil in a slow thin stream as you do.
4. Transfer to a bowl and adjust the seasoning with salt and pepper to taste. Cool to room temperature, then whisk in the lemon juice. Store in the refrigerator for up to 1 week.

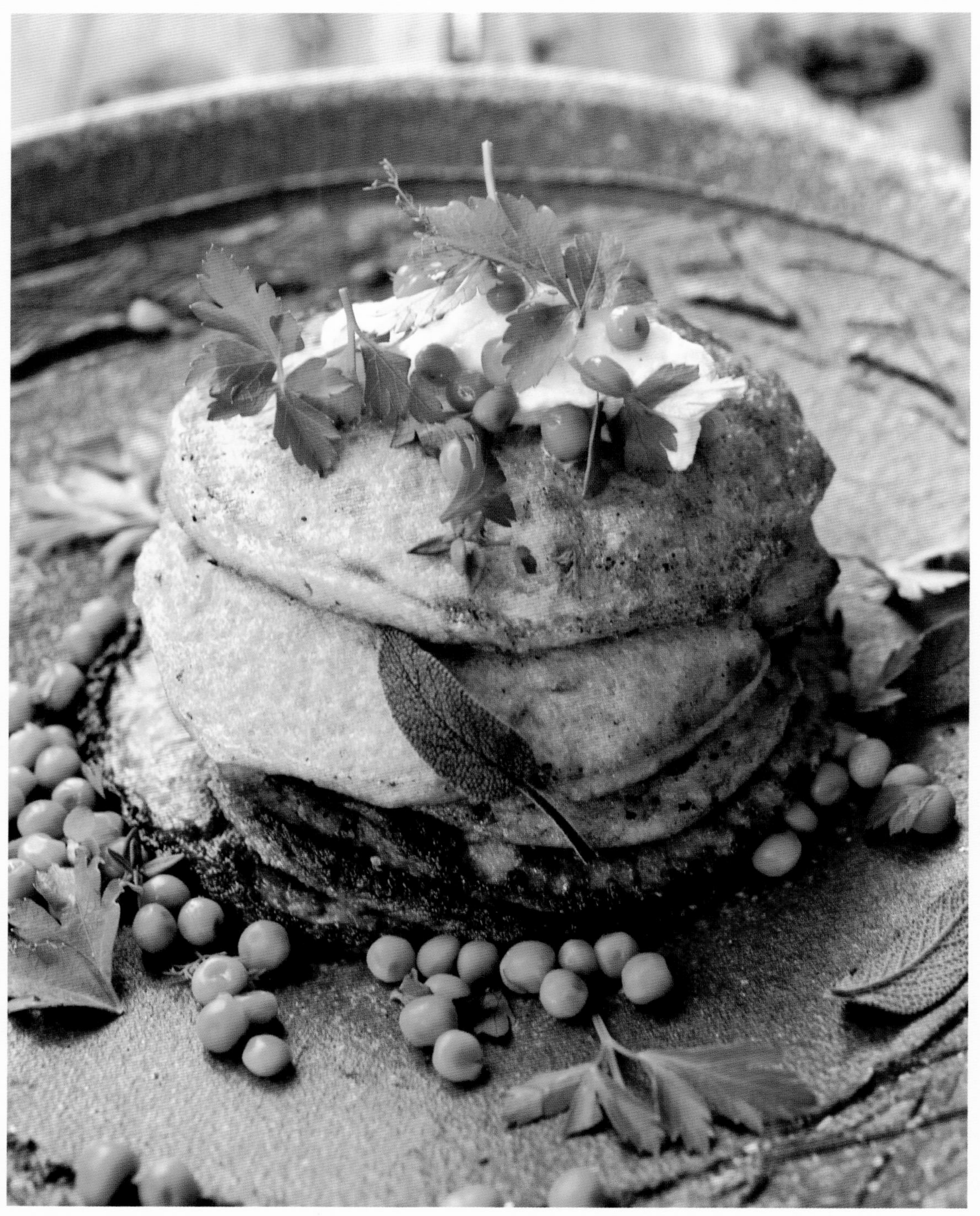

PEA PANCAKES

SERVES 4, ABOUT 12 PANCAKES

Peas grow so well on just a trellis or fence with a little bit of soil. With their intense pea flavor, this recipe is perfect as a savory appetizer, more dense and delicate than your traditional pancakes. For small canapés use 1 tablespoon of batter rather than 2. Cook them gently, low, and slow, with a cover so they don't lose their beautiful green color while they cook. A dollop of plain Greek yogurt on top and some fresh herbs bring them to a whole new level. Diced ham, caviar, and crumbled bacon would also be a perfect garnish.

PREP TIME: 1 minute
COOK TIME: 15 minutes
TOTAL TIME: 16 minutes

- ½ pound shelled sweet peas, fresh or frozen
- 1 teaspoon kosher salt
- 1 large egg
- 1 large egg yolk
- 1 cup heavy cream
- 4 tablespoons all-purpose flour
- ½ teaspoon baking powder
- 1 tablespoon lemon zest
- 1 teaspoon freshly ground black pepper
- 2 to 3 tablespoons unsalted butter
- Crème fraîche or plain yogurt (optional)
- Fresh herbs like tarragon, parsley, and chervil (optional)

1. In a medium saucepan, cover the peas with water, add the salt, and bring to a simmer. Cook until tender, about 5 minutes for fresh peas, and 1 minute for frozen. Strain and transfer to the bowl of a food processor to cool, reserving a few peas for garnish.

2. Once the peas have cooled, add the egg and egg yolk and puree. Add the cream, flour, baking powder, lemon zest, and pepper, and pulse to combine.

3. Melt 1 tablespoon of butter in a heavy-bottomed skillet over medium heat. Drop about 2 tablespoons of batter per pancake into the skillet, making sure not to crowd the pan. Cover and turn the heat down to very low and cook for about 3 minutes per side, flipping the pancakes gently. Repeat this until all of your batter is used. To avoid greasy pancakes, only add butter to the pan as needed. If the pan becomes greasy or too hot, remove it from the heat for several minutes between batches and wipe it out with paper towels.

4. Serve the pancakes warm, with a dollop of crème fraîche or plain yogurt mixed with your favorite herbs and some extra peas, if desired.

ONION COMPOTE

MAKES 1 CUP

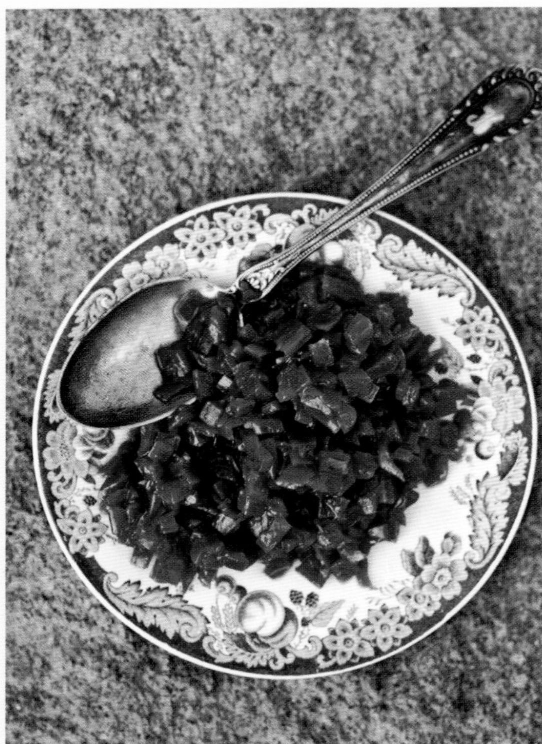

This is a great way to cook onions before you can them because the compote is so versatile for other dishes. I especially like it on pork chops or with smoked fish. When selecting a cooking wine, a cabernet or darker grape is best; pinot noir will produce a light-colored marmalade that isn't quite as dramatic, and the hue is half the fun. Also, be sure to cook the onions until they are very tender, without any bite, for the best flavor.

PREP TIME: 5 minutes
COOK TIME: 10 minutes
TOTAL TIME: 15 minutes

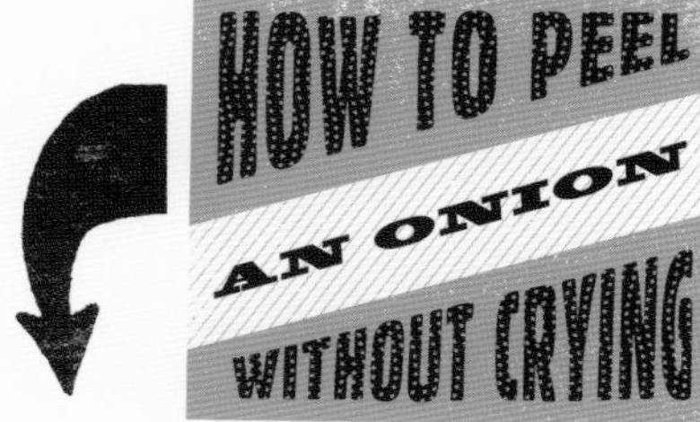

SOME MAY CALL THIS AN OLD WIVES' TALE, BUT IT HAS ALWAYS HELPED ME CONSIDERABLY. IF YOUR EYES TEND TO WEEP WHILE YOU CHOP ONIONS, PUT A TOOTHPICK BETWEEN YOUR TEETH AND CLENCH DOWN BEFORE CHOPPING.

- 1 medium white or yellow onion, minced or finely diced
- 1 cup red wine, preferably cabernet or another full-bodied variety
- 1 tablespoon raspberry vinegar
- 1 tablespoon port
- ¼ cup extra virgin olive oil
- 1 tablespoon fresh lemon juice
- Salt to taste

1. Combine the onion, wine, vinegar, and port in a medium saucepan. Bring to a boil, then reduce to a simmer and cook until all the ingredients are tender and almost all liquid is reduced, about 10 minutes.
2. Remove from the heat, transfer the mixture to a bowl, and slowly whisk in the olive oil, lemon juice, and salt to taste.
3. Let cool slightly and adjust the seasonings to taste again. Serve at room temperature. Stores in the refrigerator for up to 1 week.
4. Alternatively, you can process the compote in a hot-water bath (see page 144) for 5 minutes. It will store in a cool, dark place for up to 12 months.

MELON AGUA FRESCA

SERVES 6, ABOUT 8 CUPS

Translated as "fresh water," this beverage is commonly sold on the streets of Mexico. Sometimes you will see it made from seeds or hibiscus flowers, but my favorite is with fruit, which requires little, if any, added sugar and makes use of the garden's bounty.

PREP TIME: 30 minutes **TOTAL TIME:** 30 minutes
COOK TIME: None

- 8 cups seeded and cubed melon, such as cantaloupe, watermelon, or honeydew (about 5 pounds whole)
- 1 tablespoon agave nectar or honey
- ¼ cup fresh lime juice
- Mint leaves, lemon verbena, or other favorite herb for garnish
- Crushed ice to serve
- Lime slices for garnish

1. In a blender, process half the melon with ½ cup of water until smooth.
2. Pour the mixture through a fine-mesh strainer into a wide-mouth pitcher, using a rubber spatula or wooden spoon to press the liquid through the pulp and seeds. Alternatively, strain the mixture into a bowl, then ladle the finished drink into a pitcher. Repeat this process with the remaining melon and ½ cup water, adding the tablespoon of agave nectar or honey to the second batch.
3. Stir in the lime juice. Muddle the mint leaves in the bottom of the six glasses. Add ice, stir the contents of the pitcher, and pour the liquid into the glasses. Garnish with lime slices and whole herbs, along with some additional ice if you wish.

PUMPKIN CHUTNEY

MAKES 3 CUPS

This chutney is earthy and tangy. If you don't have pumpkin available, use your favorite fall squash—butternut or buttercup squash would both work well, and smaller squashes can grow easily in vertical gardens. The orange juice adds a gentle sweetness and should really be fresh squeezed from an orange so as not to overpower the flavor of the chutney. You will be surprised at how the chutney's taste changes for the better as it sits for several days in the refrigerator. Freeze it all winter long to serve alongside pork chops and roasted chicken.

PREP TIME: 20 minutes
COOK TIME: 35 minutes
TOTAL TIME: 55 minutes

- 2 tablespoons extra virgin olive oil
- 1½ pounds pumpkin or other fall squash, peeled and cut into ½-inch cubes, about 6 cups
- ½ cup minced yellow onion
- 1 garlic clove, minced
- Sea salt to taste
- ⅓ cup raisins
- 2 tablespoons light brown sugar
- 1 teaspoon freshly grated ginger
- 1 tablespoon white wine vinegar
- ½ cup freshly squeezed orange juice (the kind in a carton is too strong)
- Zest of 1 lime
- 1 teaspoon grated orange zest
- ½ teaspoon ground cinnamon
- Dash of cayenne pepper
- Freshly ground black pepper to taste

1. In a heavy-bottomed medium Dutch oven or stockpot, heat the olive oil over low heat. Add the pumpkin, onion, garlic, and a dash of sea salt, and sweat over low heat until the squash is slightly tender, stirring occasionally, about 10 minutes.
2. Add the raisins, brown sugar, ginger, vinegar, orange juice, zests, cinnamon, and cayenne and let simmer over low heat for about 25 minutes, stirring regularly until the ingredients are fully tender. Season with salt and black pepper. The flavors will continue to develop as it cools.
3. Serve the chutney at room temperature and store any leftovers in the refrigerator for up to 2 weeks in a sealed container. Alternatively, freeze it in freezer-safe plastic bags for up to a year.

CAULIFLOWER STEAKS

WITH PINE NUT DRESSING

SERVES 4

This is an unexpected way to serve cauliflower and it is especially beautiful to look at on the plate, a reminder that, as Grandma Pellegrini taught me, presentation is equally as important as taste. When served with this tangy and nutty dressing, cauliflower doesn't just look exciting, it tastes exciting as well.

PREP TIME: 5 minutes
COOK TIME: 20 minutes
TOTAL TIME: 25 minutes

- 2 large heads of cauliflower (bonus if you have the purple, green, or yellow variety)
- 1 tablespoon kosher salt
- ¼ cup pine nuts
- ⅛ cup golden raisins
- ¼ cup finely chopped parsley leaves
- ¼ cup extra virgin olive oil
- 4 tablespoons fresh lemon juice
- Salt and freshly ground black pepper to taste
- 2 tablespoons unsalted butter

1. Preheat the oven to 350°F.
2. With a large chef's knife, cut the cauliflower from top to bottom through the largest part of the head, into cross sections about 1½ inches thick. Depending on the size of the cauliflower you should get at least 2 per head.
3. Set the remaining scraps aside and place the 4 cauliflower steaks in one large baking dish, or two medium baking dishes. Pour water into the dish to reach a height of about ½ inch. Sprinkle the steaks with the salt and cover the dish tightly with foil. Place it in the oven for 15 to 20 minutes or until the cauliflower is tender when pierced with a knife.
4. Remove the dish from the oven and, using a spatula, carefully transfer the steaks to a plate. Let cool slightly while you make the dressing.
5. In a small bowl, combine the pine nuts, raisins, parsley, olive oil, and lemon juice. Season with salt and pepper and set aside to marinate.
6. To serve the cauliflower steaks, melt the butter in a large sauté pan over medium heat. Brown the cauliflower in the butter, about 3 minutes per side, until browned like a steak. Remove to a serving dish and drizzle with the dressing.

TURN CAULIFLOWER SCRAPS INTO A GRATIN

With the leftover cauliflower scraps make a cauliflower gratin! Steam the cauliflower pieces in a small amount of water until tender, strain the water, and put the cauliflower in a baking dish with chopped parsley, chopped garlic, and your favorite cheese. Cover with bread crumbs and more cheese and bake in a 350°F oven until golden brown on top, about 15 minutes.

BEET MARSHMALLOWS

MAKES ABOUT 16 1-INCH SQUARE MARSHMALLOWS

I love beets for their beautiful color and versatility. The juice can be used as lipstick, clothing dye, food coloring, paint, and on and on. The flavor and color even shines when incorporated into sweet treats like these marshmallows. You can really use any size dish with sides to mold them. And if beets aren't your thing, substitute the same amount of carrot juice, lime juice, grapefruit juice, or any other flavoring that you please.

PREP TIME: 15 minutes
COOK TIME: 5 minutes
INACTIVE TIME: 2 to 24 hours
TOTAL TIME: 2 hours, 20 minutes

- Vegetable oil, for greasing the pan
- ¼ cup cornstarch
- ⅓ cup powdered sugar
- 1 envelope unflavored powdered gelatin
- ⅓ cup beet juice
- ⅔ cup granulated sugar
- ½ cup light corn syrup
- Pinch of salt

1. With a pastry brush or paper towel, lightly coat a loaf pan or small baking dish with a neutral-flavored oil like grape seed or vegetable.
2. In a small bowl, sift together the cornstarch and powdered sugar.
3. Dust the baking dish with 1 tablespoon of the cornstarch mixture, making sure all surfaces are well-coated. You can leave any excess in the bottom of the dish. Set aside the remaining cornstarch mixture.
4. In a small saucepan, sprinkle the gelatin into the beet juice, and let soak for 5 minutes.
5. Place the saucepan over medium-low heat, and stir in the granulated sugar. Cook, stirring occasionally, until the sugar dissolves completely, about 5 minutes, then turn off the heat. Transfer the mixture into the bowl of an electric mixer. You'll need to scrape the liquid out of the saucepan since it's very sticky.
6. Add the corn syrup and salt, and whisk at a medium speed for about 15 minutes until the mixture is light and fluffy, like Marshmallow Fluff.
7. With a spatula, coax the mixture out of the bowl and into your prepared dish. Smooth out the surface. then let the dish sit at room temperature for 2 hours.
8. Once the mixture has set and has a uniform marshmallow consistency when pressed, wet a knife and gently slide it around the edges of the pan to loosen the sides of the marshmallow from the dish. Cut the marshmallows into any shape you please, wetting your knife every so often to make smooth cuts. You can even use a cookie cutter if you're feeling adventurous.

(continued on page 74)

9 Place a wire rack on top of paper towels. Toss each marshmallow into the remaining cornstarch mixture, shake it to remove any excess powder, and place it on the rack. Cover the marshmallows with a paper towel to prevent debris from sticking to them and let them sit at room temperature for up to 24 hours to allow the outer skin to dry. If you're feeling impatient you could skip this part, but the marshmallows will store better and be less likely to stick together afterward.

10 Store the marshmallows in an airtight container on a cool, dark shelf; they will keep for up to 1 month.

HOMEMADE TINTED LIP GLOSS

4 teaspoons coconut oil

1 teaspoon liquid vitamin E (any kind from capsule or bottle)

4 tablespoons Vaseline or petroleum jelly

½ teaspoon beet juice

If you have leftover beet juice, it can be used to color more than just food. Homemade lip gloss is quick to make and a wonderful gift or stocking stuffer. You can add slightly more or less beet juice depending on how intense a color you would like. There are all kinds of lip gloss tins and containers available online. Or if you want to be thrifty, save your store-bought lip gloss containers and refill them with your homemade concoction.

1 Combine the coconut oil, vitamin E, Vaseline, and beet juice in a small microwave-safe bowl and stir together with a spoon.

2 Microwave on high in 30-second increments until the mixture is pourable. Stir it again and spoon the mixture into lip gloss containers.

3 Let cool at room temperature or in the refrigerator.

4 Use within 3 weeks.

HERB RECIPES

ROSEMARY SYRUP

MAKES 1½ CUPS

Rosemary is one of those woody herbs that maintains its potent flavor even when dried during the winter. This syrup is a wonderful way to sweeten iced or hot tea, simple soda water, fresh lemonade, or a grapefruit cocktail. The sugar water is bursting with a sweet rosemary flavor so a little goes a long way, and of course you can switch the rosemary for so many other herbs. Lemon verbena would be magical.

PREP TIME: 3 minutes
COOK TIME: 15 minutes
INACTIVE TIME: 3 hours
TOTAL TIME: 3 hours, 18 minutes

- ½ cup (about 5 sprigs) loosely packed fresh rosemary, or 1 cup of other whole herbs
- 2 cups sugar

1. Bring 3 cups of water to a boil in a medium saucepan over medium heat.
2. Remove the pan from the heat and add the herbs. Cover and let them steep for 3 hours to strongly infuse the water.
3. Strain the liquid into a medium nonreactive saucepan, add the sugar, and bring to a boil, stirring to dissolve the sugar completely.
4. Boil to thicken, without stirring, for 10 to 12 minutes. Remove the pan from the heat. Let the syrup cool to room temperature, and bottle the syrup. It will store well in the refrigerator for 3 months.

TARRAGON
PANNA COTTA

SERVES 4

Tarragon is one of my favorite herbs—just a few pinches and it transforms a dish. This creamy panna cotta features the tarragon beautifully; it is mildly sweet with a faint anise flavor. Garnish with edible flowers such as nasturtium (see page 53), sugared flowers (see page 86), a few tarragon sprigs, and even a sprinkling of Rosemary Syrup (page 75), and you will have a lush dessert.

PREP TIME: 5 minutes
COOK TIME: 40 minutes
INACTIVE TIME: 2 hours
TOTAL TIME: 2 hours, 45 minutes

- 2 teaspoons powdered gelatin
- 1 cup heavy cream
- 1 cup whole milk
- ¼ cup sugar
- 2 tablespoons packed fresh tarragon leaves

1. In a small bowl, sprinkle the gelatin into 2 tablespoons of cold water and stir. Set aside to let bloom.
2. Place the heavy cream, milk, sugar, and tarragon in a medium nonreactive saucepan and bring to a boil. Immediately remove the pan from the heat, whisk in the gelatin, and let it bloom for 5 minutes.
3. Cover the pan and steep for 30 minutes.
4. Pour through a fine-mesh strainer into a bowl, pushing on the tarragon with a small ladle or spoon to extract all of its flavor.
5. Ladle the panna cotta liquid into 4-ounce ramekins or desired serving dishes and transfer to the refrigerator. Let cool until set.

MINT
ICE MILK

MAKES 1 QUART

This egg-free ice cream is quick and easy to make. It is a slightly sweet and refreshing after-dinner palate cleanser that makes use of summertime's fresh mint, which overruns the garden wherever it grows. Many flavorings suit this recipe, so experiment with other favorite herbs as well: spearmint, lemon verbena, or sage perhaps. And the best part is that you don't need an ice cream machine to make it.

PREP TIME: 5 minutes
COOK TIME: 10 minutes
INACTIVE TIME: 80 minutes
TOTAL TIME: 1 hour, 35 minutes

- 4 cups whole milk
- 1 cup torn fresh mint leaves
- ½ cup sugar

1. Combine the milk, mint, and sugar in a medium saucepan and bring to a boil over medium heat, stirring until the sugar has completely dissolved, about 10 minutes. Remove from the heat, cover partially with a lid, and let the milk infuse with the mint for 20 minutes.
2. Pour the mint milk into a blender and blend until uniform. Let it cool for 10 to 15 minutes, then pour the liquid into a freezer-safe container or baking pan.
3. Place in the freezer until solid and cover the container to store.
4. When ready to serve, let the ice milk sit at room temperature for about 10 minutes, then scrape with a large spoon. It will be slightly slushy, but not as slushy as a granita.

MINT ICE MILK

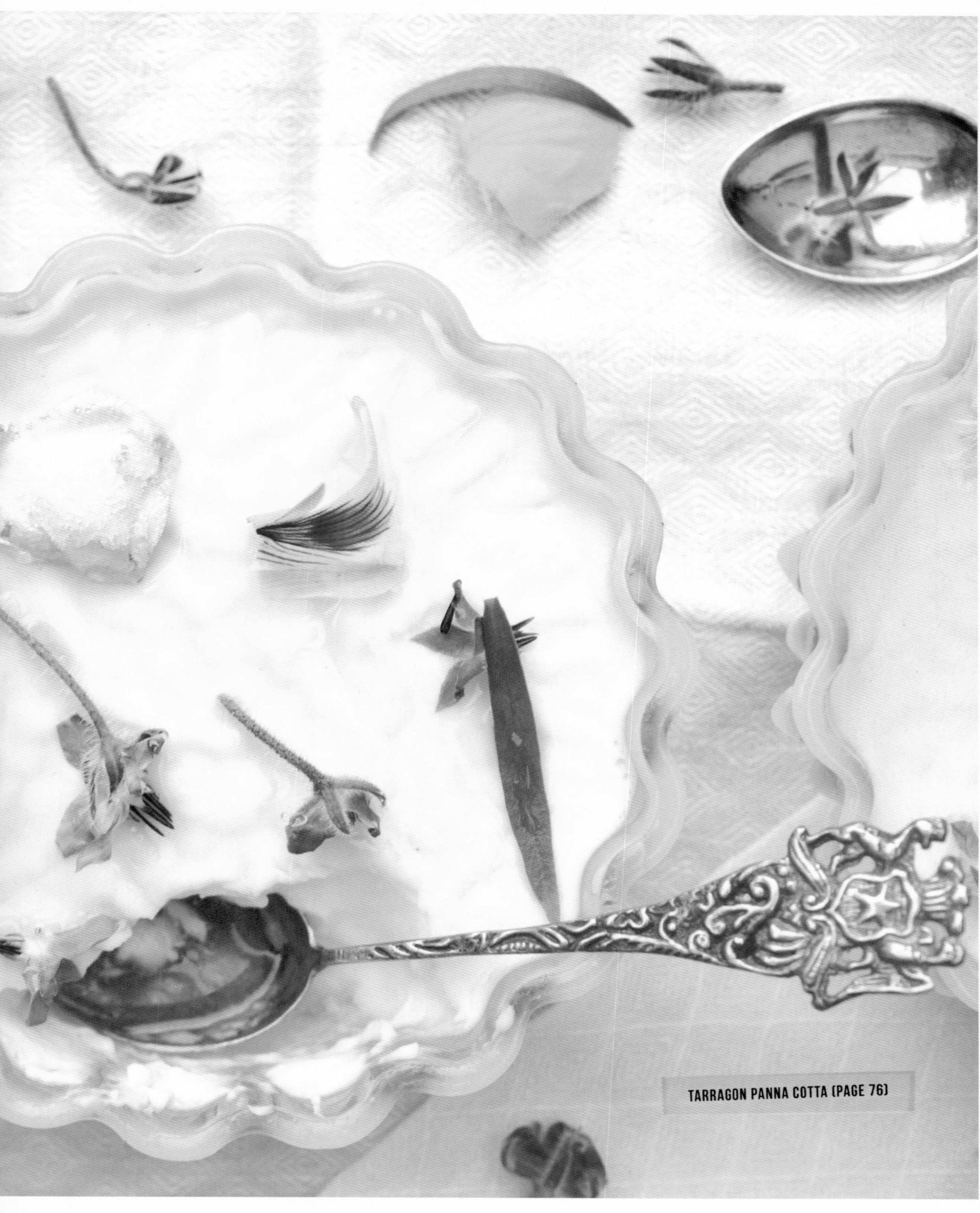

TARRAGON PANNA COTTA (PAGE 76)

LEMON BASIL

ICE CREAM

MAKES 1 QUART; SERVES 6

I can't get enough of basil in the summer; I put it in everything, even my desserts. It has an intoxicating flavor that goes well in so many recipes, from cookies to tomato sauce. Lemon zest brightens the flavor here, while the ice cream has a beautiful pale green color. If you don't have an ice cream maker see "How to Make Ice Cream Without an Ice Cream Maker" (opposite).

PREP TIME: 10 minutes
COOK TIME: 15 minutes
INACTIVE TIME: 80 minutes
TOTAL TIME: 1 hour, 45 minutes

- 2 cups whole milk
- 1 cup heavy cream
- 1 teaspoon lemon zest
- 1½ cups packed torn basil leaves
- Pinch of salt
- 5 large egg yolks
- ¾ cup sugar

1. If you are using an ice cream machine, place the churning bowl in the freezer to cool.
2. In a medium saucepan over medium heat, combine the milk and cream along with the zest, basil, and a pinch of salt. Stir gently and bring to a gentle boil, then immediately remove from the heat, cover partially with a lid, and let infuse for about 20 minutes, until warm but no longer hot.
3. In a separate medium bowl, whisk together the egg yolks and the sugar until they are light in color from the air that you've incorporated. Set aside.
4. Mix the basil milk in a blender until uniform.
5. Temper the yolks by gradually whisking in a bit of the warm liquid. Keep stirring as you pour in the milk mixture, scraping down the sides of the bowl with a wooden spoon to avoid scrambled eggs.
6. Add the tempered egg yolks to the saucepan. Stir the mixture continually with a wooden spoon over low heat until the liquid thickens to the point where you can leave a track with your finger on the back of the spoon, about 10 minutes, and remove the pan from the heat.
7. Let the custard cool for 10 to 15 minutes, then freeze it in an ice cream maker for 50 to 60 minutes, or until thick, or follow the instructions opposite. Transfer the ice cream to a plastic container and store it in the freezer, where it will become firm.

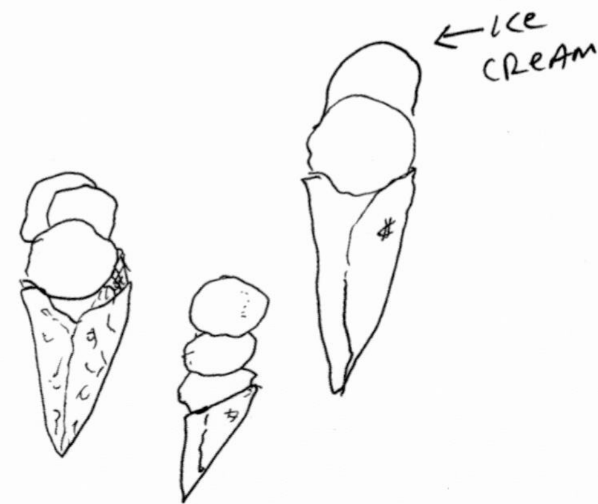

HOW TO MAKE ICE CREAM WITHOUT AN ICE CREAM MAKER

MAKES 1 QUART; SERVES 6

PEOPLE HAVE BEEN MAKING ICE CREAM SINCE LONG BEFORE THE INVENTION OF ELECTRICITY. HOW DID THEY DO IT? START WITH A CREAMY, RICH BASE FOR THE SMOOTHEST TEXTURE POSSIBLE. THEN SIMPLY BREAK UP THE ICE CRYSTALS OVER A PERIOD OF TIME BY HAND, AS THE MIXTURE IS FREEZING IN THE FREEZER.

This is a basic custard recipe to which you can add flavorings such as vanilla, mint leaves, strawberries, chocolate chips, etc. If adding herbs or fruit pieces, let them infuse in the milk as it cools. If incorporating chocolate chips, wait until the mixture is going into the freezer.

PREP TIME: 10 minutes
COOK TIME: 15 minutes
INACTIVE TIME: 2 hours, 30 minutes
TOTAL TIME: 2 hours, 55 minutes

- 2 cups whole milk
- 1 cup heavy cream
- Pinch of salt
- 5 large egg yolks
- ¾ cup sugar

1. Put a 2-quart bowl made of plastic or stainless steel in the freezer. Alternatively, you can use a deep 11 × 7-inch or similar-sized baking dish.
2. Heat the milk and cream along with a pinch of salt in a medium, heavy-bottomed saucepan over medium heat, stirring gently so it doesn't scorch. Bring it up to a gentle boil, then remove the pan from the heat and let cool for 20 minutes.
3. In a medium bowl, whisk together the egg yolks and the sugar until they are light in color from the air that you have incorporated. Temper the yolks by adding a bit of the warm milk to the yolk mixture gradually. Keep stirring continually, scraping down the sides to avoid scrambled eggs.
4. Add the tempered yolks to the saucepan and stir the mixture continually with a wooden spoon over low heat until it thickens to the point where you can leave a track with your finger on the back of the spoon, about 10 minutes. Remove the pan from the heat and let it cool for 10 to 15 minutes.
5. Pour the liquid into the chilled bowl and set it back into the freezer for 45 minutes. Remove the bowl from the freezer and use a spatula or whisk to mix in the frozen edge of the custard, then return it to the freezer. Repeat this process every 30 minutes until the custard is uniformly frozen and creamy.
6. Transfer the mixture to a sealable container and store it for up to 5 days. This type of ice cream should be eaten fairly quickly after it is made.

SAGE SUGAR

MAKES 1 CUP

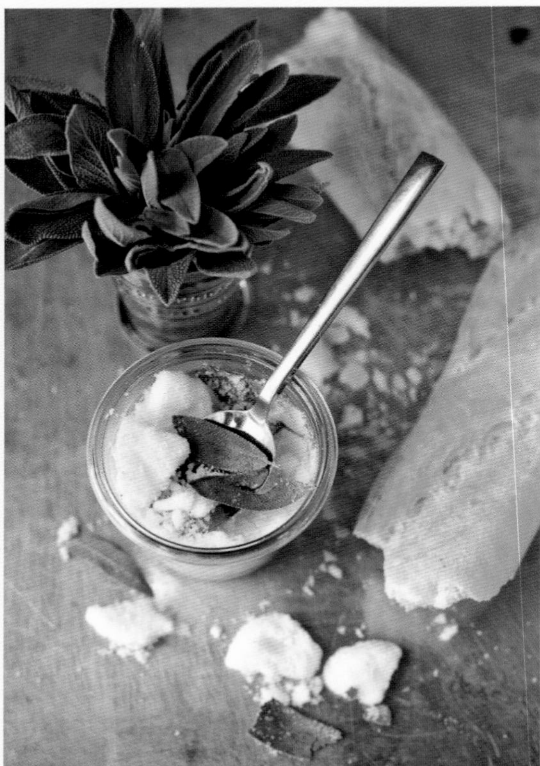

This makes a wonderful gift in an attractive jar and is versatile in the kitchen. Sprinkle it on hot buttered toast or warm scones, stir it into your tea for something special, use it on the icing of cakes or before placing cookies in the oven to bake. Also try thyme, lavender, scented geranium leaves, lemon verbena, bay leaf, and on and on!

PREP TIME: 24 hours
COOK TIME: None
INACTIVE TIME: 2 weeks
TOTAL TIME: 2 weeks, 24 hours

- About ¼ cup whole fresh sage
- 1 cup sugar

1. Pick herbs at their peak, when most fragrant.
2. Trim off any debris or brown bits, give the leaves a light rinse, and pat dry.
3. Place a layer of sage at the bottom of a 1-cup jar.
4. Evenly pour a ¼-inch layer of sugar over the sage.
5. Repeat the layers of herbs and sugar until the jar is full. Finish the top with a layer of sugar. Seal the jar and store in a cool, dark place for two weeks before using so that the sugar can fully absorb the flavor of the herbs. The sugar and herb combination will store there for up to one year.

VARIATION

Try adding spices like star anise, cinnamon stick, and vanilla bean. You can experiment with proportions, but start with a ratio of 3 star anise, 2 cinnamon sticks, and 1 split vanilla bean per cup of sugar.

7-HERB FRITTATA

SERVES 4

Grandma Pellegrini taught me this recipe after we visited an herb farm together and bought more herb plants than we knew what to do with. It is juicy and fluffy and can be cut into wedges and eaten like a pizza. Of course you can use any herbs that you have on hand. The idea is to use fresh ones, a lot of them, in all varieties. The frittata will be bursting with flavor.

PREP TIME: 10 minutes
COOK TIME: 15 minutes
TOTAL TIME: 25 minutes

- 1 tablespoon unsalted butter
- 1 tablespoon finely diced shallot
- 6 large eggs
- 1 teaspoon chopped fresh mint
- 1 teaspoon chopped fresh basil
- 1 teaspoon chopped fresh parsley
- 1 teaspoon chopped fresh thyme
- 1 teaspoon chopped fresh oregano
- 1 teaspoon chopped fresh marjoram
- 1 teaspoon chopped fresh sage
- 1 tablespoon plain yogurt
- ½ teaspoon salt

1. Preheat the oven to 325°F.
2. Melt the butter in a medium ovenproof skillet over low heat. Add the shallots and sweat them until soft, about 5 minutes, stirring occasionally.
3. Meanwhile, in a medium bowl, beat the eggs and add the herbs and yogurt. Whisk thoroughly to incorporate the yogurt into the eggs as well as possible.
4. Add the egg mixture to the skillet, sprinkle with the salt, and briefly scramble them with a wooden spoon over low heat.
5. Cover the pan and transfer it to the oven, baking it until the frittata has set, about 10 minutes. If the frittata is not ready, remove the lid and continue to bake for another 5 minutes. Once set, remove the skillet from the oven and cut the frittata into wedges. Serve warm or cold, garnished with additional herbs.

VARIATION

Try swapping in chervil, tarragon, and lemon verbena.

FLOWER RECIPES

CHIVE BLOSSOM VINEGAR

MAKES 1 CUP

Chives are delicious, but so are their blossoms, which aren't given their chance to shine often enough. To make the most of their flavor and color, cut the blossoms off of the chives as they mature to encourage new growth, and use the buds in this recipe, adding new blossoms to the vinegar all summer long. At the end of the summer you will have a bright pink, chive-flavored vinegar that is wonderful on just about everything.

PREP TIME: 2 minutes
COOK TIME: None
INACTIVE TIME: 2 to 3 weeks
TOTAL TIME: 2 weeks, 2 minutes

- 1 cup chive blossoms
- 2 cups white wine or champagne vinegar

1. Put the chive blossoms in a quart mason jar or other glass bottle, cover with the vinegar, and seal the jar.
2. Let it steep for 2 to 3 weeks and watch it turn to pink. Use the flavored vinegar in your cooking and as you run out, simply add more chive blossoms and top it off with vinegar to reconcentrate it.

FLOWER-STUDDED ICE CUBES

1 TRAY OF ICE CUBES

This technique works best in large, square ice cube molds, where the flowers and herbs are clearly visible. The larger the mold, the better, so that the beauty of the ice lasts longer as you sip. Since the art of mixology has become so popular, there are many types of ice cube molds on the market to choose from and experiment with. For ice that is especially transparent, use distilled water, that is, water that has been boiled and cooled to eliminate cloudiness and impurities. As a variation, try making the ice cubes with fresh herbs and berries.

PREP TIME: 5 minutes
COOK TIME: None
INACTIVE TIME: 3 hours
TOTAL TIME: 3 hours, 5 minutes

- Water, preferably distilled
- Edible flowers, such as nasturtiums and violets

1. Fill an ice tray a quarter of the way with water, and lay the flowers into the containers. Place the tray in the freezer.
2. After 1 hour, remove the tray from the freezer and fill it halfway with water. Return the tray to the freezer.
3. After 1 hour, add water to fill the tray to the top and return it to the freezer. Allow the ice cubes to freeze completely before using (about 1 hour).

FLOWER-STUDDED ICE CUBES

SUGARED FLOWERS

AMOUNT VARIES

If there is one thing that I learned from my grandmother it is that presentation is key, and God is in the details. These flowers are useful to have on hand to quickly beautify a dessert—to decorate cupcakes, cakes, puddings, or cheese platters.

PREP TIME: 5 minutes
COOK TIME: None
INACTIVE TIME: 24 to 36 hours
TOTAL TIME: 24 hours, 5 minutes

Flower buds, such as violets, lilac florets, nasturtiums, pansy or rose petals
1 large egg white
Superfine sugar

1. With a pastry brush, carefully dust each blossom for grit and remove the stems, making sure the flowers are perfectly dry. Lay them out on a sheet of parchment or wax paper in a warm place.
2. In a small bowl, whisk the egg white with 1 teaspoon of water until it is slightly thinned. Dip a small pastry brush in the egg white and lightly coat each flower.
3. Sprinkle the buds all over with superfine sugar. Place them on the parchment or wax paper and leave to dry for 24 to 36 hours.
4. Store the candied flowers in an airtight container, out of direct light, for up to 6 months.

HOW TO MAKE A

FLOWER PRESS AND DRY FLOWERS

AS A CHILD I USED TO LOVE TO COLLECT SUMMER FLOWERS, GREEN CLOVER, AND FALL LEAVES FOR MY FLOWER PRESS. I WOULD THEN PASTE THEM ONTO HOMEMADE CARDS OR DROP THEM INTO LETTERS BEFORE SENDING THEM OFF SO THAT THE READER HAD A LITTLE PIECE OF WHERE I WAS WRITING FROM. MOST LARGE HOME-IMPROVEMENT STORES HAVE A SCRAP WOOD SECTION, WHICH IS VERY CHEAP, AND THEY WILL EVEN CUT YOUR WOOD TO YOUR DESIRED DIMENSIONS.

Cardboard that you can cut into 4 to 6 12 × 12-inch pieces, plus extra to lay down as a surface to cut on

2 8 × 8-inch pieces of wood , ¾- or 1-inch thick (you can go a bit smaller or larger)

X-Acto knife or blade

Roll of wax or parchment paper

¼-inch drill bit

Tape

Drill

Wood block

4 ¼-inch threaded flat-end screws

4 wing nuts

Flowers

1. Lay down one piece of cardboard as your cutting surface. Place another piece of cardboard that you plan to cut onto the cutting surface, and then lay a wooden square on top of the cardboard to use as a template. Using the X-Acto knife, cut the cardboard to the same size as the square. Start by cutting out four squares of cardboard; you can always cut more later.

2. Roll out the wax paper and lay a trimmed piece of cardboard over it to use as a template. With the X-Acto knife, cut the wax paper; make six in total.

3. Trim the corners off of the cardboard squares. Use one of the templates to trim the corners off of all the wax paper squares.

4. In order to avoid drilling too far through the wood onto your work surface, measure the drill bit alongside the thickness of the stacked squares and mark the bit with tape so you don't drill any deeper than the tape. Drill a hole into the corners of both wood squares. Then you can finish on a wood block or flip the wood over to finish the hole from the other side.

5. Stack the two squares of wood, marking one corner of each piece so you know where to align them later.

6. Insert the screws through one wooden square, from the bottom up, so that the end of the screw is facing upward. Layer one piece of cardboard on the wood surface, followed by two sheets of wax paper, and then another piece of cardboard. Repeat these layers, ending with a piece of cardboard at the top. Then mount the second piece of wood over the screws, being careful to align the marked corners, and screw the wing nuts onto the screws.

7. When you are ready to press flowers, unscrew the wing nuts, remove the top layer of wood, and insert the flowers between the sheets of wax paper and cardboard. Reassemble the press and tighten the wing nuts. Allow the flowers to stay in the press for 3 to 4 days, then remove them to use on homemade note cards or however else you would like.

FIG. Nº 1a
FIG. Nº 1b
FIG. Nº 1c
ABBAYE • ABBEY
Affligem
ANNO 1074
FIG. Nº 2a
FIG. Nº 2b
FIG. Nº 3a
FIG. Nº 3b
FIG. Nº 4
FIG. Nº 5
FIG. Nº 6a
FIG. Nº 6b
FIG. Nº 7a
FIG. Nº 7b
FIG. Nº 7c

VARIATION

Instead of using lollipop molds, you could also use fresh or dried lavender with its stem as the base for the lollipop. Make the same recipe opposite through step 4. Hold the lavender stem upside down and dip the lavender bud into the sugar mixture. Lift it and dip it into a bowl of ice water. Then lay it on some greased parchment paper and repeat with the other lavender sticks. Individually wrap the sticks in plastic and store them in an airtight container in a cool, dry place for up to 1 month. Serve in glasses of lemonade or iced tea as a sugar stirrer.

FLOWER-STUDDED LOLLIPOPS

MAKES ABOUT 6 2¼-INCH LOLLIPOPS, OR 15 1¼-INCH LOLLIPOPS

These lollipops make a beautiful, whimsical party favor or holiday treat. You can switch in any edible flower, herb, or seasoning of your choice. The more beautiful the flower or herb, the more beautiful the lollipop will be. You will need to get yourself some lollipop molds to do it cleanly, but don't worry, you will want to make them again and again.

PREP TIME: 5 minutes
COOK TIME: 10 minutes
TOTAL TIME: 15 minutes

Fresh edible flowers or herbs, or dried edible flowers
1 cup sugar
½ cup light corn syrup
1 teaspoon extract of your choice (vanilla, mint, cinnamon, coconut)
2 drops food coloring, pink and purple are ideal (optional)

1. Prepare the lollipop molds by spraying them with nonstick cooking spray. Alternatively, you could brush the molds with oil. Insert a lollipop stick in each mold. Place your flowers or herbs into the molds, display-side down.
2. Combine the sugar, corn syrup, and ¼ cup of water in a small saucepan over medium-high heat. Stir until the sugar dissolves, then brush down the sides of the pan with a wet pastry brush. Bring to a boil and insert a candy thermometer.
3. Allow to boil without stirring, until a candy thermometer reaches 300°F, about 5 minutes. If you don't have a candy thermometer, use a spoon to drop a little of the hot syrup into a bowl of cold water. If the drop forms hard, brittle threads that break when bent, the syrup is ready.
4. Remove the pan from the heat and allow the syrup to sit until it stops bubbling completely. Stir in the extract of your choice, and, if desired, food coloring.
5. Working quickly, spoon the candy into the mold cavities, making sure to cover the back of the lollipop stick. If the syrup becomes too hard to pour in the process, reheat it gently on the stove, mixing it with a spatula.
6. Once the molds are filled, allow them to cool completely at room temperature. Remove the lollipops from the molds when they have completely hardened.
7. Store the lollipops, individually wrapped and in an airtight container at room temperature, for up to 1 month.

HOW TO CLEAN A CANDY-COATED POT

TO CLEAN A CANDY-COATED POT AND SPATULA, FILL THE POT WITH FRESH WATER AND BRING IT TO A SIMMER. SCRAPE THE SIDES OF THE POT WITH THE SPATULA UNTIL IT MELTS INTO THE WATER AND OFF OF THE SPATULA. TURN OFF THE HEAT AND POUR THE MIXTURE OUTSIDE IF YOU CAN, OR DOWN THE SINK IF NECESSARY.

FLOWER BUD PANCAKES

SERVES 4

A smattering of flowers in your pancakes is a beautiful presentation, perfect for a spring brunch party when you want to branch out from the usual blueberry-studded flapjacks. Try dandelions in the height of summer for a bright color, or choose another edible flower (see page 53).

PREP TIME: 5 minutes
COOK TIME: 5 minutes
TOTAL TIME: 10 minutes

- 2 cups cake flour or sifted all-purpose flour
- ½ teaspoon salt
- 2½ teaspoons baking powder
- 1 tablespoon sugar
- 1¾ cups whole milk
- 2 large eggs
- 1 tablespoon vanilla extract
- 2 tablespoons unsalted butter, melted
- 1 cup edible flowers such as dandelions and violets, plus extra for garnish
- Unsalted butter, room temperature, for serving
- Maple syrup for serving

1. Mix the flour, salt, baking powder, and sugar together in a large bowl.
2. In a separate medium bowl, whisk together the milk, eggs, and vanilla.
3. Add the wet ingredients to the dry, stirring very gently until they are just combined.
4. Add the 2 tablespoons melted butter to the batter, stirring gently until combined.
5. Heat a large greased cast-iron skillet or griddle over medium heat and pour in a ½ cup of batter. Place the flower buds gently into the batter, face up, 4 to 5 per pancake. Cook for 2 to 4 minutes until golden brown, then flip the pancake over and cook until golden brown on the second side, about 2 minutes. Serve immediately with butter and maple syrup on the side and a scattering of flowers as garnish.

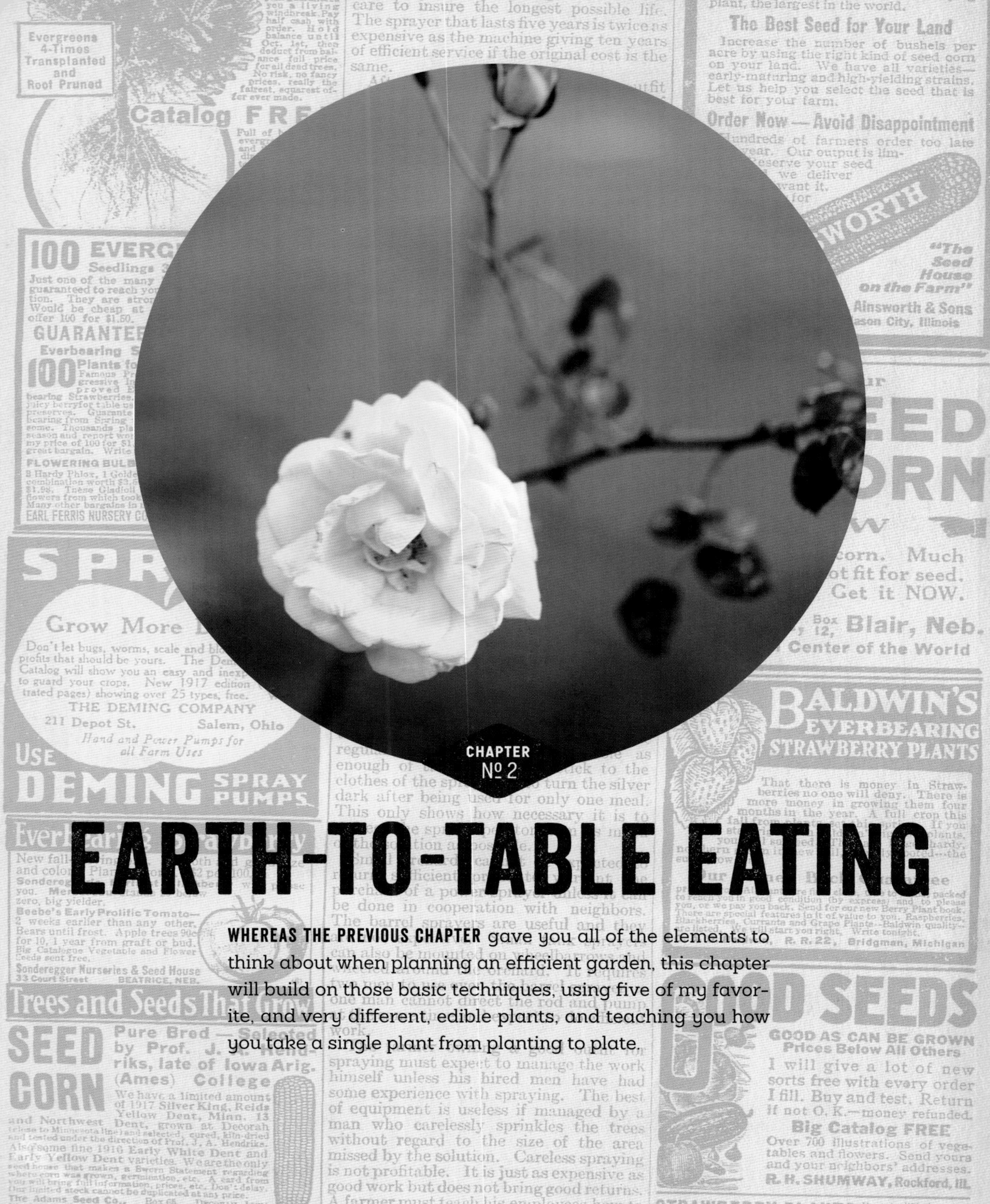

CHAPTER
No. 2

EARTH-TO-TABLE EATING

WHEREAS THE PREVIOUS CHAPTER gave you all of the elements to think about when planning an efficient garden, this chapter will build on those basic techniques, using five of my favorite, and very different, edible plants, and teaching you how you take a single plant from planting to plate.

You will learn how to eat a rose, after you have learned to choose, plant, care for, and even preserve it. You will learn how to take a single potato from the store and turn it into twenty pounds of potatoes by sprouting it and growing it in a garbage bag that can sit virtually anywhere. And if you are in the mood for adventure, you will find instructions on how to inoculate an area of your backyard or windowsill with spores to bloom your own mushrooms. At the very least you'll be inspired to tear up your grass to fit in a fig tree.

HOW TO EAT A ROSE

THEY SAY THAT ROSES ARE 70 MILLION YEARS OLD. Confucius wrote of seeing them in the garden of the Chinese emperor. Legend has it that Cleopatra wooed Antony with scores of them, and that Nero showered his guests in them. Throughout history, the scent of a rose has alleviated the coarseness of life. Today, the rose injects an elegance into our daily existence—its oils, color, and aroma transport us. They say we should take some time to stop and smell the roses. What they don't say is that we should stop and taste the roses, too. Here is how.

How to Choose a Rose

1. First do a little research and decide what your rose priorities are. Do you want low-maintenance roses that will flourish without attention, or are you willing to put in a bit more effort for something visually unique or especially fragrant?
2. The best roses are found at nurseries that specialize in them. They can also be purchased online from reputable rose growers (see some rose suggestions on page 97). Buy No. 1 grade roses whenever possible, as they are the best specimens to get you off to the right start.
3. For bare-rooted plants, the roots should be thick and fibrous, without any signs of shriveling, and the stock should be at least as wide as a thumb. There should be two or three branches growing from the stock.
4. Container roses should have healthy growth and well-proportioned branches. Remove the plant from its container and inspect the roots, making sure that they aren't bound together.

How to Plant a Rose

1. Autumn is the best time to prepare for a rose. Choose a spot that has at least five hours of sunlight every day, but also one where you can enjoy the beauty of the plant down the road.
2. Tend to the soil, adding rich compost and organic matter and working it in. Give it some time

to decompose. If the soil seems to be heavy and dense with too much sticky clay, work in some sand for proper drainage. Now let it sit and rest.

3 Some say it is okay to plant container roses in late fall. I prefer to wait until after winter and the last frost, sometime in March. For bare-rooted roses, plant them when the soil is warmer, such as late April, depending on the weather.

4 Trim any exceptionally long roots and cut off any broken roots or branches. Also snip off any leaves, buds, or hips so that the plant's energy will focus on the roots when it is planted.

5 Dig a hole deep enough to contain the roots, and let them flow in their natural direction. Bare-rooted and container roses should be planted so that the area where the first branches arise from the crown is at least three inches under the soil. Eventually the soil will settle and this bud union area will peek above ground.

6 Fill the hole with soil and press it down gently. Then soak the plant with about a gallon of water. Finish by pruning any branches back to about five inches in length, which will redirect the plants' energy downward so it can establish strong roots. The exception to this is climber roses, which you don't need to cut back at first planting.

7 Add a good supply of compost mulch around the base of the rose, which will protect it from disease and provide the right balance of nitrogen, phosphorus, and potassium along with trace minerals.

How to Care for a Rose

1 Roses are particularly sensitive to water and need it regularly to prosper. When the rose is first planted, water it whenever the top two inches of soil are dry. Keep doing this four weeks after first planting the rose, then switch to soaking the bed completely. Give them a deep soaking, one to two times per week, if there hasn't been adequate rainfall. This will encourage deep roots, which creates healthier plants.

2 Try not to wet the leaves and instead direct all of the water to the roots. Wetting the leaves will encourage the spread of disease like black spot and mildew. Watering in the morning will help any water on the foliage to dry quickly in the morning sun. Use a spray hose or watering can to gently pour water into the root area and stop intermittently to let the water soak in and prevent runoff.

3 How often you fertilize depends on what kind of fertilizer you are using, and in what region you are growing roses. If you are growing them in a warm climate, and they grow for longer in the year, you will need more fertilizer than those growing in colder climates (and for less time during the year). If you plan to use them for culinary purposes (and you should!), use organic fertilizer and apply it every ten weeks. Liquid fertilizer can be applied more frequently depending on how quickly it dissolves into the soil, but follow the guidelines given by the brand you are using. No matter what type you choose, you should begin fertilizing the plants four weeks before your flowers begin budding for spring.

4 Late winter is pruning time in most places. Starting at the base of the plant, remove all unproductive wood and prune back one-third of the remaining plant. Cut the stems particularly around

FERTILIZE WITH A BANANA PEEL

Add a chopped banana peel to the hole when planting a new rose. The potassium will fertilize the rose and deter aphids. My father makes a manure tea for his roses but I advise against this. It really stinks!

the center of the plant, to allow air circulation and light. Leave any twiggy, nonflowering growths when pruning, which will help the plant the following year.

5 In spring and summer you can begin to deadhead roses; that is, snip off the dead flowers, which will encourage new blooms. It is best to cut all the way back to a healthy bud, which will then turn around and produce new shoots. If you love rose hips, the fruit of the rose that ripens in late summer and fall, then stop cutting off the flowers by late June so the hips have time to form.

How to Dry a Rose

Drying flowers is a simple thing to do; just keep a few rules in mind:

1 First, if you want them to keep their color, dry them away from direct sunlight.

2 Second, hang them upside down in the driest environment you can muster. Use a rubber band around the stems so that when the roses begin to dry and lose volume, the band will tighten around them. Once they feel brittle to the touch they are ready to use in tea, as decoration, to put in wreaths, or to mix into homemade potpourri with other aromatic flowers like lavender. You can even encase the flowers in two sewn-together cloth rectangles and make a soothing eye pillow.

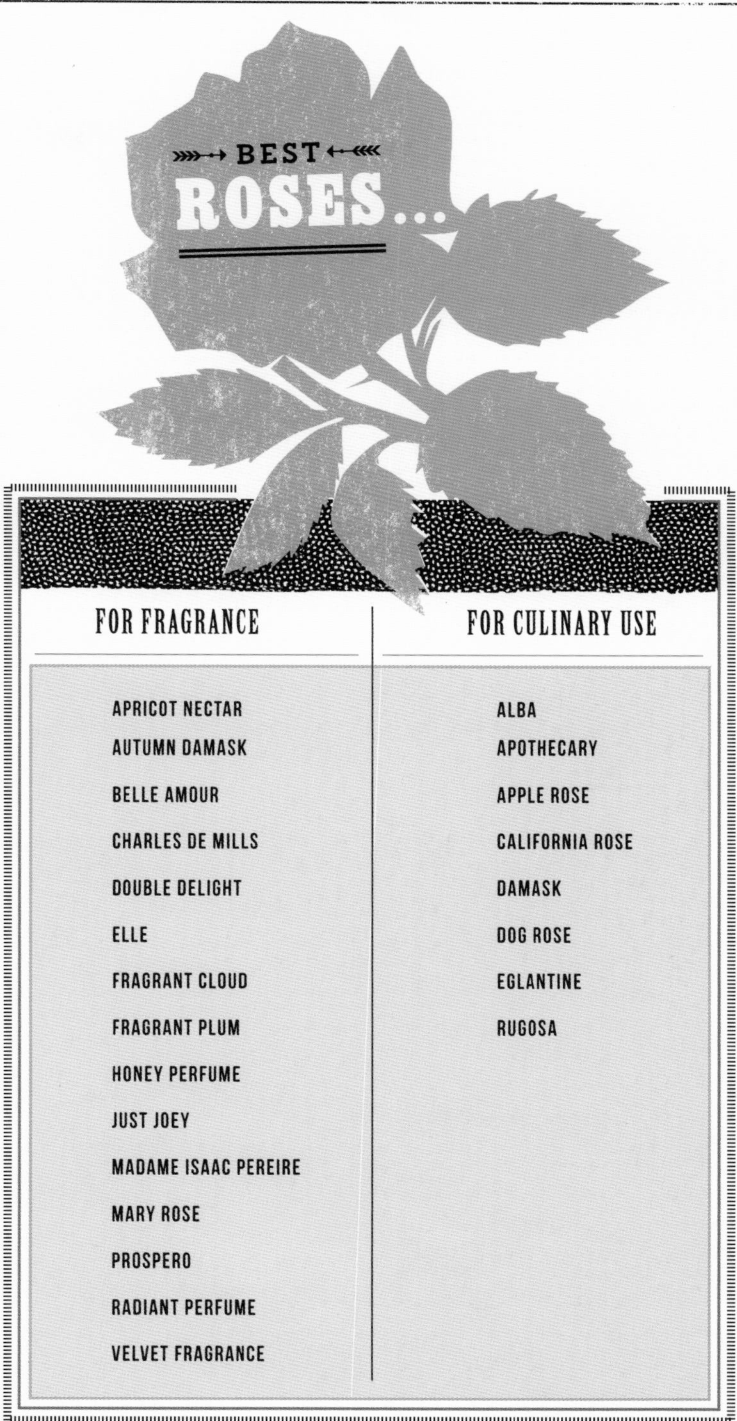

BEST ROSES...

FOR FRAGRANCE	FOR CULINARY USE
APRICOT NECTAR	ALBA
AUTUMN DAMASK	APOTHECARY
BELLE AMOUR	APPLE ROSE
CHARLES DE MILLS	CALIFORNIA ROSE
DOUBLE DELIGHT	DAMASK
ELLE	DOG ROSE
FRAGRANT CLOUD	EGLANTINE
FRAGRANT PLUM	RUGOSA
HONEY PERFUME	
JUST JOEY	
MADAME ISAAC PEREIRE	
MARY ROSE	
PROSPERO	
RADIANT PERFUME	
VELVET FRAGRANCE	

ROSE HIP—CARDAMOM TEA

HOW TO EAT A ROSE

ROSE HIP–CARDAMOM TEA

MAKES 2 CUPS

The hips of certain wild roses are the world's richest and least expensive source of vitamin C. Rose hips are easy to collect and dry yourself and store away for the cold season. This tea has an underlying natural sweetness, which eliminates the need for honey or sugar. As a variation, try using dried rose petals and a cinnamon stick.

PREP TIME: 1 minute
COOK TIME: 5 minutes
INACTIVE TIME: 4 minutes
TOTAL TIME: 10 minutes

15 rose hips
12 cardamom pods, crushed with a mortar and pestle or back of a pan

Place the rose hips and crushed cardamom pods in a teapot. Cover with 2 cups of hot water and let brew for 4 minutes. Pour into teacups and enjoy.

ROSE PETAL JELLY

MAKES 4 CUPS

This jelly is quick and doesn't require time over a pot stirring and waiting for it to thicken. As the liquid settles in the jar, it will separate into three distinct layers for quite a dramatic visual effect, making this a beautiful gift, especially if you opt for bright pink roses. Be sure to dig deep when spooning the jelly out to get all of the colors and flavors onto your scone.

PREP TIME: 5 minutes
COOK TIME: 2 minutes
INACTIVE TIME: 6 hours
TOTAL TIME: 6 hours, 7 minutes

3 cups fresh organic rose petals, white bases trimmed (they are bitter)
Juice of 1 lemon
2 cups sugar
One ¼-ounce envelope powdered pectin

1. Place the rose petals in a food processor or blender along with the lemon juice and ¾ cup of water. Blend for about 1 minute, until the mixture is very smooth, then gradually add the sugar in a slow stream as the blades spin. Continue to let the mixture blend for another minute or two to help dissolve the sugar.
2. Separately, in a medium saucepan over medium-high heat, combine the pectin with ¾ cup water and let it boil for 1 minute, stirring continually.
3. Turn the food processor on again and slowly pour in the hot pectin. Let the food processor

(continued on following page)

run for about 1 minute. The mixture will become foamy and lighter in color.

4 Immediately pour the mixture into the prepared jars with lids loosely secured. Cool in the refrigerator or leave out at room temperature until it has jelled.

5 This jelly will store in the refrigerator for up to 1 month or in a freezer-safe container for 6 months. Alternatively, you can process the rose petal jelly in a hot-water bath (see page 144) for 10 minutes. It is best when consumed within 12 months of canning.

ROSE PETAL HAZELNUT CAKE

SERVES 8

This is a simple, nutty cake good for afternoon tea. Because it is flourless and not too sweet, eating it any time of day is suitable. You can of course dress it up with whipped cream or frosting if you would like. Note: If you whisk the whites by hand, use a large, heavy whisk for efficiency and make sure the whisk and bowl are very clean and dry so that your whites form stiff peaks.

PREP TIME: 20 minutes
COOK TIME: 20 minutes
TOTAL TIME: 40 minutes

- Unsalted butter for greasing the pan
- 1½ cups hazelnut flour (or finely ground hazelnuts)
- 2 teaspoons baking powder
- 4 large eggs, separated
- ⅓ cup sugar
- ½ teaspoon almond extract
- ½ teaspoon vanilla extract
- ¼ cup heavy cream
- ½ cup fresh organic rose petals

1. Preheat the oven to 350°F. Butter an 8-inch fluted tart pan with a drop bottom and set aside. You may also use a cake pan, but if you do, be sure to use a toothpick to check for doneness.
2. In a medium bowl, combine the hazelnut flour and baking powder and set aside.
3. In a large bowl, combine the egg yolks and sugar and whisk vigorously until pale yellow. Add the almond and vanilla along with the cream and whisk again until fully combined.
4. Add the dry ingredients to the yolk mixture and mix together until uniform.
5. In a large bowl, whisk the egg whites until stiff peaks form.
6. With a spatula, fold a third of the egg whites into the batter, then incorporate the rest of the whites all at once.
7. When the batter is uniform, gently fold in the rose petals.
8. Pour the batter into the prepared pan. Place the pan in the oven on the middle rack and bake for 20 minutes or until a toothpick inserted into the cake comes out clean. Remove from the oven and let the cake cool for 10 minutes, then remove the cake from the pan and let it cool to room temperature.
9. Sprinkle the cake with powdered sugar, slather it with whipped cream or frosting, or leave it be . . . whatever you please. It will keep for about 3 days, and should be stored in an airtight container or wrapped in plastic.

ROSE PETAL HAZELNUT CAKE (PAGE 101)

HOW TO EAT A JALAPEÑO

THE JALAPEÑO HAS BECOME PERHAPS THE MOST ubiquitous and versatile pepper in the United States, with a flavor that will range from mild to hot and a color that will range from green to red depending on how long you leave it on the plant. Its uses are endless, from infusing alcohol to making salsa to spicing up Popsicles. And unlike bell peppers, hot peppers like the jalapeño are easier to bring to maturity before the first frost simply because of their smaller size. They don't require the same staking and caging to keep them from falling over, so they are decidedly more low-maintenance.

The chemical that makes hot peppers spicy is called *capsaicin* (pronounced kap-'say-i-sin), which ranges widely on the Scoville heat scale. Jalapeño peppers range in heat from 3,500 to 8,000 Scoville units, whereas the mildest hot peppers are at 100 to 900 units and the hottest at 1,500,000 to 2,000,000 units. These rules for growing and cooking jalapeños can be applied to other hot peppers—it all depends on whether you can handle the heat.

How to Plant a Jalapeño

1. If starting from seed, begin growing them indoors at least 8 weeks before the last frost. They don't like to be disturbed once planted, so they will need to germinate in soil blocks and then be gently transferred to the ground. Hardening them off outdoors is not a good idea in the case of peppers.

2. Jalapeño plants like well-fertilized, well-drained, warm soil. Planting them in raised beds is ideal because the soil warms up more quickly. Space the plants 15 to 18 inches apart. If you are container gardening, use a 16-inch pot.

3. Once the soil has warmed enough and the nighttime temperature is no less than 55°F , choose a very sunny spot where other members of the pepper family have not grown recently, and transplant the seedlings.

4. Remove any flowers that appear on the plant for about a month after the transplant, so that the plant's energy is forced into root growth.

How to Care for a Jalapeño

1. Water the plants regularly, especially while they are establishing roots and as the fruits are forming.

2. At the onset of hot weather, add compost mulch around the base to help keep the soil moist. For container plants especially, use slow-release fertilizer in late spring and again at midsummer.

How to Harvest a Jalapeño

1. Jalapeño peppers ripen 6 to 8 weeks after they are transplanted to the ground. They can be harvested when they are unripe and still add zing to your dishes, but ripe jalapeño peppers are best for drying.

2. Once they are mature, be sure to pick them, otherwise fruiting will slow down. Use a knife or clippers to cut the peppers where the stem meets the main stalk, rather than simply pulling, so as not to damage the plant.

How to String Peppers and Dry Them

Peppers can be dried in the sun and air or in the oven or dehydrator. The simplest way is to string them with a large needle and twine and let them hang in a room for several weeks. Keep the room well ventilated, because peppers can give off pungent fumes that will sting the eyes and throat, especially when hot from the sun. A portable fan will help you here. Also, use latex gloves when handling peppers—or at the very least be sure to wash your hands thoroughly after working with them, making sure to scrub under your fingernails. Don't rub your eyes after handling hot peppers. Here are the steps:

1. Inspect the peppers that you are planning to dry and discard any with soft or questionable-looking spots. Then wash them with warm water and dry them well with a towel.

2. Using a small paring knife, make a ½-inch slit along the side of each pepper. This will help the dehydrating process.

3. Use a large darning needle and run heavy kitchen twine through the eye. Then start by running the needle under the stem area of the pepper. Continue to string the peppers through the stem end and tie the ends of the string together to form a circle of peppers.

4. Hang the peppers in an airy room with low humidity and wait 3 to 4 weeks for the peppers to become brittle.

5. The dried peppers can be powdered or crumbled in a spice grinder and used in soups, stews, chilis, hot chocolate, and many other recipes. You can also rehydrate the peppers by soaking them in water. Before you do so, save the seeds so they can be used for next year's planting. The string of dried peppers also makes a beautiful homemade gift.

HOW TO EAT A JALAPEÑO

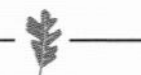

JALAPEÑO-INFUSED VODKA

MAKES 4 CUPS

This is a fun concoction to have on hand when you want to spice up a drink and give it a savory quality. You could also use a canned chipotle pepper in this recipe for a smoky flavor. Taste the liquid after several hours to gauge the taste and heat. And if you are really worried about too much heat, remove some of the seeds of the jalapeño before dropping it into the bottle.

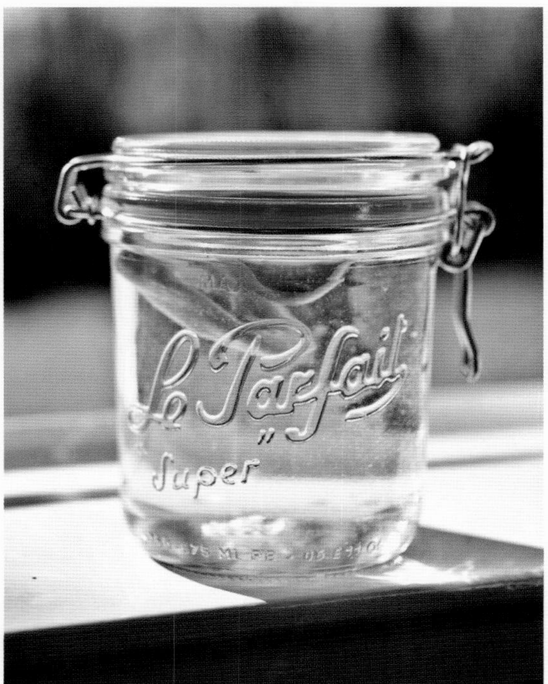

PREP TIME: 3 minutes
COOK TIME: None
INACTIVE TIME: 24 hours
TOTAL TIME: 24 hours, 3 minutes

- 4 cups vodka
- 1 jalapeño pepper, stemmed and sliced in half

1. Pour the vodka into a resealable container, such as a large mason jar. Add the jalapeño halves and reseal the jar. Shake it well, then place the jar on a cool, dark shelf.
2. After 6 hours, taste the vodka to determine if it is spicy enough for you. If not, let it brew longer, even overnight.
3. Remove the jalapeño from the jar with a fork and strain the liquid into a fresh container to remove any seeds and debris. Store it sealed in a cool, dark place for up to a year. Chill well before serving.

JALAPEÑO-BACON

MICHELADA

SERVES 1

This is an ode to Austin, Texas, the town that introduced me to this drink. It is typically made with beer, but good things are meant to evolve. This drink is savory, spicy, and rather refreshing.

PREP TIME: 5 minutes **TOTAL TIME:** 5 minutes
COOK TIME: None

- 1 lime, juice reserved
- Sea salt
- 1 ounce Jalapeño-Infused Vodka (page 107), well chilled
- 2 dashes Worcestershire sauce
- Dash of soy sauce
- Dash of Tabasco sauce
- ¼ teaspoon freshly cracked black peppercorns
- 6 ounces seltzer water
- 1 crisply rendered piece of bacon for garnish

1. Rub a lime wedge around the rim of a glass and dip the rim into salt on a saucer.
2. In the glass, combine the jalapeño vodka, lime juice, Worcestershire, soy sauce, Tabasco, and cracked peppercorns.
3. Add about ¼ cup crushed ice and the seltzer water and stir.
4. Drop the bacon strip into the beverage as a stirrer and garnish.

BEER-BATTERED

JALAPEÑO CHIPS

SERVES 6

I am fairly certain there is nothing more satisfying to eat than a fried spicy bite dipped in a tangy sauce. The good thing about this batter is that you can coat more than just fresh jalapeños in it—try olives, sliced pickles, or even pickled jalapeños to get the best of both worlds (see page 149). If you opt for straight jalapeños, a vinegar-based dipping sauce is the perfect accompaniment, but even a few dashes of vinegar will suffice. When deep-frying, I prefer to use grape-seed oil because it has a cleaner, more neutral flavor, but vegetable oil will also work. Once you have finished frying, you can strain the oil and store it in a mason jar to use again. Just be sure not to pour it down your drain.

PREP TIME: 5 minutes **TOTAL TIME:** 8 minutes
COOK TIME: 3 minutes

- 4 cups grape-seed or vegetable oil
- 2 cups all-purpose flour
- 1 tablespoon baking powder
- 1 teaspoon salt, plus more to taste
- 1 12-ounce can light beer
- 8 fresh medium to large jalapeños, sliced into ¼-inch rounds
- Freshly ground black pepper to taste

1. In a large, heavy-bottomed skillet, pour enough oil to reach about 1 to 2 inches up the side of the pan. Heat the oil to 350°F using a thermometer, or test the heat by dropping in a dollop of batter. When it's ready, the batter should sizzle immediately.
2. To make the batter, combine the flour, baking powder, and salt in a bowl. Slowly whisk the beer into the dry ingredients, blending until the mixture has a pancake-batter consistency.

(continued on page 110)

BEER-BATTERED JALAPEÑO CHIPS

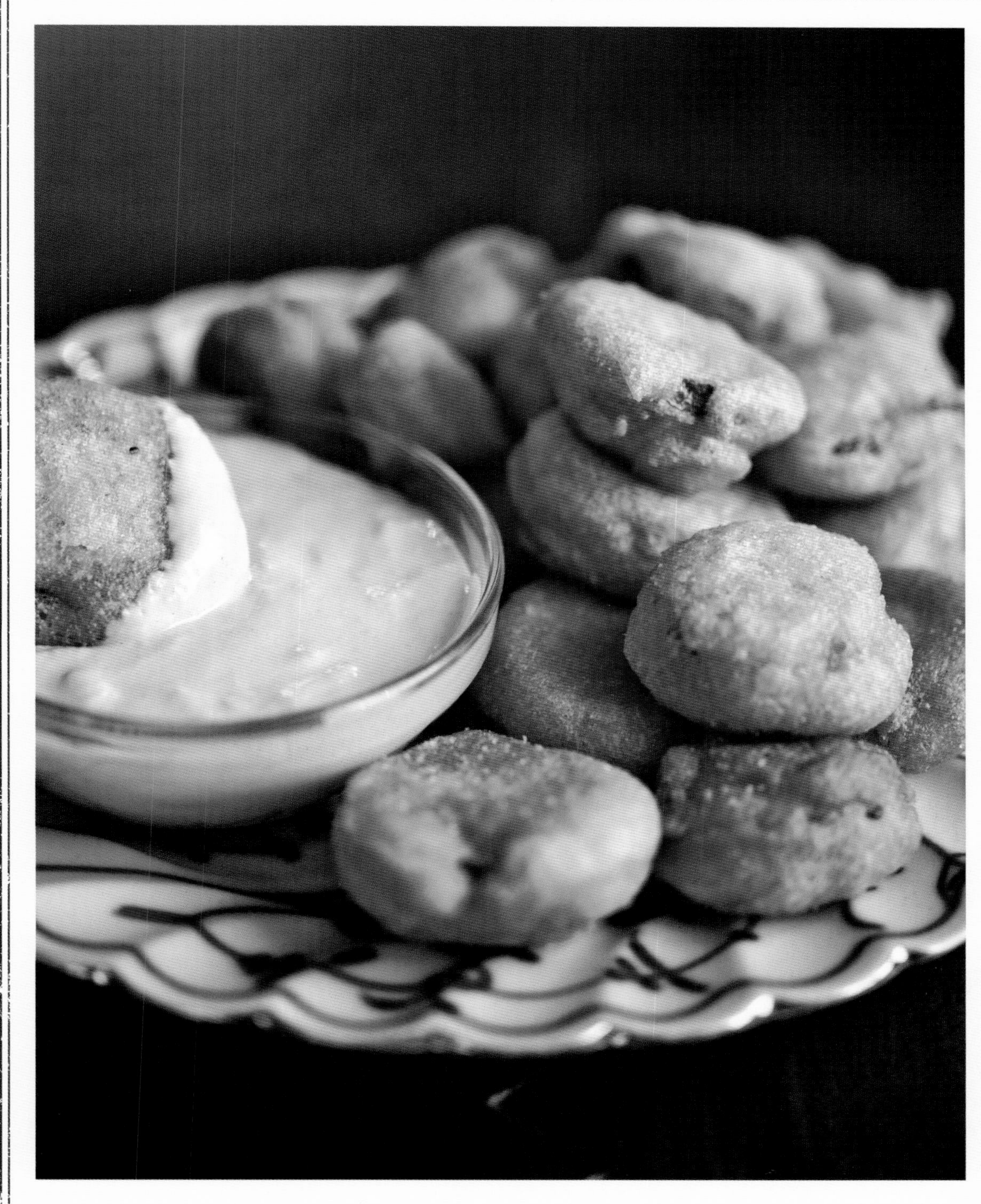

3 Line a plate with paper towels and set it aside. Using tongs, dip the jalapeño slices one at a time into the batter and then place them in the heated oil. Fry them for about 2 minutes, flipping them over after about 1 minute.

4 Place the jalapeños on the paper towels and season them with salt and pepper. Serve with vinegar, ranch dressing, or your favorite dipping sauce.

POTION Nº 3

BEER RINSE

This is a hair potion that works for all hair types.

1 After you shampoo, condition, and rinse with warm water, pour beer all over your hair.

2 For light hair use a light-colored beer, for dark and red hair use a darker beer.

3 Use about half a can for short- to shoulder-length hair and up to a whole can for longer hair, making sure you douse your hair thoroughly.

4 Don't rinse it out, just dry with a towel and complete your regular drying routine. The proteins in the beer will add a coating, which helps protect against humidity and allows hair to style and set easily. The beer will also tighten the cuticle imbrications of the hair, which allows light to reflect off of it and create shine.

5 Any beer that is left you can drink as you finish your shower, or store in the refrigerator. The carbonation will go flat as it stores, but its useful properties for hair washing will remain. You can do this weekly.

JALAPEÑO-MINT JELLY

MAKES 2 CUPS

This jelly is sweet, but it has a real kick. Serve it with lamb in lieu of the traditional apple-based mint jelly, or with cheese and crackers for a sweet, sour, and spicy combination. You can skip the food coloring in this recipe, just keep in mind that without it the result might be a more muddy color.

PREP TIME: 5 minutes
COOK TIME: 6 minutes
TOTAL TIME: 11 minutes

- 1 cup deseeded and chopped jalapeño or other hot peppers
- 1 cup deseeded and chopped green bell peppers
- 1 cup fresh mint leaves
- ½ cup cider vinegar
- ½ cup sugar
- 2 drops green food coloring (optional)
- 1 ¼-ounce packet powdered gelatin

1 Combine the jalapeños, green peppers, mint, and vinegar in a food processor and puree until liquefied. Transfer the mixture to a medium saucepan and add the sugar, 1 cup of water, and the food coloring, if desired.

2 Simmer the mixture slowly for 5 minutes, then turn off the heat and strain the liquid into a medium heavy-bottomed pot.

3 Place the pot on the heat and bring to a boil. Add the gelatin and boil vigorously for 1 minute, stirring constantly. This could boil over rapidly, so if it begins to rise too high, turn down the heat.

4 Remove from the heat. Skim any foam or impurities from the surface, then pour the jelly into a mason jar, seal with a lid, and store in the refrigerator for up to 6 months. Alternatively, process the jelly in a hot-water bath (see page 144) for 5 minutes. It will store on the shelf for 12 to 18 months.

MASON

HOW TO EAT A POTATO

WOULDN'T IT BE WONDERFUL TO TASTE A POTATO called "Pink Fir Apple"? It is uncommon to find more than a few varieties of potatoes at a market today, yet there are thousands that we have never tasted before. The range of potato flavors varies from waxy to floury, with names like "Arran Victory" and "Highland Burgundy Red." The older the variety, the more dimples or eyes it has, reflecting its history. And more eyes means they will sprout as seeds and yield more potatoes. Supermarket potatoes are bred to be smooth-skinned and perfect, and are sprayed regularly with a growth inhibitor to keep the eyes from sprouting.

Fishing through the soil for spuds you have grown yourself is like digging for gold. And they are exceptionally easy to grow not just in the garden but also in a garbage bag in a small space. They don't even want a lot of light! Plus you can have potatoes year-round: early and midseason to eat fresh, and late season to store through the winter if you like.

How to Plant a Potato

1. Plant potatoes in spring as early as several weeks before the last frost, once the soil has sufficiently dried out. Choose a spot that hasn't grown potatoes, tomatoes, or other members of the Nightshades family recently (see page 45).

2. Potatoes like to be planted deeply in loose, well-manured, sandy, moist soil. Prepare 1 pound of dirt in your garden with a combination of soil, sand, and slow-release fertilizer, in the proportions specified by the fertilizer brand's instructions. Alternatively, plant the potatoes in large containers or plastic garbage bags indoors or on a balcony.

3. Potatoes prefer a slightly acidic soil, so mixing in coffee grounds or pine needles to any soil will help, whether indoors or out. Just be sure not to overdo it, as highly acidic soil will yield small potatoes.

4. Buy seed potatoes and cut them so that each piece has one to three eyes in it. Allow them to cure for 3 to 4 days in a cool, dry place so their surfaces harden. Inspect the insides after you cut them to make sure there is no discoloration, which could be a sign of disease. Using seed potatoes to start your crop will ensure that they are disease-free and bred to stay true to type. They may even be presprouted when you receive them, which will save you time. Otherwise you can buy organic potatoes, and let them presprout to get a jump on the season by placing them in an area indoors where they will get light but not direct sun. They will produce green sprouts and take on a greenish tinge. Once sprouted, cut them into quarters so that there is at least one eye in each piece.

5. Plant them at least 8 inches deep so that the potatoes have soil above the eye to grow. You can then use the resulting potato harvest to plant again the following year.

How to Care for a Potato

For inground potatoes, have mulch or straw on hand throughout the summer to add on top of the potato bed. This will help keep weeds at bay and ensure that the potatoes don't come in contact with direct sunlight, which will turn them green and inedible.

It will also keep the soil cool, since potatoes stop growing once the soil reaches 80°F. Potatoes are drought-tolerant but thrive when watered regularly in small doses after the tubers are marble-sized. Feeding them with a supplement of bone meal is also beneficial.

How to Grow Potatoes in a Pot (or Garbage Bag)

1. Prepare the soil as you would to plant seeds, working in compost. Fill a large pot or black plastic garbage bag with the mixture. If using a plastic bag, poke small holes in the sides for air circulation and drainage.

2. Poke seed potatoes or chunks of potato with one or two eyes into the soil, eyes facing up, and cover the potatoes with 6- to 12-inch mounds of dirt. You can also include straw and leaf mulch.

3. Set the bag in a sunny spot with the bag open and the potatoes completely submerged in the soil. Water as needed to keep the soil moist. How often will vary depending on your climate, so check the soil regularly to make sure it feels sponge-damp.

4. Add more mulch as vines appear, making sure that the developing spuds aren't exposed to daylight. Once flowers appear, you can begin to reach into the mulch and harvest a few new potatoes.

5. At the end of the growing season, as the vines begin to die and wither away, dig up the mulch and harvest the full-size potatoes.

How to Harvest a Potato

Potatoes can be harvested throughout the summer and early fall, and stored through the winter.

Check their size by digging up a few tubers and if full-size for their variety, use a garden fork to dig deep and carefully around the area where you have planted and lift the tubers out of the ground. Early and midseason potatoes are ready when there are purple or white flowers blooming in the foliage above ground, but late-season potatoes can be left in the ground weeks after the tops wither.

How to Store a Potato

Once harvested, lay potatoes out in the sun for a few hours to dry, then brush off the dirt (don't wash them) before storing them. This will cure them for storage, allowing their skin to fully set. They should then be stored in a dark and dry place like a cellar, basement, or cabinet away from any heaters. An ideal temperature is between 40°F and 50°F, which is common during the winter months. Don't store them in the refrigerator or they will become too sweet.

HOW TO EAT A POTATO

APPLE CIDER POTATO SALAD

SERVES 10

This dish gets better as it sits and the flavors have time to mingle, so you can make it many hours in advance and leave it at room temperature, covered, while you go about your day. Be sure to taste it and adjust the seasonings after it cools, since every potato absorbs flavor differently, especially as it comes to room temperature.

PREP TIME: 5 minutes
COOK TIME: 40 minutes
TOTAL TIME: 45 minutes

- 1 5-pound bag of Red Bliss or other thin-skinned potatoes, skins intact
- ½ cup salt
- 1 tablespoon cayenne
- 8 to 10 cloves of garlic
- 2 bunches green onions, thinly sliced, both white and green parts
- 1 cup chopped fresh basil, plus additional for garnish
- 1 cup kalamata olives, finely chopped
- Juice of 2 lemons
- 1 cup apple cider or all-natural apple juice
- 1 cup extra virgin olive oil
- 1 tablespoon paprika, plus additional to finish
- 1 tablespoon freshly ground black pepper
- 2 tablespoons red wine vinegar
- ¼ cup coarse mustard
- 1 cup yellow or white onion, finely diced

1. Place the potatoes in a large pot and cover with water. Add the salt, cayenne, and garlic cloves. Bring to a boil, then reduce the heat to simmer over low heat until they are fork-tender, about 40 minutes. Drain and set aside to cool until just warm.
2. In a large bowl, combine the green onions, 1 cup of basil, olives, lemon juice, cider, olive oil, 1 tablespoon of paprika, pepper, vinegar, mustard, and onion. Allow to sit and macerate for a few minutes.
3. Once the potatoes have partially cooled, chop them roughly until chunky and add them to the mixture. Stir well to soak up the dressing.
4. Garnish with the additional basil and paprika and serve while still slightly warm.

ROSEMARY POTATO PUREE

SERVES 12 TO 15

These may seem like mashed potatoes, but they are much more silky and divine. They demonstrate just how malleable a potato is and how much flavor it can absorb. Having a food mill or ricer is helpful to achieve the maximum silkiness, but if you don't have either you can still get part of the way there by mashing and stirring vigorously, while slowly incorporating the cream and milk in stages. At times it may seem like you have added too much liquid, but do not fear. Let it sit, stirring occasionally, and the starch from the potatoes will absorb it.

The flavor will change as this dish cools, so be sure to taste and adjust the seasoning when it is warm, rather than piping hot. You can make this in advance. Leave the lid on and let it sit for several hours, then reheat it over low heat by adding a touch more milk and cream and stirring constantly as it reheats. This side dish is lovely when served under a stew or beef short ribs.

PREP TIME: 10 minutes
COOK TIME: 45 minutes
TOTAL TIME: 55 minutes

- 5 pounds Yukon Gold potatoes, washed, peeled, and quartered
- 3 tablespoons kosher salt
- 1 head garlic, cloves peeled
- 3 shallots, peeled and quartered
- 3 2-inch sprigs fresh rosemary
- 1½ cups whole milk, plus more for added smoothness as needed
- 1½ cups heavy cream, plus more for added smoothness as needed
- 16 tablespoons (2 sticks) unsalted butter, cut into small pieces, plus more for added smoothness as needed

1. Place the potatoes into a large pot and cover with water. Add the salt, garlic, shallots, and rosemary, and bring the water to a boil.

2. Boil until the potatoes are fork-tender, about 30 minutes. Drain the water and pass the mixture through a food mill in batches, transferring it to a mixing bowl.

3. In a small saucepan over medium-low heat, heat the milk and cream until barely simmering, then remove the pan from the heat. Slowly pour half of the milk-and-cream mixture into the potatoes, stirring as you go.

4. Incorporate the butter, alternating with the milk-and-cream mixture, until the potatoes are smooth and creamy. For added smoothness, pass the potatoes through a fine-mesh strainer in batches, pressing on the potato puree with the back of a ladle to help it pass through. Add more milk, cream, and butter as needed. Serve immediately.

POTATO, APPLE, AND PARSNIP

SKILLET TART

SERVES 4

This tart entails layers of thinly sliced potatoes laced with apple and parsnip. The amount of potato, apple, and parsnip slices you need will vary slightly depending on what size skillet you are using, but I recommend building at least five layers in the skillet, three of potato, and two of the apple-parsnip combination. Use a waxy boiling potato rather than a floury baking potato for the best texture. This pairs particularly well with a dollop of sour cream, crème fraîche, or plain Greek yogurt.

PREP TIME: 15 minutes
COOK TIME: 60 minutes
TOTAL TIME: 1 hour, 15 minutes

- 4 tablespoons (½ stick) unsalted butter, melted
- 2 medium Yukon Gold or new potatoes, peeled and sliced ⅛-inch thick on a mandolin
- 2 medium Pink Lady apples, peeled and sliced ⅛-inch thick on a mandolin
- 2 medium parsnips, peeled and sliced ⅛-inch thick on a mandolin
- Salt and freshly ground black pepper to taste
- Nutmeg to taste

1. Preheat the oven to 350°F. Rub the bottom and sides of an ovenproof 8-inch skillet with some of the melted butter. Begin to layer potato slices in a circular fan around the bottom of the skillet, overlapping by a third, until the whole surface is covered. Add a second layer of apples and parsnips, covering the surface in overlapping slices, alternating between the two. Brush the layers with butter and sprinkle lightly with salt, pepper, and nutmeg.

2. Repeat this with layers of potato, then apples and parsnips, brushing with butter and seasoning with salt, pepper, and nutmeg after each layer of apples and parsnips, until the skillet is full.

3. Brush the final layer with butter and transfer the skillet to the oven. Bake for one hour, or until the edges brown.

4. Remove from the oven and let cool slightly. Serve in wedges directly from the skillet, or if you're feeling fancy, set a plate smaller than the circumference of the skillet onto the tart and invert the tart onto the plate.

HOW TO EAT A FIG

THE BEST FIG, A FRENCH FIG GROWER ONCE TOLD ME, is one you eat from the tree. One of the world's oldest fruits, the fig comes in varieties that represent a kind of time travel, back to the earliest books of the Bible; to 2500 BC, during the reign of King Drukagina, when Sumerian scribes wrote of figs on clay tablets. They were found among tomb offerings to Egyptian dynastic kings; and with Cleopatra, who ended her life with an asp and a basket of figs. They give off an indefinable smell, a mélange of hot sun on ripe grass, raw coconut, honey, and tobacco. Our good fortune is that fig trees are perfect for container gardening because they can be rolled indoors in the colder months or kept indoors all year long if you have a really sunny spot. And their roots benefit from being constrained in a container, improving both the quality and quantity of fruit.

How to Choose a Fig Tree

While there are a lot of varieties to choose from, it is important to select a species that is suited to the climate in which you will be growing . Varieties like Chicago, Brown Turkey, or Celeste are especially good if you are looking to grow your fig tree in colder climates. Also be sure to pick a tree that is self-pollinating, because some species rely on tiny little Mediterranean flies to pollinate them (which, sadly, are indigenous to the Mediterranean and won't be available to pollinate your tree for you). Reputable U.S. nurseries will only sell self-pollinating fig trees, but make sure to double-check just in case.

How to Plant a Fig

Grow figs in full sun, or in front of a white wall that can bounce back warmth. Figs give off the most abundant and flavorful fruit when their roots are constrained, so they thrive in pots and containers—though they can grow anywhere that is sunny, sheltered, and moist (dry areas are okay, but it might cause the fruit to prematurely drop). If you are not planting your fig in a pot, prepare a bed to constrain the roots as well as possible. After you dig your hole, line the sides with slate slabs that stick out of the ground about an inch. Then line the bottom of the bed with broken bricks or rubble, which will both improve drainage and help constrict the roots. Fig trees like rich, well-drained soil that is moist. In the colder months, the trees like mulch or heavy straw placed over the shallow-growing roots.

How to Care for a Fig

Water young fig trees regularly (10 gallons of water three times per week during the first year) to make sure they become established. Once they have matured, water your trees depending on the climate of your area and how dry your soil is. If you are growing in warmer, dry regions, water your tree well at least every week or two and add mulch around the base to conserve moisture. Pay attention to your plant's leaves, because they will tell you how much moisture your plant needs: Yellow, wilting leaves are a sign of a plant that needs more or less water. Feeling the soil will tell you which it is. In addition, do the following:

» Mulch the roots with compost regularly.

» During the growing season, apply foliar sprays of seaweed extract at least once a month, which will allow the fig to absorb fertilizer through their broad leaves.

» Different cultivars will have varying cold resistance, so check the hardiness rating for your particular tree and make sure it matches your region. If you live in a temperate climate where there are hard freezes, move the tree inside before the first frost if it is in a container, or wrap the branches in burlap to keep them protected.

How to Harvest a Fig

Figs typically produce two crops per year, the first crop in the spring based on the previous year's growth, and the main crop in the fall. Unlike other fruits, figs will not continue to ripen after they are picked, so make sure they have reached maturity before you harvest them. When the fruit is ready to pluck, it will feel soft and tender when pressed together on the branch. And of course there is my favorite method: the taste test.

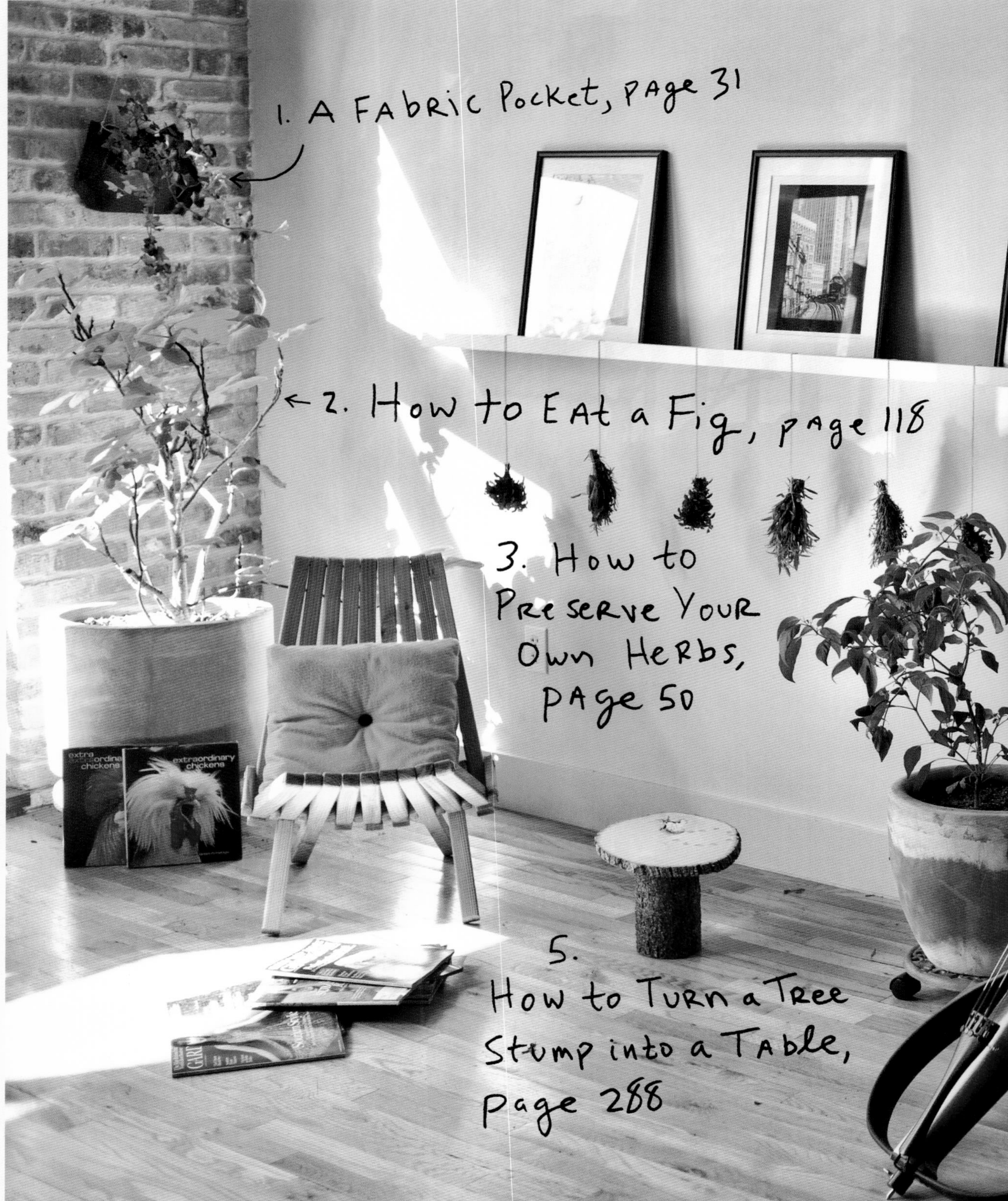

1. A Fabric Pocket, page 31
2. How to Eat a Fig, page 118
3. How to Preserve Your Own Herbs, page 50
5. How to Turn a Tree Stump into a Table, page 288
extraordinary chickens

2ND FLOOR
4. How to Eat a Jalapeño,
page 105

HOW TO EAT A FIG

LEMONY FIG JAM

MAKES 6 TO 8 CUPS

This is a chunky jam, best made with tender ripe figs. If you want a smoother effect, the smaller you cut your fig pieces, the less lumpy it will be. Ripeness will also affect how smooth the texture becomes. For fun variations, substitute white port, Grand Marnier, Limoncello, or your favorite liqueur for the water; substitute rosemary or thyme for the oregano; and substitute high-quality white or red balsamic for the lemon juice. The possibilities are endlessly delicious.

PREP TIME: 15 minutes
COOK TIME: 45 minutes
TOTAL TIME: 1 hour

- 4 pounds fresh figs, washed, stemmed, and cut into ½-inch pieces
- Zest and juice of 2 lemons
- 8 sprigs fresh oregano, leaves picked
- ½ teaspoon sea salt
- ½ cup honey

1. Combine all of the ingredients with 1 cup of water in a large, nonreactive saucepan over medium-high heat, cover, and bring to a boil.
2. Remove the lid and reduce the heat to a simmer over low heat. Stir the mixture. Let it continue to cook, stirring occasionally, until the fruit is soft and the liquid runs off the side of a spoon in thick, heavy drops, about 35 minutes. Spoon the jam into jars and allow it to cool.
3. Store in jars in the refrigerator for up to 3 months. Alternatively, process the jam in a hot-water bath (see page 144) for 5 minutes. It will keep in a cool, dark place for 12 to 18 months.

FREEZE THE DOUGH FOR LATER

IF YOU ONLY NEED ONE PIZZA, MAKE THE FULL DOUGH RECIPE, DIVIDE IT IN HALF, AND PUT ONE PART IN THE FREEZER WRAPPED IN PLASTIC. USE HALF OF THE TOPPING INGREDIENTS LISTED ABOVE FOR ONE PIZZA AND DEFROST THE SECOND DOUGH ON A RAINY DAY WHEN YOU ARE IN THE MOOD FOR SOME MORE PIZZA. THE FROZEN DOUGH WILL KEEP FOR 3 MONTHS.

FRESH FIG, FONTINA, AND THYME PIZZA

MAKES 2 PIZZAS

On New Year's Eve, my family multiplies this dough recipe and serves pizzas fresh out of the oven all night long. Because the crusts are thin and delicate, it is easy to eat a pie or two (or three!) all by yourself. Really good pizza dough is a canvas on which to drop your favorite ingredients and express your culinary creativity. It is also a good place to scatter fresh fruits from the season, figs being among my favorite because their sugars caramelize into an earthy, honey flavor. I also like to offer up some pizzas with fresh greens on top; arugula tossed in a bit of lemon juice, salt, and pepper is one of my favorite things to add to a pie when it is fresh out of the oven. It gives one the illusion of a well-balanced meal when you are leaning in for the third pizza.

You can make this dough in advance, divide it into portions, and freeze it to have on hand for another day. If you don't have fresh figs available, try soaking dried ones in water to reconstitute them, or fresh peaches and nectarines would also work well. You will notice the preheat time for the oven is an hour. This is to create even, radiant heat for a very crispy crust, but if you manage slightly less time it will still be delicious.

PREP TIME: 1 hour
COOK TIME: 20 minutes
TOTAL TIME: 1 hour, 20 minutes

FOR THE PIZZA DOUGH:

- 1½ teaspoons dry active yeast
- 1 pinch sugar
- 3 cups all-purpose flour, plus additional for the work surface
- ½ teaspoon salt
- ½ teaspoon extra virgin olive oil, plus more for greasing the baking sheets
- Wondra flour (optional)

FOR THE TOPPING:

- 2 cups grated fontina cheese
- 16 fresh or dried, reconstituted figs, sliced crosswise into ¼-inch pieces
- 1 tablespoon fresh thyme leaves
- 2 tablespoons honey
- 4 tablespoons balsamic vinegar
- 1 teaspoon coarse sea salt
- Extra virgin olive oil for drizzling onto the pizza and brushing over the crust

1. Preheat the oven to 500°F for 1 hour.
2. To make the pizza dough, in a small bowl, dissolve the yeast in a pinch of sugar and ¼ cup of warm water. Let stand until foamy, about 5 minutes.
3. In a large bowl, combine the flour, salt, and olive oil. Stir in the yeast mixture, then 1 cup of water. Work the dough into a firm ball. Cover with a moist towel and let rise until double, about 1 hour, depending on the climate.
4. Divide the dough in half and roll it out onto a floured work surface. If you have Wondra flour, that is best for rolling. Grease 2 baking sheets or pizza stones with olive oil and lay the dough into each.
5. To make the topping, distribute the fontina, figs, thyme, honey, vinegar, and salt evenly on each pizza. Drizzle with olive oil and brush it over the outer crust so that it browns nicely.
6. Bake the pizza in the oven for 10 minutes, then reduce the temperature to 400°F for about 10 minutes more. Serve hot.

FIG AND HONEY
VINEGAR

MAKES ¾ CUP

Use this vinegar on leafy greens, steamed kale, or to deglaze the drippings in a pan of roasted meat. It will add a brightness to any dish. If fresh figs aren't at your fingertips, try other fruits like strawberries. Even dried fruits like apricots and prunes will work; simply add them to the vinegar as they are.

PREP TIME: 5 minutes
COOK TIME: 5 minutes
INACTIVE TIME: 2 weeks
TOTAL TIME: 2 weeks, 10 minutes

- 1 cup quartered figs or other chopped fresh fruit, plus more for flavor
- 1 cup white wine vinegar
- 6 sprigs fresh thyme
- Honey or sugar to taste (optional)

1. Combine the figs, vinegar, and thyme in a mason jar, and store for 2 weeks in a cool, dark area.
2. After 2 weeks, taste the mixture to see if it is fruity enough for your taste. You can add more fresh fruit to fortify it if it is not flavorful enough for you.
3. Strain the liquid through a fine-mesh strainer into a nonreactive saucepan and add honey or sugar to taste, if desired. Bring to a simmer over medium heat for 2 to 3 minutes uncovered, then remove from the heat and skim off any foam.
4. Strain the liquid into a dry, sterilized mason jar. (You can easily sterilize it by running it through the dishwasher.) Store, tightly sealed, in a cool, dark place for up to 1 month.

BLISTERED FIGS
WITH MARSALA AND GORGONZOLA CREAM

SERVES 4

This simple, luscious dish can be served as an appetizer or dessert. It tastes and appears more complicated than it really is. The salty Gorgonzola tempered by the whipped cream and paired with the warm, caramelized figs is sublime.

PREP TIME: 5 minutes
COOK TIME: 25 minutes
TOTAL TIME: 30 minutes

- 8 ounces Gorgonzola, room temperature
- ½ cup heavy cream, whipped to soft peaks
- 2 teaspoons fresh lemon juice
- Zest of 1 lemon, plus additional for garnish
- 12 fresh, ripe figs
- ½ cup sweet marsala, plus more for deglazing
- 1 tablespoon fresh thyme leaves for garnish

1. Preheat the oven to 400°F.
2. In a small bowl, stir together the Gorgonzola and cream until it is lumpy yet spreadable. Add the lemon juice and zest, stir together well, and set aside.
3. Cut the stems from the figs and slice a deep cross into each fruit, vertically from the stem end, cutting about halfway down the fig. Press each fruit at its base so that it opens up like a flower.
4. Place the figs in a small baking dish or ovenproof skillet and sprinkle the marsala over them. Bake for about 20 minutes, until the fruit is meltingly tender and the edges have started to caramelize. Switch the oven to broil and bake for 5 minutes more, until caramelized.
5. Remove the figs from the oven and let them cool slightly. Place 3 figs on each serving plate. Add a dollop of Gorgonzola cream to the center of each fig. Garnish by sprinkling with some extra lemon zest and thyme over the top.

FIG AND QUINOA SALAD

WITH LEMON VINAIGRETTE

SERVES 4

Quinoa originated from the Andean region of South America about six thousand years ago. It is grown for its edible seeds but is actually not a true grain; in fact, it is in the same family as spinach and beets. Packed with incredible nutritional value, including protein, it is malleable, so it will take on so many flavors, and its subtle crunch makes it delicious when mixed in salads along with other vegetables. I have even seen it incorporated into desserts and breakfast cereal. The lemony dressing in this recipe will also stand on its own, so try making a jar of it in advance and drizzling it on other vegetable dishes when quinoa isn't on the menu.

PREP TIME: 10 minutes
COOK TIME: 15 minutes
TOTAL TIME: 25 minutes

- 1 cup quinoa, any kind
- 1 teaspoon kosher salt
- 1 teaspoon Dijon mustard
- Juice and zest of 1 lemon
- ½ teaspoon honey
- 4 tablespoons extra virgin olive oil
- Salt and freshly ground black pepper to taste
- 5 to 6 fresh ripe figs, quartered
- 3 to 4 green onions, thinly sliced, white and light green parts
- ⅛ cup roughly chopped fresh mint leaves
- ⅛ cup roughly chopped fresh parsley leaves
- ⅛ cup roughly chopped fresh chervil leaves
- ⅛ cup roughly chopped fresh tarragon leaves
- ⅛ cup roughly chopped fresh dill leaves

1. Place the quinoa in a strainer and rinse until the water runs clear.
2. In a medium saucepan with a tight-fitting lid, combine the quinoa with 1¾ cups water and the salt. Bring to a boil, lower the heat to a simmer, cover, and continue to cook for 10 minutes, stirring occasionally.
3. Once cooked, fluff the quinoa and transfer it to a bowl to cool to just above room temperature.
4. In a separate, small bowl, whisk together the mustard, lemon juice and zest, honey, and olive oil. Season with the salt and pepper.
5. Pour the lemon dressing over the cooled quinoa and add the figs, green onions, mint, parsley, chervil, tarragon, and dill. Toss and serve.

HOW TO EAT A MUSHROOM

MUSHROOMS NATURALLY CONTAIN VITAMIN D and are full of minerals and antioxidants. Mushrooms form when two spores mate and grow a network of mycelium, similar to roots. The mushroom itself is the fruit that forms when the mycelium feed on carbonaceous material found in dead organic matter like fallen leaves or a tree stump.

How to Grow a Mushroom

Mushrooms don't need a lot of sun and will actually flourish in a dark apartment. They are also perfect for damp, shady areas of the garden. The way to start as a beginner is with a full mushroom kit, which includes a plastic bag filled with a growing medium like sawdust that has been inoculated with mushroom spores. These are available in a number of places (see Find It, page 296).

If you are feeling adventurous, you can get more for your money by growing mushrooms on your own medium like a stump or log. For this, you will need mushroom plug spores, which are wooden dowels that have been colonized by mycelium. Ask the supplier of your mushroom spores which size drill bit to use and how deep to drill the holes, then drill holes into the stump about 4 inches apart. Insert the plugs and seal them with melted wax to prevent insects from invading the hole. Keep the stump moist and in a shady area, and over the next year the mycelium will colonize it and you will begin to see mushrooms sprouting from the cracks. You will have 3 to 5 years' worth of mushrooms to harvest with this method.

If drilling holes in stumps isn't your style, you can also create an outdoor bed of sawdust, wood chips, straw, or compost and inoculate it with mushroom spores. Moisten the beds every week and mushrooms will appear in about a year.

How to Grow Mushrooms on the 34th Floor

To grow mushrooms indoors, purchase a growing medium that has already been inoculated, or spores and a separate growing medium, and follow the provider's setup instructions. Mushrooms do best at a temperature of 55°F to 75°F, so take note of the temperature around your container and adjust the thermostat accordingly. If insects appear, spray the inside of a clear plastic bag with cooking oil and use it as a tent over the mushrooms.

Mushrooms will develop within weeks, but they will fruit for a shorter period of time before the inoculated medium should be discarded to a compost pile or garden. You may get a surprise and see mushrooms growing in the compost pile later.

How to Care for Mushrooms

Mushrooms require very little maintenance, which makes them ideal for a busy person who wants to invest just a little time with large reward.

Simply keep your growing medium, whether it be a log, stump, sawdust, or compost, in a shaded area and if weather conditions are dry, add water to keep the conditions moist, daily in the drier months, and less often in the rainy season. You can tell by sticking your finger in the soil: It should feel as damp as a wrung-out sponge.

How to Harvest Mushrooms

Mushrooms are most delicious when they are fully bloomed but still young, well before they harden and become woody. Simply twist them off at their base, or cut them with a small knife. Avoid leaving any of the mushroom stump in the soil or growing medium. When growing indoors especially, you want to harvest the mushrooms in time so their spores don't scatter about the house.

NO SUN? GROW MUSHROOMS

Mushrooms are the perfect edible to grow when you don't have any sunlight on hand. They will keep producing for up to five years!

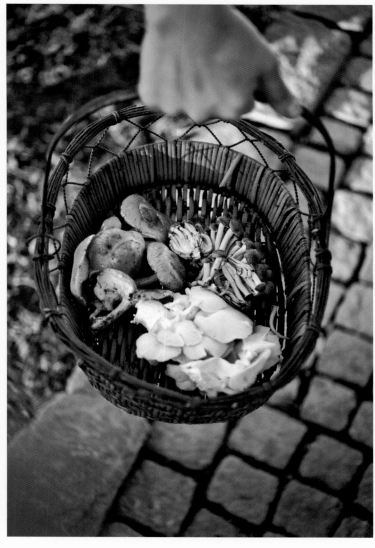

HOW TO EAT A MUSHROOM

SIMPLE SAUTÉED OYSTER MUSHROOMS

IN GARLIC AND HERBS

SERVES 6

The tendency many of us have when sautéing mushrooms and most other vegetables is to move the contents of the pan around with a spoon constantly. It is hard to simply stand idle and leave them be. In the case of mushrooms especially, it is important to drop them in the pan, distributing them evenly, and not to touch them for a solid couple of minutes over high heat. This is because you want brown bits, which produce the flavor, to form on the mushrooms and in the bottom of the pan. Then add your butter, which will deglaze the pan of its brown bits. That's when you can use your wooden spoon to scrape them up. If you begin tossing the mushrooms around too soon, they will steam and release their juices, making it impossible for any real flavor to form; instead, they will become rather soft and gray.

I recommend starting with grape-seed oil to cook the mushrooms. This will allow a much higher smoking point than olive oil so that you can brown without any bitter flavor from the oil's becoming too hot. Vegetable oil is a secondary option, though its taste isn't as neutral. When you deglaze the pan use butter, which will add a nice finishing flavor along with the garlic and herbs.

PREP TIME: 10 minutes
COOK TIME: 15 minutes
TOTAL TIME: 25 minutes

- 5 cups oyster or other mushrooms
- 4 tablespoons grape-seed or vegetable oil
- Salt and freshly ground black pepper to taste
- 2 tablespoons unsalted butter
- 2 sprigs fresh thyme
- 1 clove garlic, crushed
- 3 tablespoons chopped fresh herbs, such as dill and basil

1. Clean and dry the mushrooms well. Don't soak them in water because they are already like a sponge. Just get them damp with the spray hose from the sink or a wet paper towel. Cut the heads off the stem into pieces as desired, and cut the stems, too, discarding the very bottom portion if it is brown and dry. Certain mushrooms like the oyster tend to have tender stems while others like the shiitake are more woody and prone to dryness.

2. Heat a small amount of oil in a large sauté pan over high heat until it shimmers.

3. Drop in the mushrooms but don't overcrowd the pan. Season with salt and pepper immediately; this will release more of the mushrooms' moisture. Let the mushrooms sauté for a couple of minutes untouched so that they stick to the pan and brown. Note: If you need to work in batches, have a plate ready to transfer the sautéed mushrooms onto. The brown bits in the pan will build with each batch.

(continued on page 134)

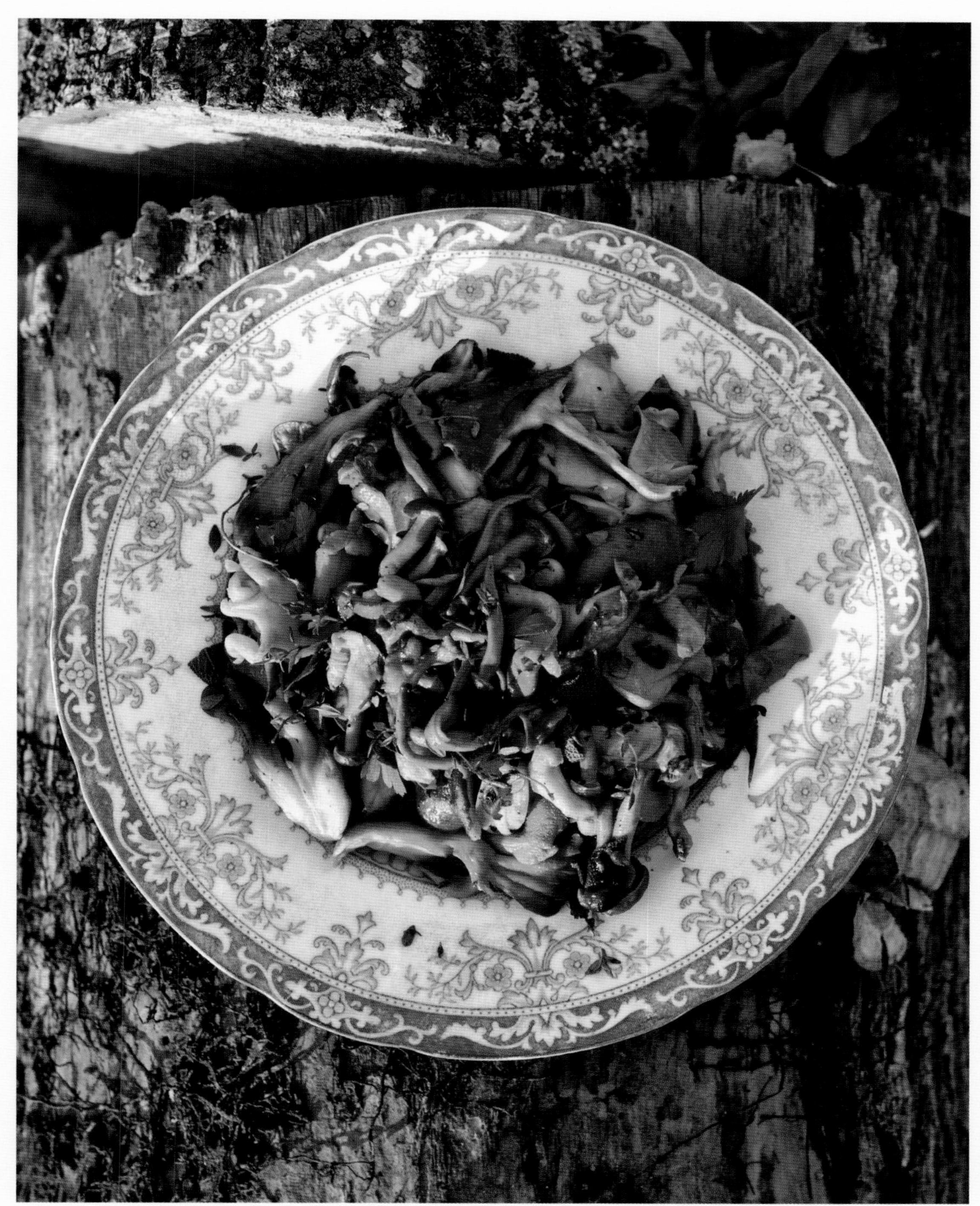

4 Add the butter to caramelize the brown bits in the pan. It is now safe to move the mushrooms in the pan with a spatula or wooden spoon. Add the thyme and crushed garlic and tilt the pan in one direction so the butter pools to one side and is infused with the garlic and thyme flavors. With a spoon baste the butter over the mushrooms. Then tilt the pan back and redistribute the mushrooms. Keep the heat high so the moisture in the mushrooms continues to evaporate, cooking until the mushrooms are well-browned, about 3 more minutes.

5 Remove the mushrooms to a rack or a plate covered with paper towels to soak up the extra moisture. To serve, toss in some chopped herbs and season with salt and pepper.

MUSHROOM STOCK

MAKES 4 CUPS

You don't hear of people making mushroom stock very often, which is too bad because it is rich and earthy, and when used in place of water for soups, stews, and rice, it absolutely transforms a meal. This recipe is also a way to make use of mushroom stems and scraps that are left over when you are cleaning mushrooms. Always save the stems. If you don't have enough to make stock initially, collect them in the freezer until you do. Use white button mushrooms to fortify the stock with flavor along with dried shiitakes and porcinis for a sublime result. This stock freezes well, so you can always have it on hand.

PREP TIME: 5 minutes
COOK TIME: 2 hours
TOTAL TIME: 2 hours, 5 minutes

- 4 cups mushroom scraps, stems, and sliced white button mushrooms
- 1 cup dried shiitakes and porcini
- 12 cups water

1 Add the mushrooms to a large stock pot and cover with water. Bring to a boil, then lower the heat to a simmer. Cover and let simmer for 2 hours, skimming the surface of the stock with a spoon every so often to remove any foam and impurities.

2 Strain the liquid and store it in airtight containers in the refrigerator for up to a week or in the freezer for up to 6 months.

PORTOBELLO MUSHROOM TARTS

SERVES 4

Portobello mushrooms are so meaty that this is a satisfying vegetarian meal on its own. The filling in this tart also makes a delicious warm dip (see Variation, opposite). For both recipes, be sure to wash the Swiss chard very well before cooking it to remove any grit.

PREP TIME: 10 minutes
COOK TIME: 20 minutes
INACTIVE TIME: 10 minutes
TOTAL TIME: 40 minutes

- 4 tablespoons grape-seed or extra virgin olive oil
- 4 Portobello mushroom caps, scraped of their spores
- Salt and freshly ground black pepper to taste
- 2 large leeks, pale green and white part, thinly sliced
- 8 cups thinly chopped Swiss chard, well rinsed of its grit
- 1 tablespoon minced garlic gloves
- ½ cup mascarpone
- 1 teaspoon fresh thyme leaves
- ¼ cup grated Parmesan

1 Preheat the oven to 400°F. In a baking dish or ovenproof skillet large enough to fit your mushroom caps, brush about 2 tablespoons of oil over the mushroom caps, inside and out, and sprinkle them with salt and pepper. Set aside.

2 In a medium sauté pan over medium heat, heat the remaining oil and sweat the leeks and Swiss chard until they are tender, stirring occasionally and sprinkling with salt to help release the juices, about 5 minutes. When tender, add the minced garlic and stir for about 1 minute, then remove from the heat. Transfer the mixture to a medium bowl and let cool for about 10 minutes. Then fold in the mascarpone and thyme.

3 Using a spoon, fill the Portobello caps with the mixture in a big mound. Sprinkle with the Parmesan, place them in the oven, and bake for 10 to 15 minutes until the tops are browned. Serve immediately.

VARIATION

LEEK AND SWISS CHARD DIP: Sauté the leeks, Swiss chard, and garlic as in step 2, then blend them in a food processor. Fold in the mascarpone and thyme, then fill an ovenproof ramekin with the mixture, sprinkling the top with Parmesan. Bake at 350°F until warm and bubbling on top, about 15 minutes. Serve with toast on the side.

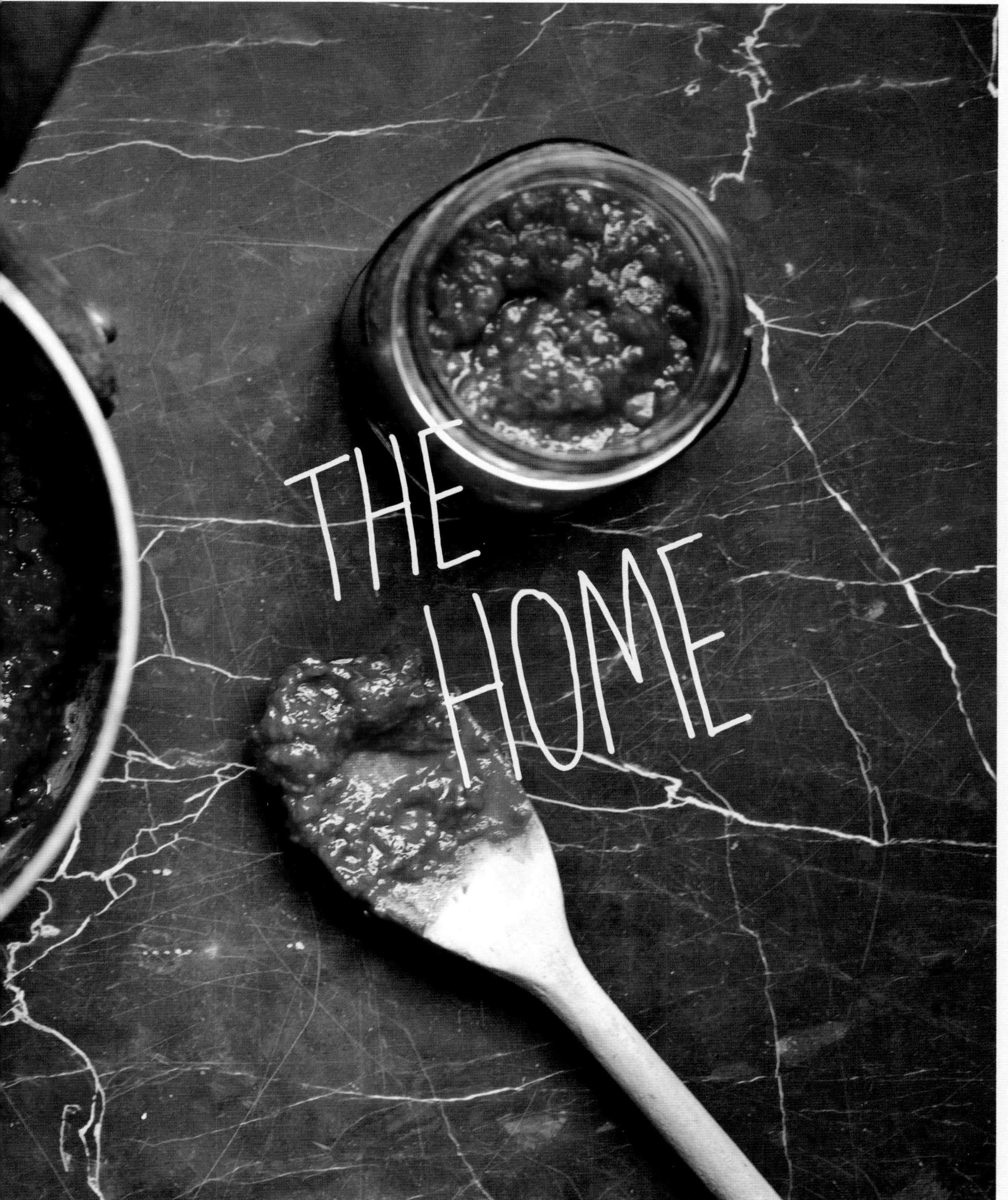
THE
HOME

CHAPTER
Nº 3

THE SELF-SUFFICIENT PANTRY

THIS CHAPTER IS FOR THOSE who want to live with true economy in mind. It is your guide to building a self-sufficient pantry, with techniques for creating a modern-day larder that makes you less reliant on the grocery store. You will learn the basic bulk staples required for a self-sufficient pantry, along with age-old food-preservation techniques: pickling, smoking, curing, jamming, and fermenting.

This section is also about avoiding food waste—learning to save your fat scraps to render fat yourself—and using your meat bones to make your own stock. When faced with left-over citrus peels or a glut of fruit at the peak of ripeness, you can make the most of them before they rot. If you do find yourself with a bowl of rotted fruit after a busy week at work, you will also find a lesson on how to trap the fruit flies that have taken up residence in your kitchen.

There are other useful lessons, like what to do with all of those bits of wine at the bottom of the bottles after a party. And in case you don't have a pantry the size of an apartment to build a self-sufficient larder, many recipes give you storage options for freezing and refrigeration in addition to instructions for how to make things shelf-stable.

FOOD STORAGE TECHNIQUES

It is most economical to buy your staples—from honey to grains and beans—in bulk and then store them yourself. Here are your main options:

» Galvanized trash bins with tight lids are a great option for whole wheat and other dried staples. They are available online in all sizes. Just be sure there is no moisture on the floor beneath the bin and if this is a concern, raise the bins up on cinder blocks.

» Plastic bins are another option but they are much more susceptible to varmints. Line the plastic bins with Mylar bags, which are effective in keeping out light and other elements that can damage your stash.

» Vacuum-packing systems are another great way to seal food for extended storage.

Temperature

Canned and boxed goods should be stored in a cool, dry place between 45°F and 65°F, either in a temperature-controlled room or in a basement or cellar. They are best kept away from vents, and off the ground to avoid pests, unexpected moisture, and heat.

Refrigerated food should be kept between 34°F and 40°F, and frozen foods should be kept well below freezing.

Labeling

You should approach your food storage with "first in, first out" in mind, meaning the oldest items should be consumed first. Each time you add a jar of canned tomatoes to the shelf, for example, it should go to the back of the line. Keep track of this by dating all of your homemade food items with a permanent marker and writing the name of what is inside. You should do this for items before you put them in the freezer and refrigerator as well.

STAPLES

FOR EVERY PANTRY

When storing foods for homesteading and self-sufficiency, moderation and variety are important. Your staples fall into three categories:

» dried foods

» canned foods

» supplementary foods

Bulk items:

ALUMINUM FOIL

ASCORBIC ACID: This is helpful when canning and preserving fruits and vegetables because it slows down the browning process. You can also use powdered vitamin C.

BAKING POWDER: It will last 18 months and is used to "fluff up" baked goods.

BAKING SODA: It lasts 2 years and is used for baking, cleaning, air freshening, and homemade body products.

BROWN RICE: It has a shorter shelf life than white rice (about 8 years versus the almost indefinite shelf life of white rice) but it has higher nutritional benefits.

CANNED FRUITS AND VEGETABLES: As long as you use the "first in, first out" rule, canned goods will not expire before being consumed. Properly canned food stored in a cool, dry place will retain its quality for at least 1 year. Canned food stored in a warm place can lose some of its quality in a few weeks or months. Moisture can also corrode lids, causing spoilage.

CANNED MEATS: These are best used within 2 years and follow the "first in, first out" rule.

CORN: Like wheat, whole corn kernels last much longer than cracked or ground corn, so grind yours by hand if you can. The storage life is 8 to 12 years.

FATS AND OILS: Olive oil stores longest when frozen in plastic bottles (4 years). Mayonnaise, canned butter, and nut butters are another good source of fat. Jarred items should be used within 6 months, but when purchased and stored in metal cans, certain oils can last up to 2 years.

FOOD-STORAGE FREEZER AND VACUUM BAGS

MASON JARS, LIDS, AND RINGS: These will allow you to preserve your vegetables and fruits without refrigeration.

MULTIVITAMINS AND OTHER FOOD SUPPLEMENTS: Stock up on supplements that are primarily only available in fresh foods. These include B-complex, vitamins C, A, D, E, K, and tablets of blue-green algae. (See also "How to Grow Sprouts," opposite.)

OATS: The storage life of whole oats depends on the variety but will range from 3 to 7 years.

POWDERED MILK: The nonfat variety stores the longest—up to 10 years; the nitrogen-packed variety stores 5 or more years.

SALT: It does just about everything, from flavoring to preserving to curing. Get both coarse and fine-grain salt.

SPICES AND DRIED HERBS: These last 6 months to 2 years, and are used for pickling, preserving, and making simple foods more exciting. Green, leafy herbs grow stale more quickly than spices like nutmeg.

SUGARS: This includes honey, maple syrup, molasses, sorghum, and regular white sugar, all of which will last almost indefinitely. Honey is the only food that never goes bad.

VINEGAR: Unopened, a bottle lasts 2 years and is used for pickling, among other things. Once a bottle has been opened, however, it is best used within 6 to 9 months.

WHEAT: Whole wheat stores for 30-plus years, much better than ground white or wheat flour, which has a short shelf life (6 to 8 months in the pantry). So for maximum efficiency buy whole grains and a hand wheat grinder.

YEAST: It is used for baking, fermentation, and converting sugar to alcohol. It lasts about 1 year on a shelf, about 5 years in the refrigerator, and almost indefinitely in the freezer.

HOW TO

GROW SPROUTS

One of the biggest challenges in creating a self-sufficient pantry is storing enough vitamins and nutrients for the long term. Sprouts are one of the most space-efficient and nutritious foods you can grow yourself when fresh, vitamin-rich fruits and vegetables are scarce. Good legumes for sprouting include: mung beans, lentils, various peas and beans, radish, alfalfa, clover, and soybeans. They are a particularly important component to add to a diet that is imbalanced because they contain vitamins B, A, K, and C, along with minerals, amino acids, and other essential nutrients. The act of sprouting these seeds, grains, and legumes makes them much more nutritious than if they were unsprouted. It also makes them easier to digest. Certain beans can be toxic when sprouted and should be avoided. They are: kidney beans, lima beans, black beans, horse beans, runner beans, and garbanzo beans. Flaxseeds and sunflower seeds should also be avoided.

4 tablespoons seeds or legumes
Quart mason jar
Cheesecloth to cover the opening of the jar
Rubber band

1. Remove any damaged seeds from the mix and discard them.
2. Place the good seeds in the jar and fill with room-temperature water to cover the seeds. Cover the jar using the cheesecloth and rubber band, and soak the seeds for 6 to 8 hours.
3. Drain the water out gently through the cheesecloth. The only water that should remain in the jar is the water that has adhered to the seeds. Set the jar aside overnight.
4. Continue rinsing and draining the seeds gently once in the morning and once in the evening so that they stay moist. After a few days, place the jar on a windowsill, which will expedite sprouting. Your sprouts will be ready in 3 to 5 days. If you have multiple jars sprouting at different stages you will have a constant supply of these energy- and nutrient-rich sprouts.

TECHNIQUES FOR PRESERVING FOOD

AS YOU SPEND TIME BUILDING UP YOUR SELF-SUFFICIENCY in a garden, all of the hoeing, weeding, sowing, and watering inevitably leads to an abundance of food during certain months . There are many ways to preserve the harvest for the cold months when you don't have the luxury of a freshly plucked pepper. The following pages teach you the preservation techniques important for storing your harvest and for building up a supply of long-lasting, high-nutrient foods for self-sufficiency. These recipes also show you how to make use of parts that are often discarded, from rinds to peels. Even if you don't have your own garden, these techniques offer a way to save money by buying items in bulk when they are on sale, and preserving them for later.

BASIC CANNING TECHNIQUE

Much of the canning equipment available today comes in sets. To buy the pieces separately, your set for the hot-water-bath method should include:

- Large pot made of aluminum or porcelain-covered steel with a lid (dimensions large enough to hold 7 quart jars with 1 inch of space at the top)
- Rack to set the jars inside the pot, with handles to make placing the rack easier
- Magnetic lid lifter (optional)
- Jar lifter
- Tongs
- Jar wrench (optional)
- Canning funnel (optional but helpful)
- Spatula or knife
- Warm, damp towel

For a pressure-canning method, you'll need all of the above as well as a pressure cooker instead of a large pot.

Whether or not you have to process your cans using the pressure-cooking method instead of a hot-water bath depends almost entirely on the acidity level of what you are canning. There are two ways food can be acidic enough to be canned using the hot-water method: Either the food itself is fairly acidic (like some tomatoes) or you have added some kind of acidic agent to the food (as is the case with pickling).

You can tell how acidic a food is naturally by looking up the standard for that type of ingredient or by testing its pH. To test the pH, take a 1- or 2-tablespoon sample and, if the food is not a liquid already, pulverize it (blend, mash, etc.) into liquid form. Then take alkacid paper, which you can get in pharmacies or on laboratory supply websites, and dip it into your sample. Take the now-colored end and compare it with the pH spectrum included with the alkacid papers. Anything above 4.6 means the food is low in acid. Anything below 4.6 means that the food is high in acid. If a food isn't naturally acidic, things like lemon juice or citric acid must be added. As a rule of thumb, foods with high acidity include tomatoes, fruits, pickles, sauerkraut, jams, jellies, marmalades, and fruit butters, and these can be processed using a hot-water bath. Foods with low acidity include red meat, poultry, seafood, and fresh vegetables, and these should be pressure-canned.

Hot-Water-Bath Method

1. Begin by washing the jars, lids, and rings under running water.
2. Fill your canner with water and place the jars on the rack, allowing the jars to simmer, covered, over medium heat at a constant temperature of 180°F until ready to use.
3. In a saucepan, add enough water to cover the lids, and simmer them over medium heat (making sure not to boil them). Like the jars, keep the lids in hot water until you are ready to use them. There is no need to heat the rings once you have washed them under running water.
4. When you are ready to fill the jars with whatever you want to can, take a jar out of the hot water and carefully ladle in your contents, leaving ¼ inch of headspace for jams and jellies. To remove any air bubbles, take a clean spatula or knife and run it around the edge of the mixture. Then use a clean, warm, damp towel to remove any contents from the jar's lip or threads. Take a lid out of the saucepan and place it on the jar, and then place a ring on top, tightening just to fingertip-tightness. Repeat with the other jars.
5. Put the filled jars back into the rack in the hot water. Adjust the rack height and the water level so there is 1 inch between the water and the top of the jars. Bring the water to a boil, cover, and boil the jars according to the processing times given by your recipe.
6. When you are finished processing the jars, turn the heat off, uncover the canner, and let it stand for five minutes. Take care not to agitate the contents by tipping, shaking, or drying the jars as you remove them from the canner. Let them sit on a heavy towel. You will often hear a popping sound, which is confirmation that the lids have sealed completely; the sound occurs when the contents cool within the jar, creating a vacuum that seals the lid.
7. After a day of resting, check each jar's lid to make sure there is a tight seal. If so, tighten the rings fully, and clearly label and date the jars. If a lid is not sealed, refrigerate the jar or reprocess it with a fresh lid.

SHELF LIFE

You will see many recipes for canning throughout this book. As a rule of thumb, the standard shelf life for canned fruits is 12 to 18 months. For canned vegetables, the standard shelf life is 1 year, and for canned meats the standard shelf life is 2 to 5 years. High-acid foods have a longer shelf life than low-acid foods.

Pressure-Canning Method

Choose high-quality fresh ingredients. If canning meat, be sure to remove the excess fat beforehand so that it doesn't inhibit a proper seal.

1. Begin by washing the jars, lids, and rings under running water.
2. Fill your canner with water and place the jars on the rack, allowing the jars to simmer, covered, over medium heat at a constant temperature of 180°F until ready to use.
3. In a saucepan, add enough water to cover the lids, and simmer them over medium heat (making sure not to boil them). Like the jars, keep the lids in hot water until you are ready to use them. There is no need to heat the rings once you have washed them under running water.
4. Add the contents to a canning jar, leaving 1 to 1¼ inches of headspace for low-acid foods.
5. To remove any air bubbles, take a clean spatula or knife and run it around the edge of the mixture. Then use a clean, warm, damp towel to remove any contents from the jar's lip or threads. Place the lids on the jars and then the rings, tightening just to fingertip-tightness.
6. Depending on what type of pressure method you are using, you will need to use a different pressure setting. For either a digital gauge or a weighted-gauge pressure canner, process pints for 75 minutes and quarts for 90 min-

utes. For a digital-gauge pressure canner, use 11 pounds of pressure between sea level and 2,000 feet, and increase the pressure by a pound after every increase of 2,000 feet. For a weighted-gauge pressure canner, use 10 pounds of pressure between sea level and 1,000 feet, and 15 pounds for anything higher.

7 At the end of the processing time, remove the canner from the heat and let the pressure drop on its own, about 30 to 45 minutes depending on the canner and size of the jars.

8 Remove the pressure regulator before opening the cover of the canner. When opening the canner, lift the lid toward you to block the steam and direct it away from you.

9 Using a jar lifter, carefully remove the jars from the canner, keeping them upright. Set them on the counter on a thick dishtowel to cool for 12 hours.

10 Check each jar's lid to make sure there is a tight seal. If so, tighten the rings fully, and clearly label and date the jars. If a lid is not sealed, refrigerate the jar or reprocess with a fresh lid.

PICKLING

PICKLING IS A USEFUL PRESERVATION TECHNIQUE because it is relatively low-cost and high-reward—with just a few ingredients (vinegar, salt) and some time, the pickling solution will kill bacteria in your food, preserving it well.

BASIC

PICKLING LIQUID

MAKES 10½ CUPS

A basic pickling liquid can be made in advance and used for just about anything. You can start with this basic ratio and then experiment by infusing the liquid with herbs, garlic, or other aromatics.

PREP TIME: 3 minutes
COOK TIME: 5 minutes
TOTAL TIME: 8 minutes

- 5 cups rice wine vinegar
- 2½ cups water
- 2½ cups sugar
- ½ cup salt

Combine all of the ingredients in a medium saucepan over medium-high heat and bring to a simmer. Stir for several minutes until the sugar and salt dissolve, then remove the pan from the heat. This liquid can be used to pickle your favorite vegetables by simply submerging them in a food-grade container and storing them in the refrigerator. You can also process them using the hot-water-bath or pressure-canning method (opposite).

PICKLED
WATERMELON RINDS

MAKES 6 TO 8 CUPS

It is rare that we think to save the watermelon rind. Next time, instead of wasting them, give them a pickle. They have a delicious crunch that pairs well with pâté and cured meats. And if you want to add a little color, throw one peeled, raw red beet into the pickling liquid for a beautiful pink rind.

PREP TIME: 30 minutes
COOK TIME: 10 minutes
INACTIVE TIME: 30 minutes
TOTAL TIME: 1 hour, 10 minutes

- Half of a medium watermelon
- 7 cups rice vinegar
- 3¼ cups sugar
- 4 tablespoons kosher salt
- ½ cup raspberry vinegar
- 1 tablespoon black peppercorns
- 2 pieces star anise
- 2 tablespoons coriander seed
- 1 tablespoon fennel seed
- 1 tablespoon ground cardamom

REUSING
PICKLING LIQUID

Once the preserved vegetables and fruits have been eaten, you can reuse the liquid to pickle or cure again. In the case of pickling, simply reheat the liquid according to the recipe instructions and repeat the process as directed.

1. Cut apart the hard green rind and soft pink flesh of the watermelon and save the flesh for another use. Remove and discard the hard green part of the rind. Trim the remaining white rind into ¼-inch batons and set them aside.
2. Combine the rice vinegar, sugar, salt, raspberry vinegar, peppercorns, star anise, coriander, fennel, and cardamom in a large saucepan. Add 2 cups of water and bring to a boil. Remove from the heat and let the mixture cool for about 30 minutes.
3. Add the watermelon rinds to clean pint or quart mason jars and ladle the liquid over them, filling to about ¼-inch from the top. You can keep the seasonings in or strain them out as you pour the liquid.
4. Store the jars in the refrigerator for up to 6 months. They will be ready to eat after several hours, but the flavor will become stronger with time; it's best if you wait at least 48 hours. Alternatively, process the rinds in a hot-water bath (see page 144) for 15 minutes. They are best when consumed within 12 to 18 months of canning.

PICKLED

PEPPERS, CARROTS, AND ONIONS

MAKES 4 QUARTS

Pickled peppers make a beautiful gift when packed in all shapes, colors, and sizes. If you have all green peppers, add some thinly sliced carrots and red onions for color and flavor. The peppers themselves are delicious chopped up and served as a condiment alongside a cheese plate, or use the whole medley of carrots, onions, and peppers on a sandwich.

PREP TIME: 10 minutes
COOK TIME: 40 minutes
TOTAL TIME: 50 minutes

- ½ tablespoon mustard seed
- ½ tablespoon coriander seed
- ½ tablespoon fennel seed
- ½ tablespoon whole black peppercorns
- ½ tablespoon cumin seed
- ½ tablespoon dried thyme
- 2 fresh or dried bay leaves (optional)
- 4 cups white wine vinegar
- 2 cups sugar
- ¼ cup salt
- About 20 jalapeño peppers or similar-sized peppers
- 2 cups thinly sliced carrots, ⅛-inch thickness (2 to 3 large carrots)
- 1 cup thinly sliced red onion, ⅛-inch thickness (1 small red onion)
- Fresh dill or other fresh herbs (optional)

1. Toast the mustard seed, coriander, fennel, peppercorns, cumin, thyme, and bay leaves, if desired, in a large pot over medium heat for about 2 minutes, stirring continuously, until they begin to exude their aroma.

2. Add the vinegar, sugar, salt, and 4 cups of water. Stir well, raise the heat to high, and bring to a boil.

3. Pack the peppers, carrots, and onions into 4 quart mason jars (or more if you have additional peppers), along with any fresh herbs, if using.

4. Pour the liquid into the jars and let it cool to room temperature with the lids loosely secured. Store the jars in the refrigerator for up to 6 months. Alternatively, process the pickled peppers in a hot-water bath (see page 144) for 10 minutes. They are best when consumed within 12 months of canning.

BASIC PICKLE DYES

Eating is a sensory experience and a large part of our enjoyment of food comes not just from flavor, but from texture and color as well. Some pickled vegetables may taste delicious but look rather drab. You can remedy this by incorporating natural pickle dyes into your recipes. Here are several dyes to try, which will brighten up the shelves of your pantry and make your pickles much more visually appetizing. The recipes below demonstrate how to use the dyes, but feel free to substitute your favorite vegetable, as the dyes will translate well.

SAFFRON

PICKLED GINGER

MAKES 1 PINT

For a bright yellow, use a few strands of saffron to liven up this jar of pickled ginger. To peel the ginger easily, scrape away the skin with a spoon. To get a very thin slice, use a mandolin or the side of a box grater. If saffron is difficult to find, or too expensive, use 1 teaspoon of turmeric for a warmer golden color. Try mixing this ginger into sandwich spreads or pair with fish as a condiment.

PREP TIME: 5 minutes
COOK TIME: 3 minutes
INACTIVE TIME: 24 hours
TOTAL TIME: 24 hours, 8 minutes

- 1 cup rice vinegar
- 3 tablespoons sugar
- 1 teaspoon kosher salt
- 1 pinch saffron threads
- 1 cup peeled, thinly sliced fresh ginger

1. In a medium saucepan over medium-high heat, combine ½ cup of water with the vinegar, sugar, salt, and saffron and bring to a simmer. Stir to dissolve the sugar and salt, about 3 minutes.
2. Place the ginger in a pint mason jar and pour the liquid over it. Let cool to room temperature, then tighten the lid and let it sit in the refrigerator for 24 hours before using. It will store in the refrigerator for up to 6 months. Alternatively, process the ginger in a hot-water bath (see page 144) for 15 minutes. This is best when consumed within 12 months of canning.

PICKLED RED BEET–

SWISS CHARD STEMS

MAKES 2 PINTS

Red beets are what make pickled Swiss chard stems bright and beautiful rather than brown and unappealing. You may want to wear rubber gloves when peeling the beets, or at the very least hold the beet with a paper towel. Red beets turn everything they come in contact with bright pink.

PREP TIME: 5 minutes
COOK TIME: 15 minutes
TOTAL TIME: 20 minutes

- 1 cup sugar
- 2 cups white or rice wine vinegar
- ¼ cup salt
- 1 teaspoon mustard seed
- 1 teaspoon black peppercorns
- 1 teaspoon fennel seed
- 1 teaspoon coriander seed
- 1 medium red beet, peeled and chopped into 1-inch chunks
- 2 cups Swiss chard stems, cut into 2-inch batons

1. In a large pot over high heat, combine 1 cup of water with the sugar, vinegar, salt, mustard seed, peppercorns, fennel seed, coriander seed, and beet, and bring to a boil. Remove from the heat and let cool to room temperature.

2. Add the Swiss chard stems to pint jars, filling them about halfway, then ladle the liquid and seasonings over them. They will store in the refrigerator for up to 6 months. Alternatively, process the chard stems in a hot-water bath (see page 144) for 30 minutes. They are best when consumed within 12 months of canning.

PINK PICKLED EGGS

MAKES 8 EGGS, PLUS ACCOUTREMENTS IN THE JAR

Pickled eggs are a special accompaniment to any salad. They also make spectacular deviled eggs. There is nothing like a bright-pink deviled egg with a creamy yellow yolk to turn heads at a dinner party. Here you use red beets to dye the eggs, but you can skip this step if you want to keep it simple.

PREP TIME: 10 minutes
COOK TIME: 45 minutes
INACTIVE TIME:: 1 week
TOTAL TIME: 1 week, 55 minutes

- 2 medium purple beets, peeled and cut into eighths
- 8 large eggs, hard-boiled and peeled
- ½ small yellow onion or 2 small shallots, thinly sliced
- ½ cup cider vinegar
- ½ cup white wine vinegar
- 4 tablespoons sugar
- 1 teaspoon kosher salt
- 1 teaspoon mustard seed
- 1 large garlic clove, crushed

1. In a small saucepan, over medium-high heat, cover the beets with water and cook until tender, about 30 minutes.
2. Drain the beets, reserving the liquid in a small bowl. There should be at least 1 cup of liquid left. If too much has evaporated, add water to bring the amount to 1 cup. Put the eggs, beets, and onion in a quart mason jar.
3. In a small saucepan, combine 1 cup of beet liquid, the cider and white wine vinegars, sugar, salt, mustard seed, and garlic, bring to a boil, and reduce to a simmer for 3 to 4 minutes to dissolve the sugar completely.
4. Pour the hot brine over the contents in the jar to cover. Cool to room temperature, seal the jar, and refrigerate for at least 1 week before serving. Stores in the refrigerator for up to 6 months. Alternatively, process the pickled eggs in a hot-water bath (see page 144) for 15 minutes. They are best when consumed within 12 to 18 months of canning.

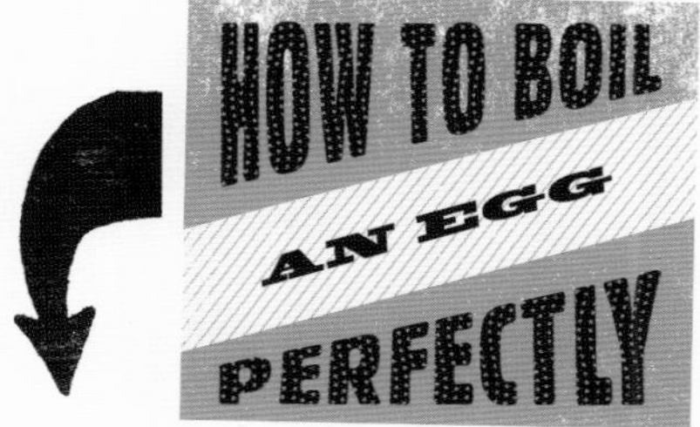
HOW TO BOIL
AN EGG
PERFECTLY

PLACE THE EGGS IN A POT OF COLD WATER AND BRING THE WATER TO A BOIL. IMMEDIATELY REDUCE THE HEAT TO A SIMMER AND LET THE EGGS COOK FOR 8 TO 10 MINUTES MORE. REMOVE FROM THE HEAT AND RUN UNDER COLD WATER UNTIL THEY REACH ROOM TEMPERATURE. THIS WILL PRODUCE A FULLY COOKED YOLK WITHOUT A BLUISH-GRAY RING.

HOW TO PEEL AN EGG WITH EASE

Fresh eggs are good for omelets and frying, older eggs are best for boiling. The whites of fresh eggs stick to the membrane more often, so the best way to ensure your eggs aren't too fresh and are easy to peel is to buy them and let them sit in your refrigerator for a week. Or you can test them by putting them in a bowl of water—the older ones will sit upright or tilt slightly while the fresh ones will lay on their sides.

1. When you peel the eggs, crack the shells all over by rolling the egg against a hard surface. This will help loosen the membrane. Then drop them in a bowl of cold water and peel them underwater.
2. If the egg still won't peel, microwave it for 20 seconds. Let it cool for another 20 seconds before removing it from the microwave, dropping it in ice water, and trying again.

SALT, SMOKE, AND TIME

SALT CURING AND SMOKING, two of the oldest techniques used to preserve food, will help your food keep longer. Curing in particular inhibits the growth of harmful microorganisms by using salt to draw water out of the protein cells through osmosis. Kosher salt is ideal for curing because it isn't heavily refined. Each grain has many faces, which helps draw out moisture. This is how it earned the name kosher salt—it is the kind of salt kosher slaughterhouses use in order to extract all of the blood from their meat so that it can be deemed kosher. A lot of people also think the flavor is more pure, so you will see it in a lot of professional kitchens. Smoke has also long been used to extend the shelf life of food well before refrigeration or chemicals were available. In the process it also adds flavor and tenderizes any cut of meat. If possible, choose a wood that is indigenous to your area: In the South use pecan, in the Southwest use mesquite, in Washington state use apple wood, and in the Midwest use the hickory tree.

PRESERVED

MEYER LEMONS

MAKES 1 QUART OR 12 MEYER LEMON HALVES

Preserved lemons are common in Middle Eastern tagines but also work nicely with fish, in braises, or even finely diced and incorporated into ice cream. When Meyer lemons are in season during the winter, I like to make a batch of these because their floral flavor translates well when preserved. A little goes a long way.

You can reuse an old pickle jar or any clean glass jar you have on hand and fill it with lemons and salt. That is all you need to make them—well, that and a little patience. When you are ready to use the lemons, remove the amount needed, rinse them in cold water, and remove and discard the pulp. Chop the rind and use in your desired recipe.

PREP TIME: 10 minutes
COOK TIME: None
INACTIVE TIME: 4 weeks
TOTAL TIME: 4 weeks, 10 minutes

3 to 4 cups kosher salt
5 to 6 Meyer lemons, cut in half horizontally or vertically
2 star anise, or other preferred flavoring

1. Pour an inch of salt into a 1-quart mason jar, then begin adding the lemons, making sure they fit snugly and alternating with a lot of salt along the way. Add the star anise as you go, and continue to add salt and lemons until the jar is completely full. Bang the jar on the counter a few times to remove air and help things settle. Top with salt and cover the jar.

2. Place the jar in a cool, dark cabinet for at least 1 month, preferably longer. If it becomes very liquid, add more salt to the top. They will store in a cool, dark place for up to 6 months.

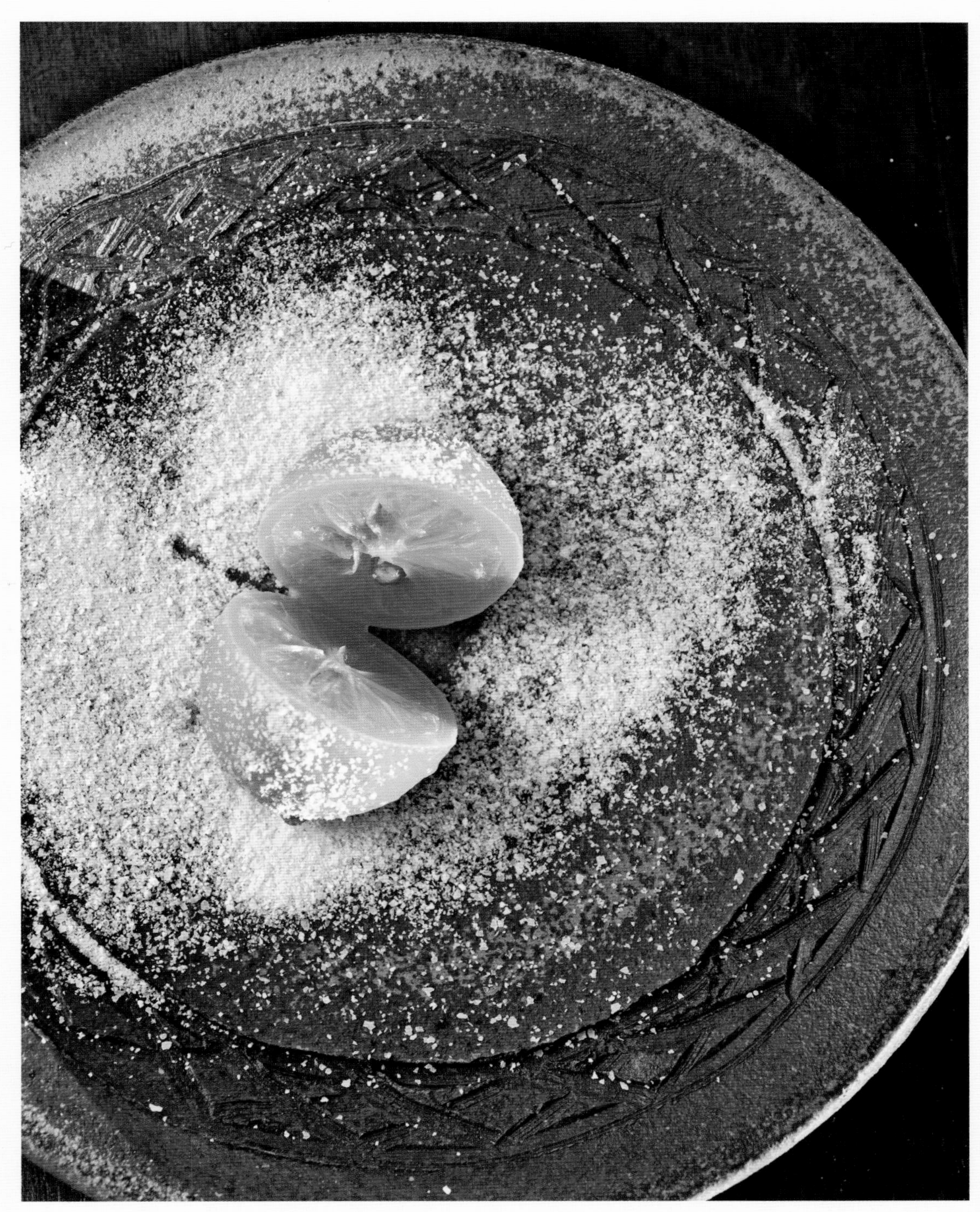

SPICED
KEY LIMES

MAKES 1 CUP

Sometimes in the colder months, we need a little spice in life to keep things lively. And sometimes when we cook at that time of year, it is easy to get into a rut and feel like we are making the same things over and over again. What I love about this recipe is that it is an instant way to add intrigue to any of the dishes in your standard repertoire. Have a favorite chicken or fish or pheasant dish? These spiced beauties will turn them into something entirely new. Key limes are only available in the winter, so if you would like to try this with regular limes, simply cut them in half and use fewer, or a slightly larger jar for which you can increase the ingredients proportionately.

PREP TIME: 10 minutes
COOK TIME: None
INACTIVE TIME: 4 weeks
TOTAL TIME: 4 weeks, 10 minutes

- 4 to 5 whole key limes
- 10 whole cloves
- Juice of 5 key limes
- ⅓ cup kosher salt
- 1 2-inch cinnamon stick
- ½ teaspoon black peppercorns
- 1 star anise
- Extra virgin olive oil

1. Wash the key limes well and slice them in half horizontally. Make an incision in each half of the rind with the tip of a paring knife and insert a clove.
2. Place the limes in a small bowl with the key lime juice and salt. Then add the cinnamon stick, peppercorns, and star anise and toss. Pour the entire contents into a pint mason jar, cover, and allow the key limes to ripen at room temperature for 7 days. Shake daily to distribute the salt and flavorings.
3. After 7 days, add the olive oil to cover the limes and age them 3 to 4 weeks at room temperature before using. They will store in a cool, dark place for up to 6 months.

SMOKED SALTS

MAKES ½ CUP SALT

You don't need a smoker for these; just a stovetop, a wide, deep pot or wok, and some wood chips. Smoked salts are expensive at the store and can be made at home in 20 minutes with regular table salt. Coarse sea salt is a great option if you have it. Mix the smoky results with lemon zest, dried chili peppers, dried herbs, or even roasted garlic for a special finish to dishes from seafood to scrambled eggs. You can experiment with various wood chips to see what you like, then store them in small jars.

PREP TIME: 1 minute
COOK TIME: 20 minutes
TOTAL TIME: 21 minutes

- ½ cup salt

1. Line the bottom of a wok or wide, deep pot with aluminum foil and place 1 cup of wood chips on top.
2. Lay another piece of foil gently above it, leaving plenty of air. Pour your salt evenly on the surface and place the lid on the pot.
3. Turn the burner on medium heat and let the salt smoke for 20 minutes. You may want to turn your stove vents on, though it won't become overwhelmingly smoky. If the smoke seems too intense, turn down your heat.
4. After 20 minutes, turn off the heat and leave the covered pot as is for 5 minutes to let the smoke subside. Remove the lid and top piece of tin foil and pour the salt into a storage jar with a lid to keep by your stove.

GRAVLAX

SERVES 12

Salting was the only widely available method of preserving food until the nineteenth century, and salt pork and salt beef were common staples for sailors on long journeys. Cured salmon is often called *gravlax*, a word that comes from Scandinavia. *Grav* means "grave," and *laks* means "salmon." In the Middle Ages, the fishermen of that region salted and fermented their salmon in the sand—a little grav for their laks. Today we do it in a similar way, minus the actual sand. Salmon is buried in a mixture of salt and sugar and cured for a few days. The salt and sugar serve as a highly concentrated brine, after which you have the option of smoking the salmon or eating it simply cured. Try to use wild Alaskan salmon rather than farmed salmon; it is both tastier and better for you.

PREP TIME: 20 minutes
COOK TIME: 20 minutes
INACTIVE TIME: 48 to 72 hours
TOTAL TIME: 48 hours, 40 minutes

- 3 lemons
- 3 limes
- 2 oranges
- 1 tablespoon ground coriander
- 4 cups kosher salt
- 2 cups sugar
- 1 tablespoon whole black peppercorns
- 2 pounds salmon, boneless and skinless, at least 1½ to 2 inches thick

1. Use a grater to remove the zest from the lemons, limes, and oranges.
2. In a 9 × 13-inch nonreactive baking dish, mix the zest with the coriander, salt, and sugar. Set aside.
3. Heat a small pan over medium-high heat until it is hot but not smoking. Toast the peppercorns until they exude their aroma, about three minutes. Place the toasted peppercorns on the counter or a cutting board, and use a heavy-bottomed pan to crush them (you could also use a mortar and pestle). Add the cracked peppercorns to the cure and mix.
4. Bury the salmon in the mixture snugly.
5. Cover the dish in plastic, place a weight on top, and store in the refrigerator for 24 hours to cure. Check the firmness of the fish by pushing aside the cure and pressing it with your finger. It should indent only slightly. It will likely need an additional 24 hours, but if it feels quite stiff, then remove it from the salt.
6. Remove the salmon from the cure, rinse well with water, and pat dry. You can slice it thinly, about ⅛-inch thick, and eat it this way, or refrigerate for 24 hours on a rack so the surface becomes tacky and will absorb smoke more readily. Then smoke it for 20 minutes, or use the method described in "How to Smoke Meat Without a Smoker" (page 160).

HOW TO SMOKE MEAT WITH FRESH HERBS

If you have an outdoor grill or even want to try the stovetop method (see page 160), adding fresh herbs will impart an especially wonderful aroma to your foods.

1. Get your smoker going so that the coals are giving off a low radiant heat of about 200°F to 250°F.
2. Gather a bunch of highly aromatic herbs with strong oils, such as rosemary, sage, oregano, and thyme. Tie them in a bundle with twine or simply bunch them, and using tongs, carefully tuck them in to the coals or wood chips.
3. Place your meat on a grill rack above the coals and close the lid. Allow it to smoke and the meat will soak up the aroma of the herbs as it does.

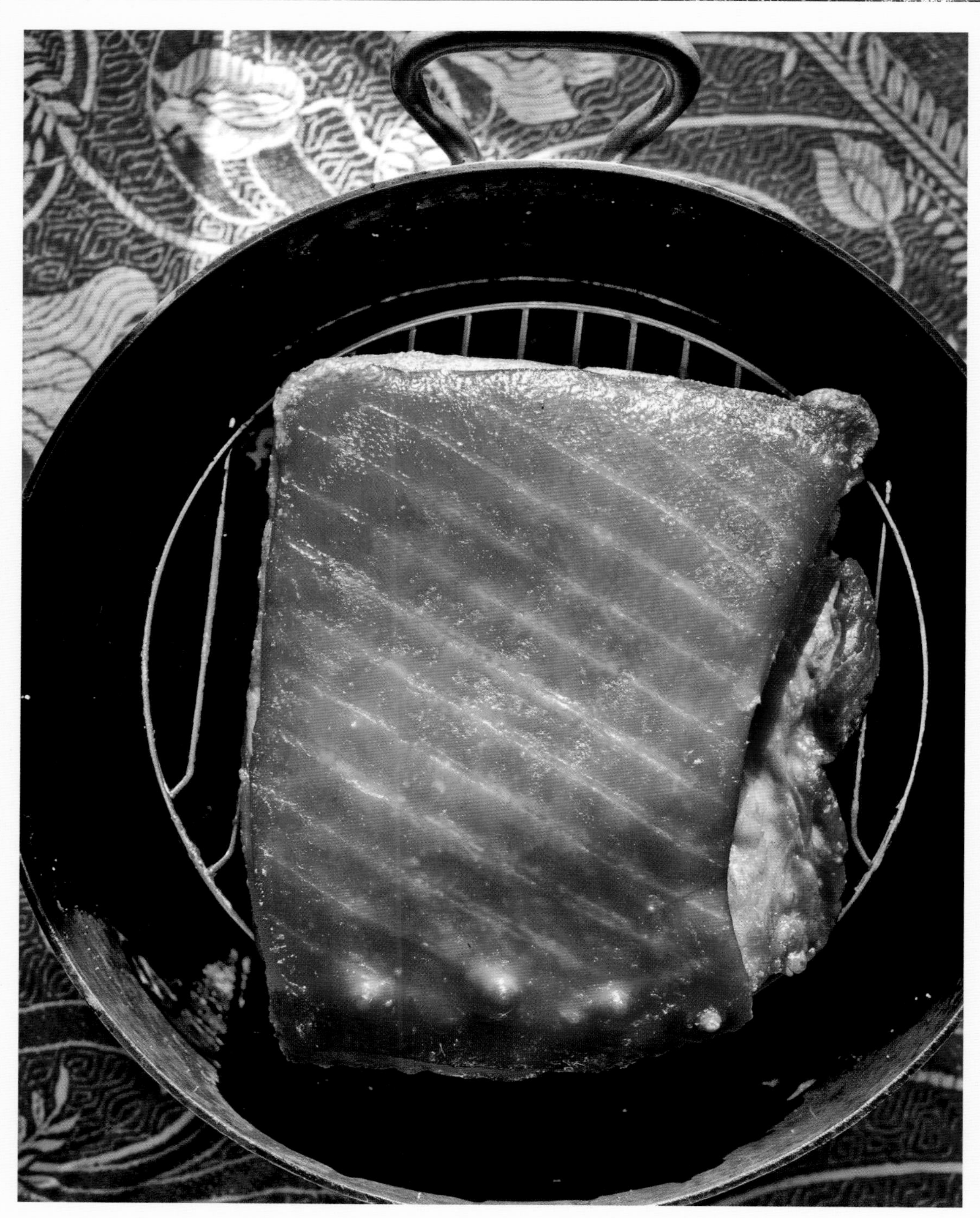

BROWN SUGAR BACON

MAKES 2½ TO 4 POUNDS BACON

I know people who are vegetarians, except for bacon. The sheer, irreplaceable majesty of pork is a delicacy too precious to pass up. There are so many tasty parts to a pig, but I think hands down the most crowd-pleasing and easy to make is bacon. When you prepare it yourself, you can enjoy its true versatility beyond the typical store-bought strips—cut it into batons, known as lardons, for classic French dishes, or into thicker cubes for soups, stews, and beans, or gently grill a whole slab at once and serve it as a main course. If you make a cure in advance, you can store it in a sealed container indefinitely so that you will always have it on hand to whip out at a moment's notice.

PREP TIME: 15 minutes
COOK TIME: 45 minutes
INACTIVE TIME: 1 week
TOTAL TIME: 1 week, 1 hour

FOR THE BACON:

- 3 to 5 pounds pork belly, skin on if you plan to smoke it, skin off if you don't
- ¼ to ½ cup dry cure

FOR THE DRY CURE:

- 2 cups kosher salt
- 1 cup light brown sugar
- 3 tablespoons plus 1 teaspoon pink salt #1 (this is used in many types of cured meat products to keep them safe, and can be found on Amazon or other online sites)

1. To make the bacon, trim the pork belly of any dry meat and glands and discard them. Neaten the edges of the pork belly and set aside.

2. To make the dry cure, combine the kosher salt, brown sugar, and pink salt in a small bowl. Place the pork belly in a large, nonreactive baking dish or sheet tray covered in plastic, and cover the pork with the dry cure, coating all sides evenly and thoroughly and pressing it into all the cracks and crevices.

3. Place the baking sheet in the refrigerator, loosely covered in plastic, for 5 to 7 days, turning the pork belly over once a day to make sure it cures evenly, until the meat feels firm throughout when pressed with your fingers. The thicker the belly, the longer it will take to become firm. The pork will release a lot of liquid as it cures, so it is important that the cure stay in contact with the meat the whole time. You may need to press the cure directly back onto the meat or add additional cure if the original cure becomes too liquid before the meat is ready.

4. When the pork belly is ready, rinse and dry it thoroughly.

5. If you want to smoke your bacon, let it sit in the refrigerator on a rack overnight to dry out and form a pellicle on the skin. This will allow for better smoke adhesion. Alternatively, use a fan for several hours to speed up the process. When ready to smoke, preheat a grill or smoker to 200°F and burn wood chips, such as apple wood or hickory, for at least 30 minutes, then add the bacon. If you have a stovetop smoker, follow the directions that come with it; if you don't have a smoker at all, use the method described on page 160. Hot-smoke the meat until it reaches an internal temperature of 150°F. You can monitor this without opening the smoker by using a meat thermometer with a cord and a 6-inch metal probe inserted into the thickest part of the meat.

6. While the fat is still warm, immediately remove the skin with a sharp knife and discard it. Serve immediately, or you can keep the bacon in the refrigerator for up to 2 weeks or cut it into manageable sizes, wrap it in plastic, and store it in the freezer for up to 3 months.

HOW TO SMOKE MEAT WITHOUT A SMOKER

A NICE SMOKED CHICKEN OR SLAB OF BACON SHOULDN'T BE RESERVED FOR THOSE WHO HAVE AN OUTDOOR SPACE AND A SERIOUS SMOKER. SEASON YOUR MEAT TO YOUR LIKING AND USE THIS ALTERNATIVE METHOD TO IMPART EXCELLENT FLAVOR.

Wood chips like apple wood, hickory, mesquite, or pecan

Small pot

Aluminum foil

Large wide pot or wok with a lid

Round cake rack with legs, or another shape that fits inside your pot

Seasoned meat

Meat thermometer with a cord attached to a 6-inch metal probe

Sauce

1. Soak your wood chips in water in a small pot for 30 to 60 minutes, then drain them.

2. Lay a piece of aluminum foil at the bottom of your pot or wok, followed by the wood chips. Then place the rack inside the pot, so that it sits several inches above the wood chips, and lay your seasoned meat on the rack. Place the probe of the thermometer inside the thickest part of the meat, making sure it doesn't touch any metal. Run the wire from the pot and ensure that it is plugged into the digital monitor, which should be set next to the pot. This will allow you to monitor the internal temperature of the meat without opening the seal and losing smoke.

3. Cover the pot with a lid, completely sealing the vessel on all sides. Use aluminum foil as well if necessary to get a good seal. The more tightly it is sealed, the smokier your meat will be.

4. Set your stovetop burner on medium-high heat and cook the meat to the desired internal temperature. Turn on an oven vent or open a window to keep the room from smelling especially smoky.

5. To give it a finishing glaze, remove the lid, brush it with the sauce of your choice, and smoke it for a few minutes more.

CORNED BEEF

SERVES 8 TO 10

No one is certain how the technique of corning beef really came about, but most theories assume that it was first used to preserve meat; these days, we still corn beef for the flavor, but most processes call for keeping the brisket in the refrigerator for a few days while the meat brines. To corn beef without refrigeration, you will need to find a place where the temperature is as cool as a normal fridge (about 40°F to prevent the growth of any bacteria in the meat), so if you prefer this option this recipe is best made in the winter months.

If you see meat on sale, take the opportunity to buy it in large quantities and corn it to make it last. This technique is best used on tougher, less expensive cuts of meat with muscle and connective tissue that need to be braised until tender—brisket, for example. Once you have corned it, however, you shouldn't freeze it since the brine will make it mushy. You can, however, freeze the meat right after buying it and then brine it at a later date once you are ready to defrost it. To cut through the salty result of corning, serve it alongside a strong, coarse mustard. Also be sure to rinse the meat well after brining and before cooking.

PREP TIME: 15 minutes
INACTIVE TIME: 10 days
COOK TIME: 2 hours, 30 minutes
TOTAL TIME: 10 days, 2 hours, 45 minutes

- 8 cups cold water
- ¾ cup kosher salt
- ⅛ cup sugar
- ½ teaspoon black peppercorns, cracked
- ½ teaspoon mustard seed, cracked
- ½ teaspoon coriander seed, cracked
- 1 fresh or dried bay leaf
- 2 whole cloves
- 1 cinnamon stick
- 2 cloves garlic, crushed
- 2½ to 3 pounds beef brisket
- 2 yellow onions

1. In a large nonreactive pot, heat 2 cups of water with the salt, sugar, peppercorns, mustard, coriander, bay leaf, cloves, cinnamon, and garlic over medium heat, and whisk together until the salt and sugar have mostly dissolved, about 5 minutes.

2. Remove from the heat and add the remaining 6 cups of cold water, which will lower the temperature, making it cool enough to add the brisket without cooking it. Place the brisket in a large plastic brine bag or a large nonreactive bowl and pour in the brine. If using a bowl, weigh down the meat with a plate so that it is completely submerged.

3. Place the meat in the refrigerator to brine for 10 days. Remove the brisket and rinse well; discard the brine. The meat is now corned and ready to be cooked.

4. Place the meat in a large, heavy-bottomed pot and barely cover it with water. Slice and add the onions, turn the heat to high, and bring to a boil. Reduce the heat to medium-low, cover the pot, and simmer for 2½ hours, or until the meat is tender. Slice the meat across the grain and serve it with Hot Pink Sauerkraut (page 189) and mustard.

CORNED BEEF (PAGE 161)

with HOT PINK SAUERKRAUT (PAGE 189)

THE ART OF DRYING FOODS

FOODS DON'T LOSE ANY NUTRITIONAL VALUE when stored in their dehydrated form, so this technique allows you to keep a well-balanced pantry that won't expire. When foods are dried, their flavors often intensify, which means that you can also use less, prolonging your food stores even further. Home dehydrators are a useful tool in helping you convert fresh food into a form for long-term storage. But there are plenty of ways to dry foods with an oven or even the sun if you are feeling adventurous. When you end up with a glut of fruit or meat especially, drying is a great way to store it and have healthy snacks on hand.

CRANBERRY CHEWS

MAKES 2 CUPS

These dried fruits are one of my favorite homemade gifts. They have a great tartness to them, which make them rather addictive. When cranberries are fresh around the holidays, you can buy these in large quantities and dry them for later use, or put them in small plastic gift bags, which you can get at a craft store, and secure them with a bow. Cranberries are also available frozen, or you can opt for strawberries, blackberries, and so on. If choosing a different berry, taste them when fresh and depending on their sweetness, use less sugar.

PREP TIME: 5 minutes
COOK TIME: 30 minutes
INACTIVE TIME: 8 hours
TOTAL TIME: 8 hours, 35 minutes

2 cups fresh cranberries, rinsed and picked over
1½ cups raw sugar, plus more for dusting
Vegetable oil for greasing the pan

1. Combine the cranberries, sugar, and 1¼ cups water in a medium saucepan over low heat, and stir to dissolve the sugar. Gently simmer until the liquid foams and thickens and the cranberries burst, about 30 minutes.

2. Meanwhile, preheat the oven to 200°F. Line two sheet pans with parchment and lightly brush with oil. Alternatively, line the sheet pans with Silpats.

3. Remove the cranberries with a slotted spoon and spread them evenly over the pans. Discard the liquid. Separate the individual berries as best you can with a fork. Place in the oven and let dry about 8 to 10 hours or until only slightly tacky.

4. Gently peel the cranberries off the parchment or Silpats into bite-size pieces with your fingers. Roll the pieces in sugar to keep them from sticking together. They will store at room temperature in an airtight container for up to 6 months.

PINEAPPLE CHIPS

MAKES 2 CUPS

These chips are light and healthy and can be made from many fruits in addition to pineapple; pears would be another good option. You will want slices that are about 1/8-inch thick, or as thin as possible without breaking the fruit up. Use a mandolin slicer if you can; inexpensive Japanese versions are available in most kitchen supply stores. An apple corer is also a good tool to have, or you can cut the pineapple into segments and carefully cut the core out with a sharp paring knife. If you want to spend a little more money, you can buy precored pineapple at the grocery store.

PREP TIME: 10 minutes
COOK TIME: 2 hours
TOTAL TIME: 2 hours, 10 minutes

- 1 fresh pineapple
- Vegetable oil for greasing the tray

1. Preheat the oven to 200°F.
2. Cut off the top and bottom of the pineapple and sit it upright. Remove the rind with a knife by cutting slices off the sides from top to bottom. Then use an apple corer or handheld corer to remove the core. Since the pineapple is longer than the corer, cut it into segments and then push the corer through the center of each segment. Thinly slice the pineapple using a mandolin or serrated knife, as thinly as your slicer will allow without breaking the pineapple ring.
3. Lay a piece of parchment paper on a 13 × 18 cookie sheet and spray or brush it lightly with vegetable oil.
4. Arrange the pineapple slices in a single layer on the parchment. You will have enough to fill three half-sheet pans if you would like.
5. Place the cookie sheet in the oven and dry the slices for about 2 to 4 hours depending on their thickness. The slices will be a deep-golden color and slightly pliable. Check the fruit pieces every 30 minutes to make sure they don't become too brown and brittle. They will be slightly pliable when ready but still golden. As they cool off, they will crisp up. Store in an airtight container for up to 1 month.

DUCK BREAST
PROSCIUTTO

SERVES 8

Curing meat was widespread among historical civilizations because it prevented waste and guaranteed a food supply in case of a poor harvest. The French and Italians were the first to raise this skill to an art form. Local craftsmen formed guilds and produced a range of cooked or salted dried meats, which varied from region to region.

Simple to make at home, duck prosciutto is a perfect way to store meat when you don't have time to cook it, and you just can't fit another thing in your freezer. All that it requires is salt, cheesecloth, and some twine, and a cool room with good relative humidity. If you aren't sure of the humidity, you can get a small inexpensive humidifier to control it; it is useful to have around in the dry months anyway. The flavor of duck prosciutto is gamier and richer than pig prosciutto, and the color is a deeper red. But it still has that signature chewy, delicate, salty flavor. Try to find the thickest duck breasts you can; the ones from a whole duck tend to be thin, making it harder to cut slices from the dried product. Serve this prosciutto with pear, crackers, cheese, or just by itself.

PREP TIME: 5 minutes
COOK TIME: None
INACTIVE TIME: 5 to 7 days
TOTAL TIME: 5 days, 5 minutes

- 2 cups kosher salt
- 2 duck breast fillets, skin on, about 2 pounds total
- ½ teaspoon freshly ground black pepper

1 Pour half of the salt into a large nonreactive container that will hold the breasts snugly but without touching. Then place the duck breasts on the salt, skin side up. Pour the remaining salt on top and pack it well with your hands. Cover the container with plastic and place it in the refrigerator for 24 hours.

2 Remove the breasts from the salt, rinse them well under water, and pat them dry. They should be a deeper red and feel firm to the touch.

3 Dust the breasts with pepper and wrap them individually in cheesecloth. Tie one end with a piece of kitchen twine about 6 inches long, which you can use to hang them from.

4 Hang the breasts in a cool place (50°F to 60°F) for 5 to 7 days until the flesh is stiff but not hard throughout. Remove from the cheesecloth and slice paper-thin on a mandolin to serve. These will keep refrigerated and wrapped in plastic for about 1 month.

TERIYAKI TURKEY JERKY

SLIM JIMS

MAKES ABOUT 30 6-INCH STRIPS

Jerky is protein-rich, so it's especially good for traveling or hiking. There are two ways to make it, either by slicing turkey breast and marinating it as with the Salmon Jerky (opposite), or by seasoning a mixture of ground meat, forming it into shapes, and drying it Slim Jim–style. This recipe shows you how to do the latter version, and your house will smell like heaven. But if you would like to slice turkey or chicken into strips, you can use all of the same ingredients below with 2 pounds of turkey breast and the addition of 1 cup of pineapple juice, and let the meat soak overnight before dehydrating as described below.

PREP TIME: 10 minutes
COOK TIME: 5 to 7 hours
INACTIVE TIME: 8 to 24 hours
TOTAL TIME: 13 hours, 10 minutes

- ¾ cup soy sauce
- 3 tablespoons honey
- 2 tablespoons red wine vinegar
- 1 teaspoon freshly grated ginger
- 1 teaspoon garlic powder
- 1 teaspoon cayenne pepper
- 2 pounds ground turkey, ideally dark meat

1. In a small bowl, whisk together the soy sauce, honey, vinegar, ginger, garlic powder, and cayenne pepper. Set aside.
2. In a medium bowl, add the turkey and pour the sauce on top. Stir until well incorporated. Cover in plastic and refrigerate overnight, or for at least 8 hours.
3. Preheat the oven to 200°F. Grease a baking sheet lined with foil or parchment.
4. Using a jerky gun or pastry bag fitted with a ½-inch round tip, pipe the jerky mixture onto the baking sheet in 6-inch lengths, leaving about 2 inches of space between each strip.
5. Place the tray in the oven and let the strips dry until they are pliable, 5 to 7 hours, turning them over halfway through. They will store in a plastic container for up to 2 weeks.

SALMON JERKY

MAKES ABOUT 24 STRIPS

Salmon jerky is one of my favorites when wild salmon is in its prime season. Slightly addictive and very satisfying, it is perfect for a summer picnic, a hike, or a long airplane ride. Fresh strips of protein are soaked in a marinade or brine, then traditionally hung to dry in the sun or dehydrated and smoked over slow, dry heat, with the addition of a few seasonings.

PREP TIME: 10 minutes
INACTIVE TIME: 12 hours
COOK TIME: 2 hours
TOTAL TIME: 14 hours, 10 minutes

- 1½ pounds wild salmon, skinned, with pin bones removed
- ¼ cup sugar
- ⅛ cup kosher salt
- 1 teaspoon freshly grated ginger
- 2 tablespoons red chili garlic paste
- Oil to brush the racks

1. Using a sharp slicing knife, cut the salmon against the grain into ¼-inch-thick flat strips. Make the strips as uniform as possible to ensure even drying. Set aside.
2. In a large resealable plastic bag, combine the sugar, salt, ginger, and garlic paste, and stir to create a uniform paste. Place the salmon strips in the cure and toss them to coat thoroughly. Seal the bag and place it in the refrigerator for 12 hours.
3. After 12 hours, remove the racks from the oven and preheat it to 200°F. Completely cover the racks with aluminum foil and brush them with oil.
4. Take the salmon from the refrigerator and arrange the strips across the oven racks, leaving ½-inch of space between the strips.
5. Place the racks in the oven and dehydrate the salmon for about 3 hours. When it is ready it will be darker in color, and slightly pliable before breaking when bent.
6. Let the strips air-dry further until they are firmer and only slightly pliable to the touch. Blot any oil or moisture with a paper towel. Store in an airtight container for 3 months.

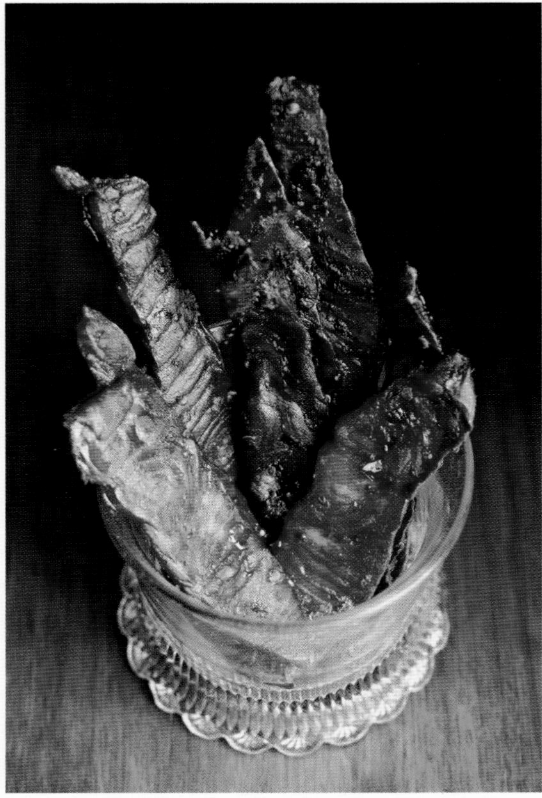

PRESERVING AND JAMMING

PRESERVING AND JAMMING FRUITS, ESPECIALLY THROUGH CANNING, turns seasonal items into year-round pleasures. These are important self-sufficiency skills as they help increase your fruit stores.

To pectin or not to pectin? That is the question. My answer: It depends on how much sugar you like to add to your preserves and jams. I favor a minimalist approach to sugar because it detracts from the flavor of the fruit and lowers the nutritional value. Fruits like quince and apple are high in pectin so they will jell even without sugar. For fruits like raspberries and strawberries, a little extra pectin will help you create a bright, sweet, and tart flavor without a lot of added sugar.

QUINCE

FRUIT CHEESE

SERVES 25

The Spanish call this *membrillo*, a paste made from the slowly cooked quince fruit. The French call this preparation *pâte de fruit*, and you can make it with many other fruits with a little patience and a food mill. Quinces can be found in the fall and look like they are a cross between an apple and a pear. They aren't good to eat raw, but when cooked they have a floral aroma and turn a deep blush red. You can leave this fruit paste out on the counter and it will remain stable at room temperature without refrigeration. Try a slice with Manchego cheese, which is a popular combination in Spain.

PREP TIME: 5 minutes
COOK TIME: 1 hour, 45 minutes
INACTIVE TIME: 6 hours
TOTAL TIME: 7 hours, 50 minutes

10 quinces, cut into eighths, with seeds and peels intact
1 750-ml bottle fruity white wine
Juice of ½ lemon
2 cups sugar
Vegetable oil for greasing tray

1 In a large pot over medium heat, combine the quinces, wine, lemon juice, sugar, and 4 cups water and bring to a simmer. Cover, reduce to low heat, and gently poach the quinces, turning them over several times to ensure even cooking, until they are soft and nicely blush in color, about 60 minutes.

2 Pass the quince mixture through a food mill or ricer into another large pot, and cook the puree over high heat, stirring constantly, until the color takes on a deeper blush and the puree holds stiff peaks to a spatula, about 45 minutes. Remove from the heat and set aside.

3 Cover a half-sheet tray with parchment and brush it with oil. Then spread the quince paste evenly, 1 inch deep, using a spatula or pastry scraper to smooth the top, into the tray. Cover the fruit paste with plastic and place in the refrigerator for at least 6 hours before serving. To store it, wrap it in plastic and cut slices or cubes from it to serve.

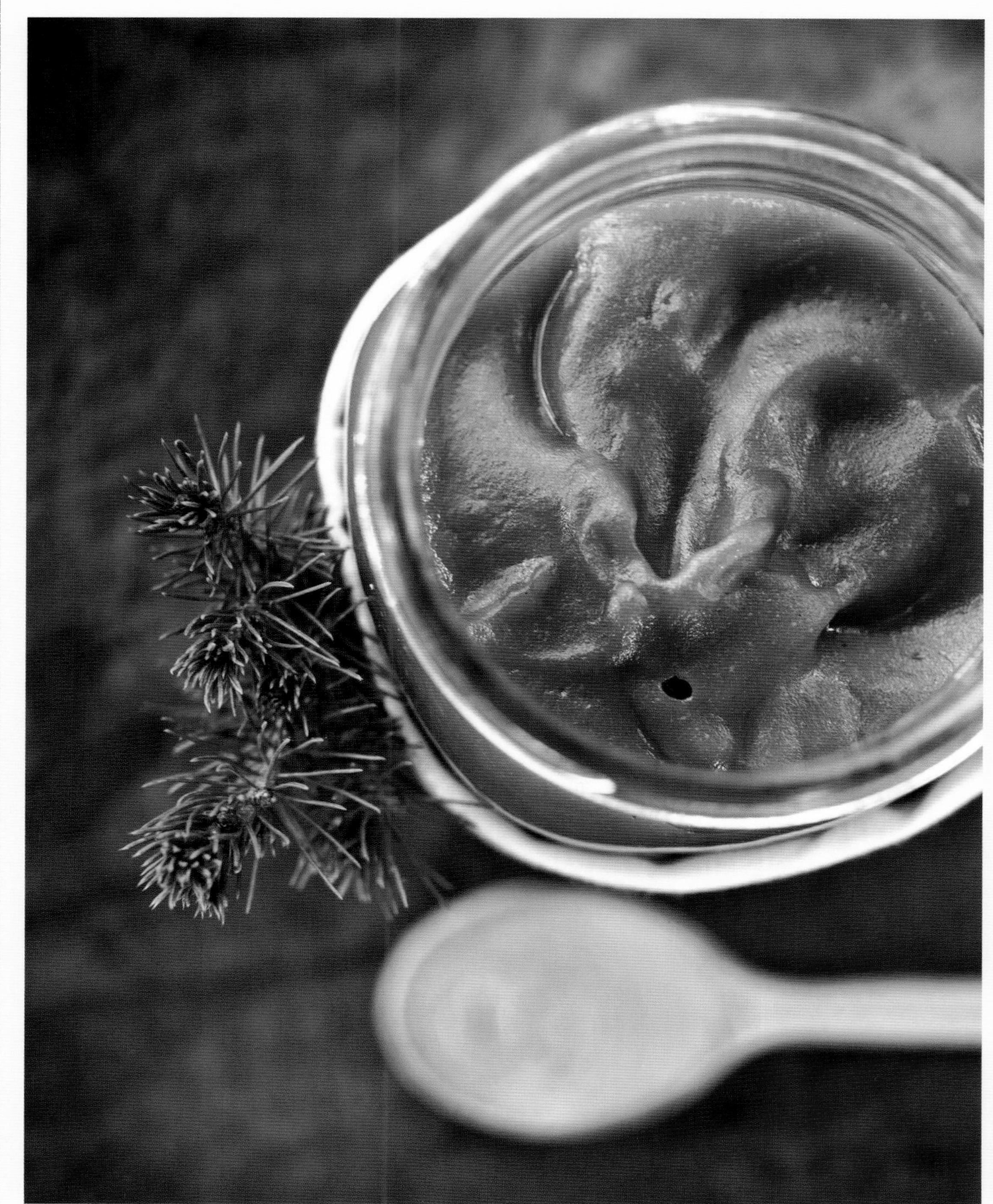

APPLE BUTTER

MAKES 3 PINTS

Apple butter is best when made with fresh, tart fall apples. As the apples cook, the water evaporates, leaving behind the natural sugars and a potent apple flavor, which will continue to develop as the apple butter sits in the refrigerator. Serve this spread on crackers or morning toast with a slice of cheddar cheese. If you don't have a food mill but want to give this recipe a try, you will need to peel and core the apples before cooking them, then puree them in a food processor or blender in between the two cooking phases.

PREP TIME: 15 minutes
COOK TIME: 2 hours
TOTAL TIME: 2 hours, 15 minutes

- 6 pounds apples, half Granny Smith and half Pink Lady or Fuji varieties, quartered (skin and seed intact)
- 3 cups apple cider
- ¼ cup cider vinegar or white wine vinegar
- 1 teaspoon salt
- 4 cloves
- ½ teaspoon ground allspice
- 1 cinnamon stick

1. Combine the apples, cider, vinegar, and salt in a large pot with 1 cup of water. Cover and simmer over medium-high heat until the apples start to become soft, about 20 minutes. Remove the lid, decrease the heat to medium-low, and let the mixture bubble until the liquid is reduced to almost nothing and the apples are very soft, about 40 minutes.

2. Pass the contents through a food mill into another large pot. When using a food mill, turn the knob in the opposite direction every so often to scrape away any sediment clogging the pores of the mill. This will ensure that the apples pass through easily.

3. Add the cloves, allspice, and cinnamon stick, and cook over medium-low heat, stirring often, until the apple puree thickens and turns a deep brown. This may take up to 60 minutes depending on the moisture in the apples. Toward the end you will need to stir continually so that the developing sugars don't burn. If the mixture spatters too much, lower the heat further. (It is also useful to have a fine-mesh spatter screen to place over the top to ensure you don't get burned.)

4. Turn off the heat and remove the cinnamon stick. Ladle the apple mixture into a blender and puree until smooth. For extra-smooth butter you can then pass the mixture through a fine-mesh strainer.

5. Ladle the butter into pint mason jars and let it cool before placing the lids on and putting them in the refrigerator, where they will store for up to 6 months or in a freezer-safe container for 1 year. Alternatively, process the apple butter in a hot-water bath (see page 144) for 10 minutes. It is best when consumed within 12 months of canning.

BLOOD ORANGE MARSALA
MARMALADE

MAKES 4 CUPS

Blood oranges, which are in season in the winter months, lend this marmalade a dark-red or deep-orange color, and a wonderful bitterness to balance out the sweet. If blood oranges aren't available, Seville oranges have a bitterness and pectin that will work equally well. They are slightly larger so you will need fewer, about eight to ten.

PREP TIME: 15 minutes
COOK TIME: 1 hour, 40 minutes
INACTIVE TIME: 20 minutes
TOTAL TIME: 2 hours, 15 minutes

- 12 small blood oranges, rinsed
- 32 cups cold water
- 3 cups sugar
- 1 tablespoon dry marsala wine (optional)

1. Place the oranges in a large pot and cover with 8 cups of cold water. Bring to a boil for 5 minutes, then remove from the heat. Pour off and discard the water. Repeat this process two more times so that the oranges have been blanched three times total.

2. Cover the oranges a fourth time in 8 cups of cold water and let them simmer, untouched, over low heat for about an hour, until the peel can be easily pierced with a fork. Remove from the heat.

3. Transfer the oranges into a large bowl with a slotted spoon and let them cool until they are easy to handle. Reserve the orange water in the pot for later. While the oranges are cooling, place 2 or 3 tasting spoons in the freezer (they will be used to check whether your marmalade has jelled).

4. Cut the oranges in half and scoop out the inner flesh, pith, and seeds with a spoon and reserve them in a bowl. Set the peels aside.

5. Set a fine-mesh strainer over the pot of orange water and add the orange flesh, pith, and seeds. Press with a spatula or large spoon to extract as much liquid as possible. Then gather the flesh, pith, and seeds in some rinsed cheesecloth, tie it with twine, and set it inside the pot of liquid.

6. Slice the peel into strips that are ⅛-inch thick and ½-inch long and place them into the pot of liquid. Turn the heat to low and simmer the orange liquid and sachet for about 10 minutes.

7. Add the sugar and bring the mixture to a boil for 30 minutes, or until it thickens and reaches a setting point. To test this, remove one of the tasting spoons from the freezer and add a drop of marmalade to it (do not dip it in the pot), then place it back in the freezer. After 5 minutes remove it and hold it vertically to see if the marmalade runs or is set. If it runs, let the mixture cook on the stove for another 5 minutes and try again with another frozen spoon.

8. Remove the pot from the heat and skim any foam from the surface. Let it sit in the pot for 20 minutes to cool, then stir in the marsala wine, if desired. Ladle the marmalade into jars and store them in the refrigerator for up to 6 months. Alternatively, process the marmalade in a hot-water bath (see page 144) for 10 minutes. It is best when consumed within 12 months of canning.

RASPBERRY JAM

MAKES 1 TO 2 CUPS

Many of the commercial jams you buy have large quantities of sugar in them because it costs less than fruit. The joy of making your own jam is that you have the chance to preserve the bright fruit flavors rather than overwhelm them with sugar. Pectin will help you achieve a jammy consistency. The cooking process is much faster when using pectin as well.

I err on the side of tart, since the slightly sour makes your mouth water a bit and keeps you wanting more. Every fruit is different, so taste your berries, see how sweet they are, and adjust the amount of honey or sugar you add accordingly as it cooks. If you use pectin, note the directions on the box. I use Pomona's Universal Pectin, which may call for a slightly different amount than other varieties.

PREP TIME: 3 minutes
COOK TIME: 30 minutes
TOTAL TIME: 33 minutes

- 4 cups fresh raspberries
- 2 tablespoons honey
- 1 teaspoon no-sugar-needed, powdered pectin, such as Pomona's Universal Pectin

1. Add the raspberries to a medium saucepan, cover, and cook over medium heat. Stir them often as the liquid releases.

2. After the raspberries have broken down to a puree (about 15 minutes), stir in the honey and pectin. Reduce the heat to low and let the mixture simmer gently, stirring often, until it has a jam consistency, about 15 minutes. Ladle the jam into 1-cup jars and let them cool before sealing. They will store in the refrigerator for up to 6 months. Alternatively, process the raspberry jam in a hot-water bath (see page 144) for 5 minutes. It is best when consumed within 12 months of canning.

PRESERVING WITH FAT

MANY PEOPLE LEAVE FATS AND OILS out of a basic food storage effort, but they are actually essential to a well-prepared pantry because they create a digestive balance. They also improve the taste and texture of food.

Preserving food in oil creates a barrier against moisture, making the items less appealing to bacteria and prolonging the edible life of fresh proteins like fish. Oil and fat present a particular food-storage challenge, however, because as they age, they oxidize and become inedible, particularly when exposed to heat, oxygen, or light. As a result, all unopened, store-bought fats should be stored in dark, cool, or even cold conditions, no more than 70°F, and rotated using the "first in, first out" rule.

There are many different sources of animal fat, good for different types of cooking, that you can render yourself. There is leaf lard, taken from the fat around pig kidneys and inside the loin. It makes the most perfect flaky piecrusts, and for that it is considered the highest grade of lard. Then there is the next highest grade, called fatback, the hard fat between the back skin and muscle of the pig. You can use that for cooking the way you would butter or olive oil. Then there is the soft caul fat surrounding the digestive organs, perfect as a wrapping for lean meats or in pâtés. A little fat in your food will leave you much more satisfied.

There are plenty of vegetarian fats that deserve a spot in your pantry as well. Cold-pressed extra virgin olive oil has the longest shelf life of all vegetable oils, up to two years, particularly when stored in a metal can over a plastic jug or glass bottle. Vegetable-based oils will keep up to a year in any pantry but remember, the darker the oil, the shorter its shelf life. Nut butters like peanut butter can keep up to a year. Ghee, or clarified butter, is another great option. True ghee will have a shelf life of up to two years, and can be used anywhere you would use butter or for deep-fat frying (without the milk solids of butter, ghee can cook at higher temperatures without smoking). Coconut oil is a solid saturated oil that can have an extremely long shelf life if kept at a temperature below 70°F. It also has the added bonus of boosting your immune system's ability to attack viruses and bacteria.

HOW TO

RENDER FAT

MAKES 1 CUP

Learning to render from animal skin will ensure that you always have fat available to you. It is the process of slowly cooking fat scraps in water until the water evaporates and the liquid fat is left. A butcher will also save fat scraps for you if you ask them, and they will sometimes even give them to you for free. Or, simply save your duck, chicken, or pork fat as you trim your meat through the months, and store the scraps in the freezer until you have at least a pound. You will need a fine-mesh strainer or some cheesecloth to strain the fat once it has been rendered.

This recipe is based on 1 pound of fat, but if you have more, simply plan to increase the amount of water and cooking time. All of the leftover crispy pork skins that remain in the pan once the fat is rendered can be saved and incorporated into cornbread for a delicious cracklin' bread.

PREP TIME: 1 minute
COOK TIME: 1 hour, 15 minutes
TOTAL TIME: 1 hour, 16 minutes

1 pound duck, chicken, or pork fat trimmings

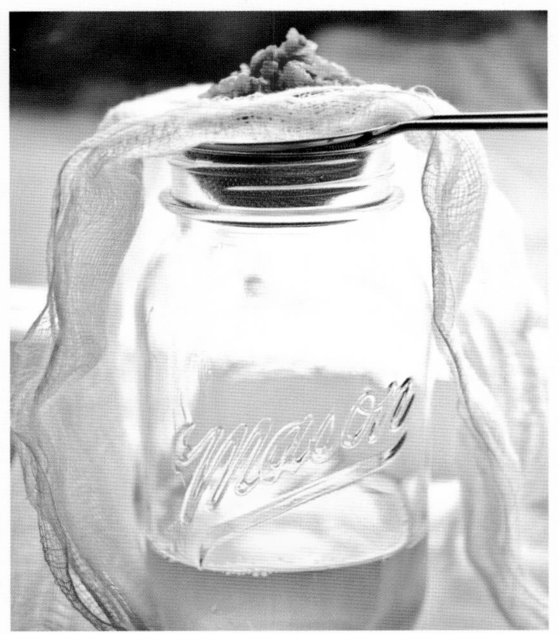

1. Place the fat in a medium skillet or pot and add water so it reaches about halfway up the sides of the fat. Set the burner to its lowest setting and let the liquid simmer, uncovered and undisturbed.

2. When it starts to look as though the simmer is dying down, watch the fat carefully. As the water evaporates, the bubbles will come closer to a boil and the remaining liquid will turn dark-gold. This will take anywhere from 60 to 90 minutes depending on the moisture content of the fat and the level of heat. Be careful at this stage, as there may be spattering as the last bits of water burst from the skins. A spatter screen would be useful here. Stir occasionally to prevent the fat from sticking to the bottom of the pan.

3. When the boiling bubbles suddenly become even smaller, just back to a bare simmer, all the water is gone. Remove the skillet from the heat immediately and pour the fat through a fine-mesh strainer into a mason jar. Let cool to room temperature, and place in the refrigerator for 1 month or the freezer for 6 months.

PORK RILLETTES

MAKES 6 CUPS MEAT, 8 CUPS WITH FAT

For the most vibrant flavor in this rich-tasting pork, grind the spices yourself in a coffee or spice grinder. Serve these rillettes with toasts and pickled condiments to balance out the fattiness, or stir them into a pan of scrambled eggs in the morning. A glass of wine with strong tannins, such as Shiraz or cabernet, also complements their flavors. You can make this ahead of time and refrigerate it for up to 1 month by keeping the meat covered with a layer of fat such as what is already in the jar or by adding olive oil. If you don't want to render the fat yourself, rendered pork fat is available at farmers' markets, online, and in some specialty or butcher shops.

PREP TIME: 15 minutes
COOK TIME: 3 hours
INACTIVE TIME: 8 hours
TOTAL TIME: 11 hours, 15 minutes

- 2 teaspoons cracked black peppercorns
- ½ teaspoon ground coriander
- ½ teaspoon ground cinnamon
- 2½ tablespoons kosher salt
- ½ teaspoon ground nutmeg
- 3 pounds trimmed boneless pork butt, cut into 2-inch pieces
- 10 sprigs fresh thyme
- 6 garlic cloves, peeled and smashed
- 4 cups rendered pork fat, melted (see page 177)

1. Add the peppercorns, coriander, cinnamon, salt, and nutmeg to a large mixing bowl and mix well. Add the pork and toss until well combined. Add the thyme and garlic cloves, cover the bowl in plastic, and place it in the refrigerator overnight.

2. Preheat the oven to 300°F. Place the pork in a 9 × 13-inch baking dish and cover with 2 cups of melted fat. Cover the baking dish with aluminum foil and place it in the oven. Let it cook for about 3 hours, or until the meat can be easily pulled apart with a fork. Remove from the oven and let cool. Using two forks, shred the meat while it is still in the baking dish. Using a large spoon, scoop the meat and fat into mason jars or crocks. Discard the thyme stems as you do.

3. Cover the tops of the jars with the remaining 2 cups of fat, let come to room temperature, and seal with a lid. Store well sealed in the refrigerator or cool basement for up to 1 month.

TUNA

PRESERVED IN OIL

SERVES 2

This preserving technique for tuna is a must-have when you want to preserve the shelf life of high-quality tuna in your midst. It falls somewhere between fresh and canned tuna; the Italians called it *conservata*, the old tradition of preserving protein in olive oil. It is usually imported from Spain or Italy and sells for as much as $50 a pound, which is especially unnecessary given how easy it is to make yourself. It goes especially well on toast or over a salad.

PREP TIME: 5 minutes
COOK TIME: 10 minutes
INACTIVE TIME: 24 hours
TOTAL TIME: 24 hours, 15 minutes

- 1 pound tuna steak
- 1½ cups extra virgin olive oil, plus more to fill the jar
- 1 teaspoon sea salt
- 1 clove garlic, crushed
- 3 sprigs fresh thyme plus any other aromatics, such as fresh bay leaf, fresh sage, fresh rosemary, lemon peel, or red pepper flakes

1. Rinse the tuna and pat it dry. Cut it into smaller 1- to 2-inch portions to fit all of it snugly into a small saucepan.
2. Add the tuna and oil to a small saucepan along with the salt. Over low heat, cook until bubbles start to come to the surface, about 10 minutes, without letting the oil simmer or bubble too much. The tuna will become opaque and stiff when pierced with a fork. Remove from the heat and stir in the garlic and thyme. Add any other aromatics as desired.
3. Pour the contents of the pan into a quart mason jar. Let it cool to room temperature, cover, and let it infuse overnight before serving. Fill the jar with more oil as needed until the fish is covered.
4. Store in the refrigerator for up to 2 weeks. Let the fish and oil come to room temperature before serving.

PRESERVED

SALMON IN A JAR

MAKES 1 CUP

If you have a piece of fresh fish you can prolong the shelf life even further by using both salt and oil, while also flavoring it with aromatics. It can be stored in the refrigerator for 6 months and makes a beautiful hostess gift in a nice jar. Serve it with crusty bread and be sure to save the oil in the jar to drizzle on salads—it is sublime.

PREP TIME: 10 minutes
COOK TIME: None
INACTIVE TIME: 36 to 48 hours
TOTAL TIME: 36 hours, 10 minutes

- 1 16-ounce salmon fillet, skin removed
- 4 tablespoons kosher salt
- 2 tablespoons sugar
- 6 shallots, thinly sliced
- 6 garlic cloves
- 2 fresh or dried bay leaves
- 6 sprigs fresh thyme
- 4 fresh sage leaves
- 1 tablespoon black peppercorns
- 1 tablespoon coriander seeds
- 2 tablespoons champagne vinegar
- 1 cup extra virgin olive oil, or enough to cover

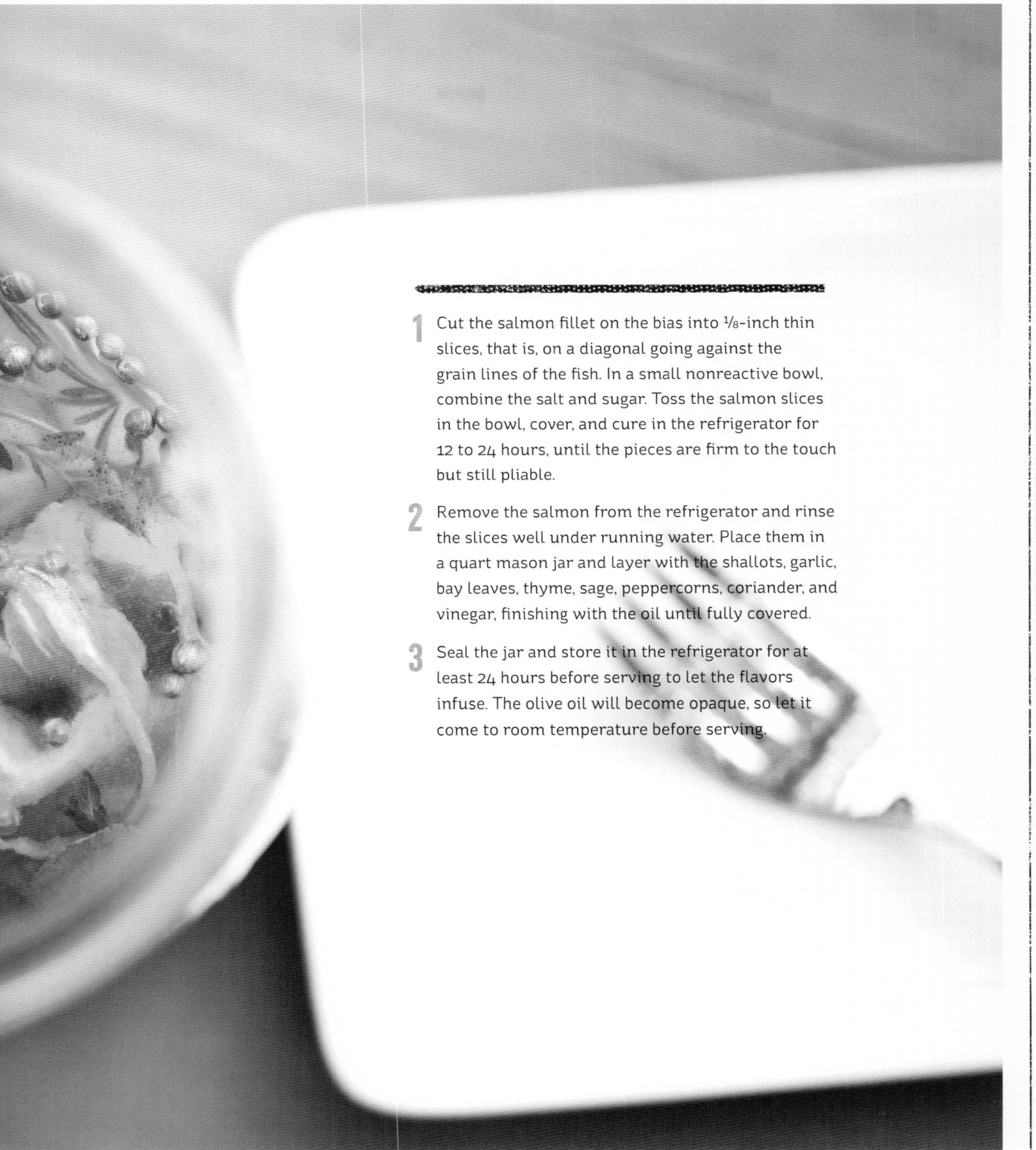

1 Cut the salmon fillet on the bias into ⅛-inch thin slices, that is, on a diagonal going against the grain lines of the fish. In a small nonreactive bowl, combine the salt and sugar. Toss the salmon slices in the bowl, cover, and cure in the refrigerator for 12 to 24 hours, until the pieces are firm to the touch but still pliable.

2 Remove the salmon from the refrigerator and rinse the slices well under running water. Place them in a quart mason jar and layer with the shallots, garlic, bay leaves, thyme, sage, peppercorns, coriander, and vinegar, finishing with the oil until fully covered.

3 Seal the jar and store it in the refrigerator for at least 24 hours before serving to let the flavors infuse. The olive oil will become opaque, so let it come to room temperature before serving.

EGGPLANT CARPACCIO

MAKES 8 CUPS

Thin slices of delicate eggplant are wonderful on an antipasto platter or served on a sandwich with fresh mozzarella. They have a little tang and absorb the flavors of the aromatics from the olive oil. Be sure to save the oil to drizzle on foods once the eggplant is gone.

PREP TIME: 20 minutes
COOK TIME: 90 seconds
INACTIVE TIME: 26 hours
TOTAL TIME: 26 hours, 21½ minutes

- 8 cups eggplant, cut into ⅛-inch slices (about 3 medium eggplants)
- ½ cup kosher salt
- 2 cups balsamic vinegar (use white balsamic if using white or light purple eggplant)
- 2 teaspoons red pepper flakes
- 4 fresh or dried bay leaves
- 4 garlic cloves
- 1 red bell pepper, seeded and cut into thin strips (optional)
- 4 cups extra virgin olive oil

1. In a large bowl, combine the eggplant with the salt and toss thoroughly. Let sit for 2 hours, stirring occasionally so that the salt continues to distribute evenly.

2. Pour off and discard the liquid from the bowl. Rinse the eggplant and pat dry.

3. In a large, heavy-bottomed pot, heat the balsamic vinegar to a simmer over low heat and then drop in the eggplant slices in 3 separate batches, boiling each for 30 seconds. Remove the slices with a slotted spoon and transfer them to mason jars. If using pint jars, divide the ingredients into fourths; if using quart jars, divide the ingredients in half. Add the red pepper flakes, bay leaves, garlic, and a few strips of red pepper, if desired, to each jar as you fill it. Then pour the olive oil over each jar. Seal the jar with a lid and shake to distribute the liquid evenly.

4. Let the jars rest for at least 24 hours before serving. You can store these in the refrigerator for up to 1 month. Simply let the oil come to room temperature again before serving.

ALMOND BUTTER

MAKES 1½ CUPS

Nut butters, a high-protein snack, can be made at home in five minutes or less. You can riff on this recipe by roasting the almonds first in an oven for a stronger flavor, or adding any other flavorings, from cocoa powder to cayenne. If almonds aren't your thing, try cashews, pine nuts, or—of course—peanuts.

PREP TIME: 5 minutes
COOK TIME: None
TOTAL TIME: 5 minutes

- 2 cups dry roasted almonds
- 1 teaspoon honey
- ½ teaspoon sea salt

1. Place the almonds in a food processor and begin to blend them.
2. Pour in the honey and salt as it spins. The almonds will go through various stages and will become a lumpy paste right before the oils release and render the almonds smooth, about 5 minutes. You will want to stop the food processor once to scrape down the sides.
3. Turn off the food processor and transfer the almond butter to a mason jar. Store in the refrigerator or a cool basement for up to 6 months.

MAKE HOMEMADE ALMOND FLOUR

THIS METHOD CAN ALSO BE USED TO MAKE HOMEMADE ALMOND FLOUR; SIMPLY PULSE IT FOR LESS TIME UNTIL YOU GET A FINE-GROUND POWDER.

GARLIC CONFIT

MAKES 2 CUPS

Start any large feast like Thanksgiving by making this garlic confit the day before. You will find it tremendously useful to rub on turkey and incorporate into stuffing, slip under chicken skin, serve with sliced tomatoes for breakfast, or spread on crackers as an appetizer. It makes everything taste delicious.

Although garlic is available year-round, the fresh kind in the summer has large cloves that are especially sweet and juicy, and that is the best time to preserve it. If you like you can also add aromatics like red pepper flakes, dried peppers, or herbs of your choosing.

PREP TIME: 15 minutes
COOK TIME: 30 minutes
INACTIVE TIME: 30 minutes
TOTAL TIME: 1 hour, 15 minutes

- 2 cups (about 5 heads) freshly peeled garlic cloves
- 6 sprigs fresh thyme
- 2 fresh or dried bay leaves
- 2 cups grape-seed or extra virgin olive oil

1. Combine all of the ingredients in a medium saucepan and simmer over low heat until the garlic is tender but not browned, about 30 minutes. Note: If the oil begins to bubble too vigorously, turn the heat off temporarily and the oil will still continue to cook the garlic; this is especially important if using olive oil, which has a low smoke point. Once the bubbling slows down considerably, turn the heat back on.
2. Let the mixture cool for at least 30 minutes, then, using a slotted spoon, transfer the garlic and herbs to a quart mason jar. Pour the oil on top and let it cool completely. Store it in the refrigerator or a cool basement for up to 1 month.

GARLIC CONFIT

HOW TO MAKE GARLIC PASTE IN UNDER 30 SECONDS

GARLIC PASTE DOESN'T NEED TO COME FROM THE GROCERY STORE. YOU CAN EASILY MAKE IT YOURSELF. USE FRESH GARLIC THAT YOU HAVE PEELED YOURSELF RATHER THAN THE PREPEELED KIND, WHICH HAS LESS MOISTURE. TRY THIS IN ONE OF YOUR DISHES TODAY—LIFE IS BETTER WITH A LITTLE GARLIC IN IT.

Garlic cloves, freshly peeled
Salt to taste

1. Set the garlic cloves on a cutting board and chop them roughly with a chef's knife, until they are about uniform.
2. Add a copious amount of salt, about 1 tablespoon for every 6 cloves of garlic, then chop the garlic some more to incorporate the salt.
3. Press the flat side of your knife back and forth against the cutting board like you are a master brick worker, moving your trowel and cement. Repeat, and you will have a lovely dollop of garlic paste.

FIG. № 1a

FIG. № 1b

FIG. № 1c

FIG. № 2a

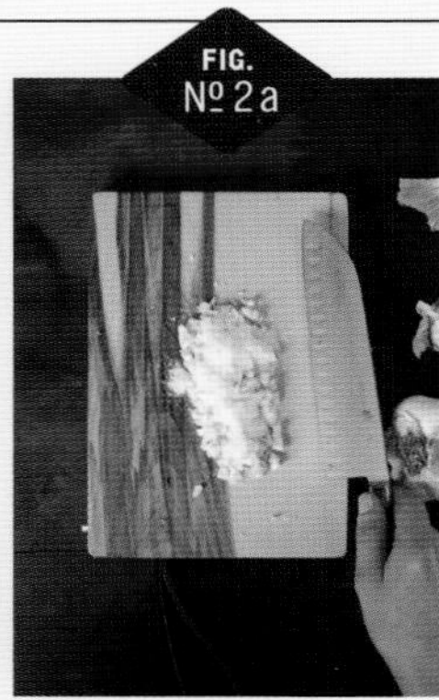

FIG. № 2b

FIG. № 3a

FIG.
№ 3a

FERMENTING

DURING THE FERMENTATION PROCESS, sugars within food are converted to acids, making the food less susceptible to spoiling, not to mention tastier. In many cases, fermentation also helps enhance the nutritional value of the food and makes it easier to absorb and digest, as well as increases the vitamin levels and promotes beneficial flora in the body, all important factors in any life situation.

HOT PINK SAUERKRAUT

MAKES 6 TO 8 QUARTS

Any kind of cabbage will work for this recipe, but whether you mix purple and green cabbage, or use just purple cabbage, you will end up with bright pink sauerkraut. You can start a new batch before the previous batch runs out by using what remains from the crock, repacking it with fresh salted cabbage, and pouring the old juices over the new. This will serve as an active starter culture and give your new batch a head start in the fermenting process. If you develop a rhythm like this you will always have sauerkraut on hand. This recipe is only mildly salty. If you like assertive cabbage you can season it more.

PREP TIME: 10 minutes
COOK TIME: None
INACTIVE TIME: 3 days
TOTAL TIME: 3 days, 10 minutes

5 pounds (about 2 small heads) purple cabbage
8 tablespoons sea salt mixed with 8 cups of water
Caraway seeds, juniper berries, shredded carrots, or any flavoring element you want to try (optional)

1. Chop or grate the cabbage finely or coarsely, however you prefer. Place the sliced cabbage in a nonreactive bowl or ceramic crock alternating with the salt water as you go. This draws moisture out of the cabbage and creates the brine in which the cabbage will ferment.
2. Add your desired flavoring elements, fold into the cabbage, then cover the bowl with a cloth or towel to keep dust and flies away.
3. Over the next 24 hours, check that the brine is above the cabbage. Simply add more salt water (a ratio of 1 tablespoon sea salt mixed into 1 cup of water) if necessary.
4. Let the cabbage ferment in the crock and continue to check it every 2 days. The kraut will become tangy after a few days, at which point you can begin eating it, but it will become stronger over time. Take it from the crock to eat as needed but leave the rest in the crock, fully submerged, to continue to develop. Keeping it in a cool place is beneficial because it will slow the fermentation, which will preserve the kraut for longer. The volume will reduce over time, and a bloom may appear at the surface. This is simply a reaction to contact with air and can be skimmed off. If you find that the brine begins to evaporate, just add more salted water. You can continue to add fresh cabbage to this brine to ensure a constant supply.

KIMCHI

MAKES 6 TO 8 CUPS

This fermented, pickled cabbage is a staple in Korean foods. Its wonderful spiciness pairs well with sandwiches, bowls of soup, or a heaping plate of ribs. You can mix in various other vegetables—daikon is a popular one. Just like with sauerkraut, it's possible to use some old kimchi from a previous batch as a starter for your new batch.

PREP TIME: 10 minutes
COOK TIME: None
INACTIVE TIME: 4 days, 4 hours
TOTAL TIME: 4 days, 4 hours, 10 minutes

- 2 heads Napa cabbage
- ¾ cups coarse sea salt
- 3 tablespoons fish sauce
- 5 to 6 green onions (white and tender green parts), cut into 1-inch lengths
- 1 cup shredded carrot (you can do this quickly in a food processor or slowly by hand)
- ½ small white onion, minced
- 5 cloves garlic, pressed
- 2 teaspoons honey
- 1 teaspoon ground ginger
- 5 tablespoons red chili paste or Korean chili powder

1. Cut the cabbages in half lengthwise and trim the ends of their thickest part. Rinse and cut them into 2-inch square pieces. Place the cabbage in a ceramic crock, nonreactive bowl, or large mason jar and sprinkle with the salt. Mix thoroughly with your hands to ensure it is evenly coated. Cover the container in plastic wrap and let it sit for 4 hours.

2. Rinse the salt from the cabbage and strain the cabbage through a colander. Return it to the crock and stir in the fish sauce, green onions, carrot, white onion, garlic, honey, ginger, and chili paste. Combine until the cabbage leaves are thoroughly coated.

3. Seal the container with a lid or plastic wrap and let it sit in a cool, dry place for 2 to 4 days. Check it daily; when it starts to bubble, it is time to refrigerate it. Refrigerate for several hours before serving, and store in the refrigerator for up to 1 month.

KEFIR

MAKES 6 CUPS

This liquid is intensely good for you, a drinkable yogurt full of beneficial bacteria, and even better when flavored at the breakfast table with fruit purees (try it with Raspberry Jam, page 175). You will need a digital food thermometer to make sure you activate the bacteria successfully. You can make kefir with coconut milk, rice milk, sheep's milk, goat's milk, or soy milk but it won't get as thick as with cow's milk.

PREP TIME: 1 minute
COOK TIME: 5 minutes
INACTIVE TIME: 18 hours
TOTAL TIME: 18 hours, 6 minutes

4 cups whole cow's milk
1 5-gram package kefir starter culture (can be found online or at health food stores) or 2 cups of kefir

USE OLD KEFIR TO MAKE NEW

YOU CAN REUSE THE KEFIR CULTURE MANY TIMES AS A STARTER BEFORE YOU NEED TO BEGIN ANEW: 2 CUPS OF KEFIR FROM A PREVIOUS BATCH WILL FERMENT 1 QUART OF NEW KEFIR.

1. Heat the milk in a saucepan over medium heat until the surface just begins to foam, stirring often so that it doesn't scald, about 5 minutes. Remove from the heat and let it cool to between 73°F and 117°F.

2. In a bowl, combine the starter culture with 1 cup of the cow's milk and whisk together. Whisk in the remaining milk.

3. Ladle the mixture into mason jars and seal the lids to fingertip tightness. Set aside. Time and temperature affect the thickness and flavor of kefir. In warmer temperatures it may be ready to drink in 18 hours; in cooler temperatures it will take longer, so observe the thickness and creaminess every 8 hours or so. Left too long at room temperature it will turn cheesy and sour, so checking its progress is key. It should be creamy, like a drinkable yogurt, thicker than milk, with a sour perfume. Shake it well and refrigerate it once it has reached this pivotal state to slow down the culture. You can drink it immediately or wait for it to chill. It can be stored in the refrigerator for 12 months, and several years in the freezer.

PRESERVING WITH ALCOHOL

ALCOHOL, WITH ITS HIGH ACIDITY, is a veritable germ-killing machine. Because of this, preserving with alcohol is a near surefire way of ridding your food of any bacteria and ensuring food safety. Preserve fruits or make cordials and infused liquors with it. You are left in many cases with a one-two punch of boozy fruit to use in desserts and flavored alcohol for an exciting cocktail.

MARASCHINO CHERRIES

MAKES 1 PINT JAR

These cherries are a great dessert staple to have on hand. All you will need to get next is some sprinkles and some ice cream. Or some vermouth, bourbon, and a martini glass. Which will it be? If you can get your hands on a cherry pitter the result will be most similar to the store-bought kind of maraschinos. If you want to be really laborious about it, use a paring knife instead. Alternatively, you can be naughty and leave the pits in; just be sure to tell your guests about the pits before serving them. Another lazy girl's method: Pitted cherries are sometimes available in the frozen foods section of the grocery store. After the pitting is done, these are very simple to make, and more flavorful than the traditional saccharine ones.

PREP TIME: 15 minutes
COOK TIME: 5 minutes
INACTIVE TIME: 24 hours
TOTAL TIME: 24 hours, 20 minutes

- 2 cups Bing cherries, fresh or frozen and thawed
- ½ cup sugar
- 1 teaspoon kosher salt
- Juice of 1 lemon
- 1 tablespoon almond extract
- 1¼ cups cherry liqueur, Maraschino if you can find it!
- ¾ cup grenadine

1. Wash and pit the cherries using a paring knife or cherry pitter. Leave the stems on if possible. Set them aside.
2. In a medium saucepan, combine the sugar, ½ cup water, and salt. Place over medium-high heat and bring to a simmer. Stir until dissolved, then turn off the heat and add the lemon juice, almond, cherry liqueur, and grenadine and stir.
3. Spoon the cherries into a pint mason jar and pour the hot liquid over them. Allow the jar to cool to room temperature, then cover with a lid.
4. Let sit for 24 hours before using. Store in the refrigerator for up to 2 weeks. Alternatively, process the cherries in a hot-water bath (see page 144) for 20 minutes (15 minutes for pint jars). They are best when consumed within 12 to 18 months of canning.

SHIRLEY TEMPLE'S ALL GROWN UP

MAKES 2 DRINKS

Here is one way to make use of your homemade maraschino cherries, based on a favorite childhood drink of mine. I recommend it with extra cherries on top. You deserve it.

PREP TIME: 3 minutes
COOK TIME: None
TOTAL TIME: 3 minutes

- 1 cup (8 ounces) seltzer water
- ¼ cup (2 ounces) whiskey or bourbon
- 1 teaspoon grated fresh ginger
- 1½ tablespoons grenadine syrup
- 6 Maraschino Cherries (page 192)
- Crushed ice

1. Combine the seltzer, whiskey, ginger, grenadine, and 3 of the maraschino cherries in a mixing glass and stir vigorously.
2. Add crushed ice to your favorite glass and pour the mixture over. Top with 3 maraschino cherries, or more, and serve.

APRICOT BRANDY

MAKES 12 APRICOTS AND 2 CUPS OF BRANDY

Apricots are hard to get year-round, so preserve them when you can. The result of this recipe will be deliciously boozy apricots. Eat the fruit separately, warmed through slightly, and serve with ice cream, Greek yogurt, or a simple drizzle of heavy cream. If you don't have fresh apricots substitute 2 cups of unsulphured, unsweetened dried apricots. They will become reconstituted, soft, and custardy.

PREP TIME: 1 minute
COOK TIME: None
INACTIVE TIME: 1 month
TOTAL TIME: 1 month, 1 minute

- 12 small fresh apricots, washed
- 2½ cups brandy
- ¼ cup superfine sugar

1. Place the fruit whole, or cut into pieces, in a quart mason jar.
2. Pour over the brandy and sugar, making sure all the fruit is covered. Seal the jar and shake to dissolve the sugar.
3. Place the jar in a cool, dark place for 1 month, shaking it several times a week. Then you can begin to strain out the fruit and eat it as well as use the alcohol as desired. It will keep for 6 months in a sealed container in a cool, dark place.

AVOIDING WASTE

IT IS EASY TO WASTE FOOD when we are busy. Leftovers end up sitting in the refrigerator, eating out becomes convenient, and late-night meetings mean that groceries don't always get consumed in time. Here are some ways to become thriftier with your food that is a bit over the hill, as well as ideas on how to make the most of the summer glut of produce when it appears in farmers' markets at great prices. Cooking with economy is even more important when you are only working with a few basic ingredients because it adds variety and flavor to simple foods that would otherwise be monotonous.

RED WINE

POPSICLES

MAKES 10 POPSICLES

After a party there are often myriad bottles of wine with a little bit left in the bottle. Or you may open a bottle of wine one night, and not have a chance to finish it the next night before it oxidizes. Taste it and if it is no longer drinkable but hasn't turned to vinegar, turn it into this sweet grown-up treat by reducing the liquid and adding flavorings. If you don't have Popsicle molds, use small paper cups. If you can't get Popsicle sticks, large wooden skewers cut to size will work in a pinch.

PREP TIME: 5 minutes
COOK TIME: 15 minutes
INACTIVE TIME: 8 hours, 20 minutes
TOTAL TIME: 8 hours, 40 minutes

- 3½ cups red wine (equivalent to one 750 ml bottle)
- Peel of 1 orange
- 4 cardamom pods, crushed
- 6 whole cloves
- 8 black peppercorns, crushed
- 1 cinnamon stick
- ½ cup sugar

1. Heat all the ingredients in a medium saucepan over medium-high heat. Stir, lower the heat, bring to a simmer, and reduce the liquid until you have one cup remaining, about 15 minutes. Reducing it to this point is important because the freezing point of wine is lower than water, so the alcohol content must be cooked down. Remove from the heat and let the liquid cool for 20 minutes. Remove the cinnamon stick.
2. Stir in 3 cups of water.
3. Carefully ladle the liquid into Popsicle molds, place a Popsicle stick in each one, and freeze overnight.

RED WINE BATH THERAPY

Pour 1 cup of leftover wine into the bathtub and settle in. The resveratrol in the wine is a powerful antioxidant that softens and firms skin. Vinotherapy at its finest!

TURN LEFTOVER COFFEE INTO...

COFFEE ICE CUBES

Have leftover coffee in that pot? Don't toss it in the sink. Instead, pour it into ice cube trays and freeze it overnight. Adding it to your iced coffee will keep it cold without diluting it, which is especially nice in the summer months. As a variation, pour leftover hot chocolate into the ice cube trays for frozen chocolate deliciousness, which will add a mocha flavor to your iced coffee.

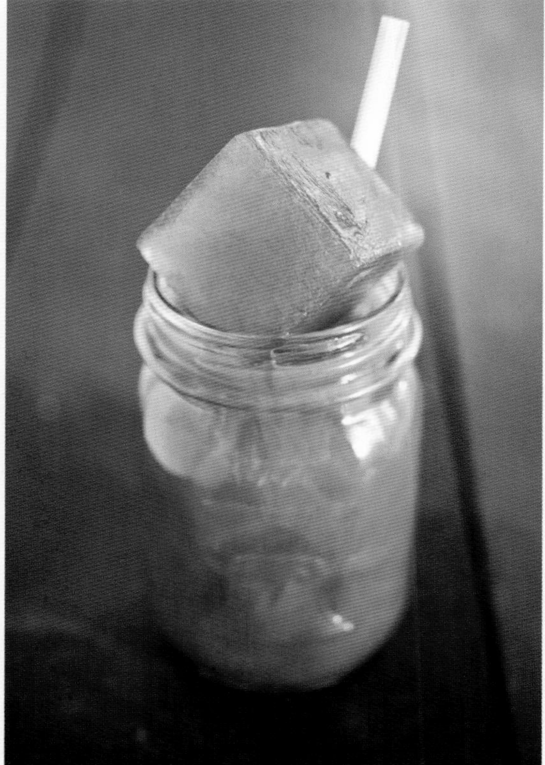

TURN EXCESS TOMATOES INTO...

TOMATO JAM

MAKES 2 CUPS

In summertime especially, there are great deals to be had on beautiful, juicy tomatoes. This tomato jam is earthy and sharp from the addition of coffee beans. You can play with the balance to suit your tastes, keeping in mind that the flavors will continue to develop as it stores. If, while making this recipe, you notice that your tomatoes aren't juicy, add ½ cup water to the pot. I especially love this jam served over steak.

PREP TIME: 10 minutes
COOK TIME: 2 hours
TOTAL TIME: 2 hours, 10 minutes

- 3 to 4 pounds of tomatoes, cut into small ½-inch pieces
- ¼ cup sugar
- 1 fresh or dried bay leaf
- 1 canned chipotle pepper
- 25 coffee beans tied into a sachet of cheesecloth
- ¼ cup white wine vinegar
- ½ teaspoon Worcestershire sauce
- ½ teaspoon fresh lemon juice
- Pinch of salt

1. Combine the tomatoes, sugar, bay leaf, and chipotle pepper in a medium heavy-bottomed saucepan. Cover and bring to a simmer over medium heat. Check after 10 minutes. If a lot of liquid has formed, remove the lid and let it begin to evaporate. If there isn't much liquid, leave the pan partly covered.

(continued on page 200)

2 Reduce the heat to low and cook for 1½ hours or more, reducing and stirring occasionally until the tomatoes have a jammy consistency, then stir more frequently to ensure the jam at the bottom of the pot doesn't burn. About 15 minutes before you estimate it will be done, when the tomatoes are soft but not quite jammy, add the sachet of coffee beans along with the vinegar.

3 Remove from the heat and let cool completely. Remove and discard the sachet and transfer the jam to quart mason jars. Season with Worcestershire, lemon juice, and salt to taste. The jam will store in the refrigerator for up to 2 weeks. Alternatively, process the tomato jam in a hot-water bath (see page 144) for 10 minutes. It is best when consumed within 12 to 18 months of canning.

$$ SAVE MONEY, BUY "SECONDS" $$

When you are making a recipe that requires a lot of produce, like tomato sauce, ask the farmer at your local farmers' market for seconds, which are bruised or blemished pieces available at a lower price. Then cut out any nasty bits and proceed with cooking.

TOMATO WATER

MAKES 1 CUP

Tomato water is a wonderful flavoring liquid to have in the kitchen. Use it to dress salads, to drizzle over a toasted baguette or pasta, or to toss into a room-temperature grain or bean salad. It is also wonderful in Panzanella Salad (page 205).

PREP TIME: 10 minutes
COOK TIME: None
TOTAL TIME: 10 minutes

- 2 large tomatoes
- ¼ red onion, thinly sliced
- 2 cloves garlic
- 1 cup fresh basil leaves
- ½ cup fresh cilantro leaves
- ½ cup fresh parsley leaves
- 2 tablespoons white wine vinegar
- ½ teaspoon sea salt

1 Cut the large tomatoes into quarters and add to a blender along with the onion, garlic, basil, cilantro, parsley, vinegar, and salt. Puree the mixture for several minutes until it reaches the consistency of a smoothie.

2 Set a fine-mesh strainer over a medium bowl and line it with a piece of cheesecloth. Sieve the mixture through the strainer, using a spatula to press it until all of the liquid is extracted.

3 Pour the tomato water into a mason jar or freezer-safe container. Store it in the refrigerator for up to 2 days—shake before using—or freeze for up to 3 months.

TURN EXCESS PEACHES INTO . . .

PEACH BUTTER

MAKES 2 CUPS

By not using much sweetener and cooking the peaches slowly for a long period of time, you allow their natural sweetness to emerge as their own sugars caramelize. The result is a very rich and peachy flavor. Spread it on toast, scones, muffins, or eat it by the spoonful.

PREP TIME: 5 minutes
COOK TIME: 55 minutes
TOTAL TIME: 60 minutes

4 to 6 cups ripe fresh peaches, sliced into eighths
Juice of ½ lemon
1 teaspoon honey or agave

1. In a medium heavy-bottomed pot, cook the peach slices with ¼ cup of water over medium heat and cover with a lid, stirring often, until they are very soft, about 10 minutes.
2. Carefully transfer the peach mixture to a blender and puree on high for about 60 seconds, until the flesh and skins of the peaches are completely pureed.
3. Return the puree to the pot over medium heat, add the lemon juice and honey, and continue to stir for 30 to 45 minutes, until the mixture is thick and forms a ribbon when dripping from a spatula. As you stir the mixture will spatter, so it is wise to use a spatter screen over the top or at the very least a large piece of paper towel. As bubbles form and spatter, stir constantly to prevent the mixture from scorching the bottom of the pot. Remove from the heat and let the puree come to room temperature.

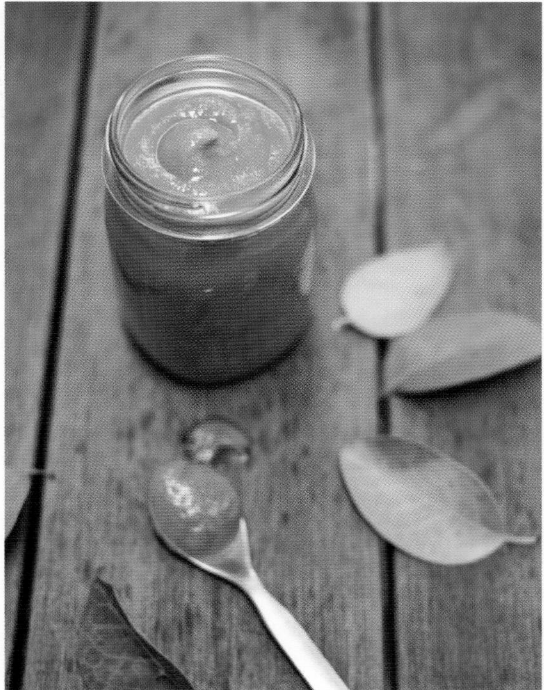

4. Spoon the peach butter into mason jars or a freezer-safe container. It will store for up to 6 months in the refrigerator or up to 1 year in the freezer. Alternatively, process the peach butter in a hot-water bath (see page 144) for 10 minutes. It is best when consumed within 12 to 18 months of canning.

HOW TO TRAP FRUIT FLIES

To make a trap with a plastic water bottle, punch holes in the sides and drop in pieces of fruit to the bottom of the bottle. Add slightly soapy water to almost the top of the bait. The fruit flies will enter . . . and not come out. Empty and rebait the container daily until your fruit fly problem is no more.

PEACH WHISKEY

HOT SAUCE

MAKES 3 CUPS

One way to make the most of very ripe or abundant fruit is to incorporate it into savory dishes. Or if juicy, ripe peaches are out of season, use frozen, no-sugar-added peaches available in the grocery store. You will find that the flavor in this recipe changes and develops as it cools and sits in the refrigerator. The heat will become slightly milder as well.

PREP TIME: 15 minutes **TOTAL TIME:** 40 minutes
COOK TIME: 25 minutes

- 2 tablespoons red or white wine vinegar
- ¼ cup serrano or other medium-spicy pepper, seeded and diced
- 2 tablespoons canned chipotle, roughly chopped
- ½ cup yellow onion, finely diced
- ½ cup carrot, finely diced
- 2 cups ripe peaches, diced (about 2 large peaches)
- ¼ cup whiskey
- Juice of 1 lemon
- ½ cup loosely packed light brown sugar
- ¼ teaspoon ground cumin
- 1 tablespoon salt

1. In a medium saucepan, heat the vinegar with 1 cup of water and add the serrano, chipotle, onion, carrot, and peaches. Let them simmer over low heat, covered, for 20 minutes to soften.
2. Add the whiskey, lemon juice, brown sugar, cumin, and salt to the saucepan. Stir and return to a simmer for 3 to 5 minutes, or until the diced peppers are tender. Remove from the heat.
3. Puree the mixture in a blender or food processor until smooth, then transfer it to a quart mason jar and let it cool to room temperature before screwing on the lid. Store in the refrigerator for up to 1 year.

TURN EXCESS BERRIES
INTO . . .

CHAMPAGNE, STRAWBERRY, AND BLACK PEPPER

FRUIT ROLL-UPS

MAKES 12 RECTANGULAR FRUIT ROLL-UPS

This recipe celebrates imperfect, overripe strawberries. These are grown-up fruit roll-ups, but could be made universal by taking out the peppercorns and swapping the Champagne for water. If you buy a split (miniature bottle) of Champagne or sparkling wine, you won't be left with a whole big bottle to finish, just a few extra sips as you cook. A quick way to crack the peppercorns is to set them on a cutting board and press on them with the back of a pan. Placing the peppercorns between pieces of parchment paper will help you transfer the shards more easily. They add a really nice heat and intrigue to this snack.

PREP TIME: 10 minutes
COOK TIME: 10 to 12 hours
TOTAL TIME: 10 hours, 10 minutes

- 3 cups sliced very ripe strawberries
- ½ cup Champagne
- 1 teaspoon cracked black or pink peppercorns
- ¼ cup sugar (optional, depending on the sweetness of your fruit)
- Vegetable oil for greasing the pan
- Cornstarch for dusting

1. Preheat the oven to 150°F to 200°F. If your oven doesn't go this low, simply set it to the lowest temperature.
2. In a medium, heavy-bottomed pot, add the strawberries, Champagne, peppercorns, and sugar.

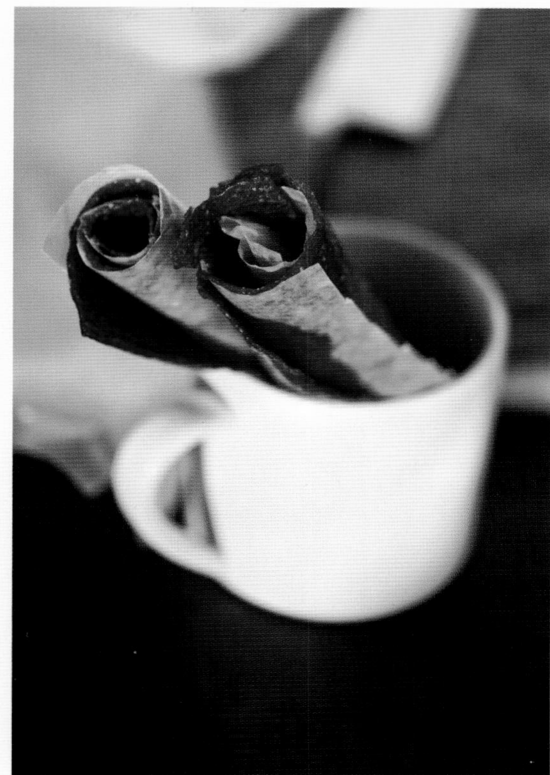

Bring to a simmer over low heat and stew until the berries are soft, about 10 minutes.

3 Transfer the berry mixture to a blender and puree for about 10 seconds, so that the black pepper stays visible.

4 Cover an 8 × 13-inch baking sheet with plastic, parchment paper, or a silicone baking mat. The temperature of the oven is low enough not to affect the plastic. Note: Wax paper will not work; it will stick. Very lightly spray or brush the lined sheet with vegetable oil, then spread the fruit puree onto the sheet tray with an offset spatula or knife to ⅛- to ¼-inch thickness. Place the sheet in the oven for 5 to 6 hours or until the surface is tacky but uniform enough that you can flip the fruit.

5 Cover another baking sheet with plastic, parchment paper, or a silicone baking mat and brush it with oil. Invert the fruit leather onto the second sheet, and remove the first lining (which will now be on top). Place the fruit leather back in the oven for another 5 to 6 hours until the surface is tacky, uniform, and pliable. If it becomes too brittle at any point, simply brush water onto any dry spots with a pastry brush to rehydrate them.

6 Let the sheet tray cool to room temperature. Then, using scissors, cut the fruit leather into 2 × 4-inch strips or your desired size. If you are cutting them on parchment paper, cut the paper as well and use it to roll around the fruit leathers to prevent them from sticking together. Dust each piece with cornstarch to also prevent sticking as you do. Store in a cool place in an airtight container for up to 1 month.

BLUEBERRY
SYRUP

MAKES 1¼ CUPS

This quick alternative to traditional maple syrup will give your guests a nice surprise. If blueberries aren't available, any small berry will work: Red currants, blackberries, and raspberries add a nice tartness to balance the sweetness of the maple.

PREP TIME: 1 minute
COOK TIME: 5 minutes
TOTAL TIME: 6 minutes

- 1½ cups blueberries
- ½ cup maple syrup
- Pinch of salt
- ½ teaspoon fresh lemon juice

1. Combine the blueberries and maple syrup in a small saucepan. Cover and bring to a simmer over low heat. Let simmer for 5 minutes, until the blueberries are soft and broken down, stirring occasionally.
2. Remove from the heat and add the salt and lemon juice. Serve immediately. To store, pour the syrup into a mason jar or freezer-safe container. It will keep in the refrigerator for up to 6 months or in the freezer for up to 1 year. Alternatively, process the blueberry syrup in a hot-water bath (see page 144) for 15 minutes. It is best when consumed within 12 to 18 months of canning.

TURN STALE BREAD
INTO . . .

CHOCOLATE BREAD PUDDING
WITH BRANDY SAUCE

SERVES 15 TO 20

Stale bread should never be thrown out; there are so many possibilities for it. This luscious dessert is one option, along with a brandy and butter sauce that will make it custardy and wonderful. If you prefer fruit to chocolate, you can use berries instead, in which case you will want about 8 cups. This recipe will still work well if your bread happens to be fresh.

PREP TIME: 5 minutes
COOK TIME: 1 hour, 15 minutes
TOTAL TIME: 1 hour, 20 minutes

FOR THE PUDDING:

- 1 tablespoon unsalted butter
- About 10 cups sweet bread, such as challah, torn into 1½-inch pieces (about 2 medium loaves, stale is preferred)
- 1½ cups bittersweet chocolate chips
- ¼ cup cocoa powder
- ½ cup brandy
- 2 cups sugar
- 2 cups whole milk
- 1 cup heavy cream
- 7 large eggs
- ½ teaspoon salt
- 1 teaspoon ground cinnamon

FOR THE SAUCE:

- ½ cup (1 stick) unsalted butter
- ¾ cup powdered sugar
- ½ cup brandy

1. To make the pudding, preheat the oven to 350°F. Grease a 9 × 13-inch baking dish with the butter.
2. Place the bread into the baking dish, alternating with the chocolate chips so they are evenly distributed.
3. In a large bowl, combine the cocoa powder, brandy, sugar, milk, cream, eggs, salt, and cinnamon and whisk together. Pour over the bread in the baking dish and evenly distribute. Press the surface with a spatula so that the bread soaks up the liquid evenly.
4. Place the baking dish in the oven and cook for 75 minutes, until golden brown.
5. Meanwhile, to make the sauce, melt the butter in a small saucepan over low heat. Whisk in the sugar and brandy, then turn off the heat. Once the bread pudding is out of the oven, pour the sauce over it to soak in. When ready to serve, add a scoop of your favorite ice cream as well.

PANZANELLA SALAD

SERVES 4

In this recipe for panzanella salad also lies a recipe for homemade croutons, which you can either make in advance and store for a future salad, or blitz in the food processor and turn into bread crumbs. I love this salad on a hot summer's day with freshly picked tomatoes.

PREP TIME: 15 minutes
COOK TIME: 20 minutes
TOTAL TIME: 35 minutes

- 1 stale baguette or loaf of bread
- 2 tablespoons extra virgin olive oil, plus additional for sprinkling
- 2 cloves garlic
- ½ teaspoon sea salt
- ½ teaspoon freshly ground black pepper
- 3 large heirloom tomatoes (the more colorful the better!)
- 1 cup heirloom cherry tomatoes
- 2 cups Tomato Water (page 200) or the juice of 4 large tomatoes
- 1 cup arugula
- ½ cup small, fresh basil leaves

1. Preheat the oven to 325°F. Cut the baguette lengthwise and drizzle all sides with olive oil. Then rub the baguette on all sides with the garlic.
2. Cut the baguette into 1-inch cubes and place them into a 9 × 13-inch baking dish. Add the salt and pepper and toss. Bake for 20 minutes until lightly golden, then remove from the oven to let cool.
3. Slice the heirloom and cherry tomatoes into bite-size pieces. In 4 shallow bowls, combine ½ cup of tomato water with the tomatoes, arugula, and basil leaves. Drizzle with olive oil and add a few croutons just before serving.

TURN LEFTOVER BONES INTO . . .

CHICKEN STOCK

MAKES 4 CUPS

Homemade chicken stock is a rich base for soups, stews, rice, and much more. Whenever you have leftover roasted or raw chicken bones they should be tossed into a pot and covered with water for stock, or at the very least frozen for a future stock. This is truly liquid gold and when used instead of water it will make every recipe taste better.

PREP TIME: 10 minutes
COOK TIME: 1 hour, 40 minutes
INACTIVE TIME: 1 hour
TOTAL TIME: 2 hours, 50 minutes

- 2 tablespoons grape-seed oil
- 1 chicken carcass, or equivalent in chicken, duck, or turkey bones
- 2 cups chopped celery, with the leaves
- 1 cup peeled and chopped carrots
- 1 cup chopped yellow onion
- 1 cup chopped leek, well rinsed
- 1 cup dry white wine, like chardonnay

1. Heat the oil in a large, heavy-bottomed pot over high heat. If the bones have not already been cooked, add the bones, browning them on all sides, about 10 minutes.
2. Lower the heat to medium and add the celery, carrots, onion, and leeks and brown them, about 5 minutes. Pour off any grease, then pour in the wine to deglaze the pan, scraping up any browned bits on the bottom of the pan with a wooden spoon. Pour in enough water to cover the carcasses and vegetables.
3. Bring to a boil and lower the heat to a simmer. Skim off any foam that forms on the surface.
4. Simmer, partly covered, for 1½ hours, or until the liquid is full-flavored. Skim the surface with a spoon occasionally to remove and discard impurities that float to the top.
5. Ladle through a fine-mesh strainer and let cool to room temperature for about an hour. Store in the freezer, dated and well labeled, in freezer bags or airtight plastic containers for up to 1 year. Alternatively, store in the refrigerator for 5 to 7 days.

HOW TO QUARTER A CHICKEN

BUYING A WHOLE CHICKEN IS MORE ECONOMICAL THAN BUYING ITS PARTS. YOU CAN EASILY QUARTER IT YOURSELF AT HOME AND THEN ROAST THE CARCASS AND TURN IT INTO CHICKEN SOUP AND STOCK (AT LEFT). MASTER THESE FEW STEPS TO QUARTER YOUR OWN CHICKEN AND YOU WILL STRETCH YOUR DOLLARS MUCH FURTHER. YOU CAN COOK THESE PARTS ALL AT ONCE, OR YOU CAN STORE SOME IN THE FREEZER FOR UP TO 9 MONTHS.

1. Lay your chicken breast-side up on a cutting board, with the legs facing you.
2. Gently pull one leg away from the breast and, using a sharp knife, cut at the loose skin in swift, long motions to reveal the joint. Grab the leg with your hand and bend it back so that the joint pops and is revealed. Use your knife to cut through the joint and skin along the back, and cut through as close to the spine as possible; ideally you will be cutting away the oyster, which is the round,

tender bit of meat along the spine, along with the leg. Repeat this with the other leg.

3 Cut the breast by running your knife along the breastbone from the neck opening to the bottom opening. Work the tip of the knife in long, swift motions along the breastbone, slowing pulling back the meat with your other hand until it is only hanging on to the wing. Using the heel of your knife, press down and cut through the joint of the wing and release the whole breast with the wing attached.

4 If you wish, you can then cut these quarters into eighths. For the breast, simply cut horizontally on a bias halfway between the wing and pointed end of the breast. For the leg, separate the drumstick from the thigh at the natural seam and bend of the leg.

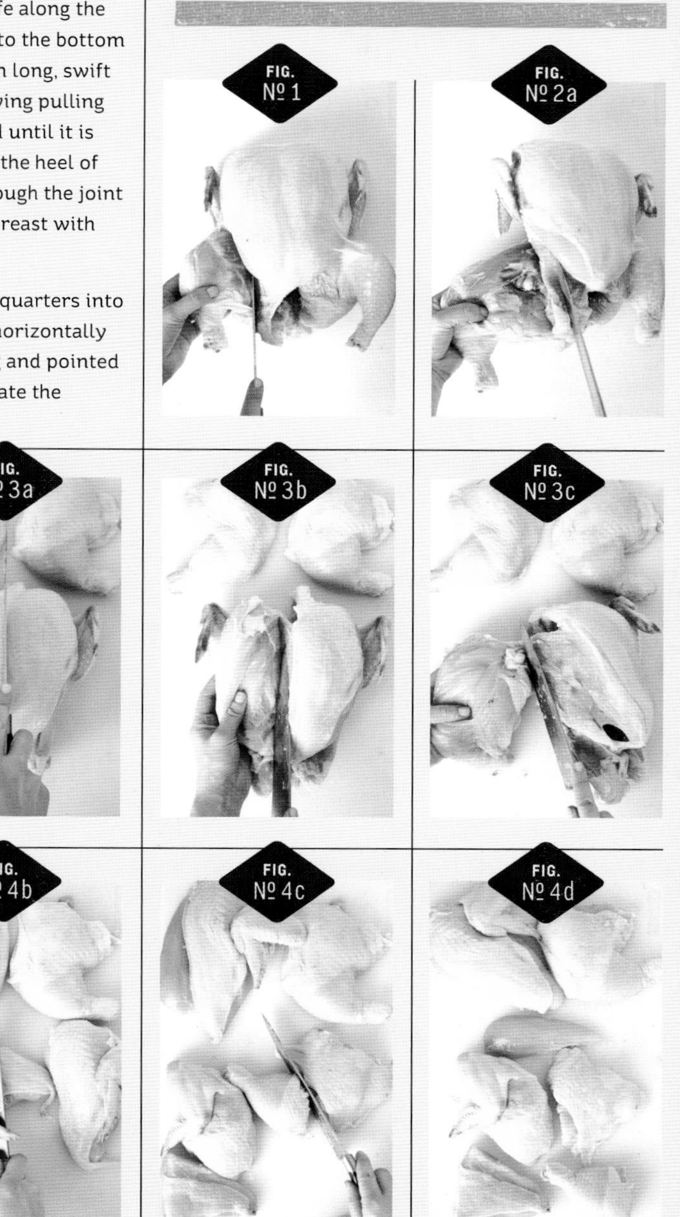

BEEF STOCK

MAKES 4 CUPS

Slightly richer and darker than chicken stock, beef stock is easy to make with leftover bones from roasts and steaks. Butchers will sell these bones to you for very little money. Simmering a pot of stock on the stove makes the house smell delicious when you are entertaining.

PREP TIME: 10 minutes
COOK TIME: 3 hours, 30 minutes
INACTIVE TIME: 1 hour
TOTAL TIME: 4 hours, 40 minutes

- 5 pounds beef bones, or equivalent in other red-meat bones
- 2 tablespoons grape-seed oil
- ¼ cup tomato paste
- 3 carrots, peeled and chopped
- 1 large yellow onion, chopped
- 3 cloves garlic, roughly chopped
- ½ 750 ml bottle full-bodied red wine, such as cabernet
- 2 sprigs fresh thyme
- 1 sprig fresh rosemary
- 2 fresh or dried bay leaves
- 3 or 4 sprigs fresh parsley
- ½ tablespoon black peppercorns

1. Preheat the oven to 400°F. Place the bones on a sheet tray, drizzle with the oil, and roast for 20 to 30 minutes, or until golden brown.
2. Remove the bones from the sheet tray and place them in a large stockpot.
3. Add the tomato paste, carrot, onion, and garlic, and let sweat, stirring occasionally over medium heat, until the onions become soft and translucent, about 5 minutes. Add more oil if necessary.
4. Pour in the red wine and simmer for 5 minutes. Add the thyme, rosemary, bay leaves, parsley, and peppercorns. Cover with water and bring to a boil.
5. Simmer over low heat, partly covered, for 2 to 3 hours, skimming off any foam or fat that forms on the surface. Taste as you go. When it is ready, the stock should be full-flavored.
6. Ladle the liquid through a fine-mesh strainer into freezer bags or airtight containers and let cool to room temperature for at least an hour. Store in the freezer, dated and well labeled, for up to 1 year. Alternatively, store in the refrigerator for 5 to 7 days.

HOW TO WRAP MEAT FOR THE FREEZER

THE KEY TO STORING AND FREEZING MEAT EFFECTIVELY IS IN HOW YOU WRAP IT. FREEZER BURN, THE MOST COMMON CAUSE OF WASTED MEAT IN THE FREEZER, IS THE PROCESS OF DEHYDRATION, WHICH HAPPENS WHEN MEAT ISN'T WRAPPED PROPERLY. MOST PEOPLE DON'T REALIZE IT, BUT EVEN ICE EVAPORATES IN THE FREEZER OVER TIME (EVER NOTICE HOW ICE CUBES GET SMALLER AS THEY SIT THERE?). HERE IS HOW TO PROTECT THE MEAT TO MAINTAIN ITS MAXIMUM FLAVOR AND FRESHNESS.

1. Remove any store wrapping.
2. Place the meat in the center of a piece of plastic wrap on a flat surface.
3. Encase the meat with plastic by folding over one side and pressing out all of the air. Repeat with the other side, pressing out any air again. You will have two "wings" of plastic available on the other sides.

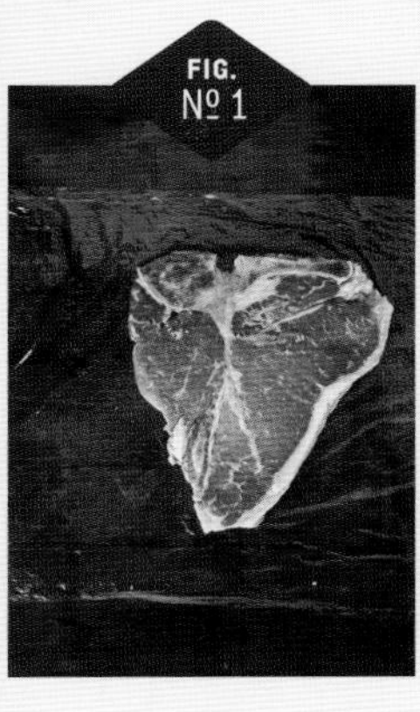
FIG. № 1

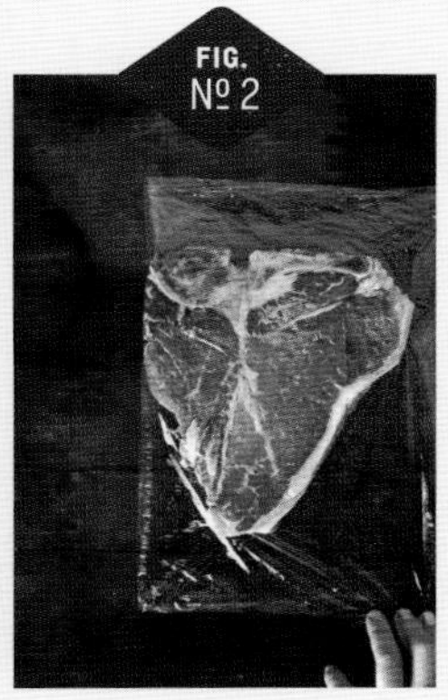
FIG. № 2

FIG. № 3

FIG. № 4

FIG. № 5

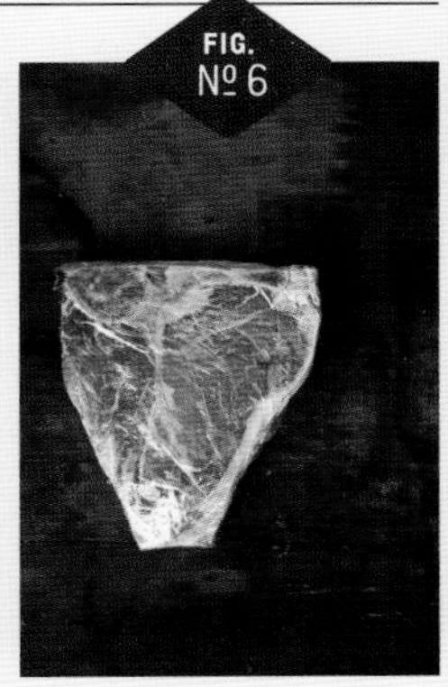
FIG. № 6

4 Fold the first wing over the meat and the second overlapping the first so you have a fully encased piece of meat.

5 Repeat this process with a second piece of plastic so you have a double coating.

6 Put the plastic-wrapped meat in a resealable plastic bag, pressing out any air as you seal it.

7 Label the bag clearly with a permanent marker with the date it was frozen and the contents of the bag. You may think you will remember what is in it, but you will be glad you labeled it 6 months from now. Make sure you practice "first in, first out" and use first what you froze first.

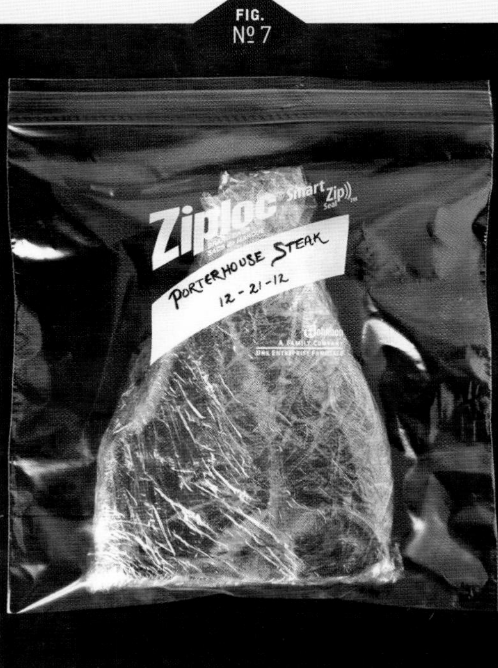

FIG. № 7

TURN PEELS AND PODS INTO . . .

SPICED
LEMON OIL

MAKES 2 CUPS

We tend to use the juice of the lemons and discard the rind, even though the rind has a lot of value. When you have citrus fruit, peel the rinds with a vegetable peeler and drop the peels in a jar. Store the citrus in the refrigerator and use the juice as needed.

I use grape-seed oil in this recipe because it has a cleaner flavor than vegetable oil and a less assertive flavor than olive oil. It is the perfect vehicle to absorb the lemon flavors of the peel and lemongrass. Use this over salad, in cakes and muffins, or to brighten the flavor of vegetable and fish dishes.

PREP TIME: 5 minutes
COOK TIME: None
INACTIVE TIME: 24 hours
TOTAL TIME: 24 hours, 5 minutes

Peel of 2 lemons
Peel of 1 lime
1-inch piece of fresh ginger, peeled
Piece of lemongrass, smacked with the back of a knife to release the flavor and cut into 2-inch pieces
2 cups grape-seed oil

1. Combine the ingredients in a quart mason jar and shake well.
2. Set the jar in a warm place, such as above a stove, on a fireplace mantel, or near a radiator.
3. Let the oil infuse for 24 hours, then strain it into another jar and discard the peels, lemongrass, and ginger. Seal the jar and store it in the refrigerator for up to 1 week.

HOMEMADE
VANILLA EXTRACT

MAKES ONE 200 ML BOTTLE OF VANILLA EXTRACT

This is a good recipe to make when you find yourself baking with vanilla bean and have a leftover pod after scraping out all of the inner pulp. Vanilla beans can be exceptionally expensive, so they shouldn't be wasted even after they have been scraped of their insides. Instead, use this recipe, where vodka will extract the vanilla flavor and you will end up with homemade vanilla extract. Another money-saving tip: Instead of buying a small jar and vodka, buy a small bottle of vodka and drop the vanilla bean right in it. Attractive bottles are useful when you want to make a lovely gift with a homemade label.

PREP TIME: 1 minute
COOK TIME: None
INACTIVE TIME: 8 weeks
TOTAL TIME: 8 weeks, 1 minute

1 vanilla bean, split in half (with or without inner pulp)
1 200 ml bottle of vodka (if using a larger bottle, use more vanilla bean)

1. Cut the vanilla bean into 2-inch pieces and drop it into the bottle of vodka.
2. Store it in a cool, dark place for 6 weeks, shaking it about once a week. After 8 weeks the vanilla will be full-flavored and you can stop shaking it. You can continue to leave in the bean and the flavors will develop slightly more. It will keep indefinitely.

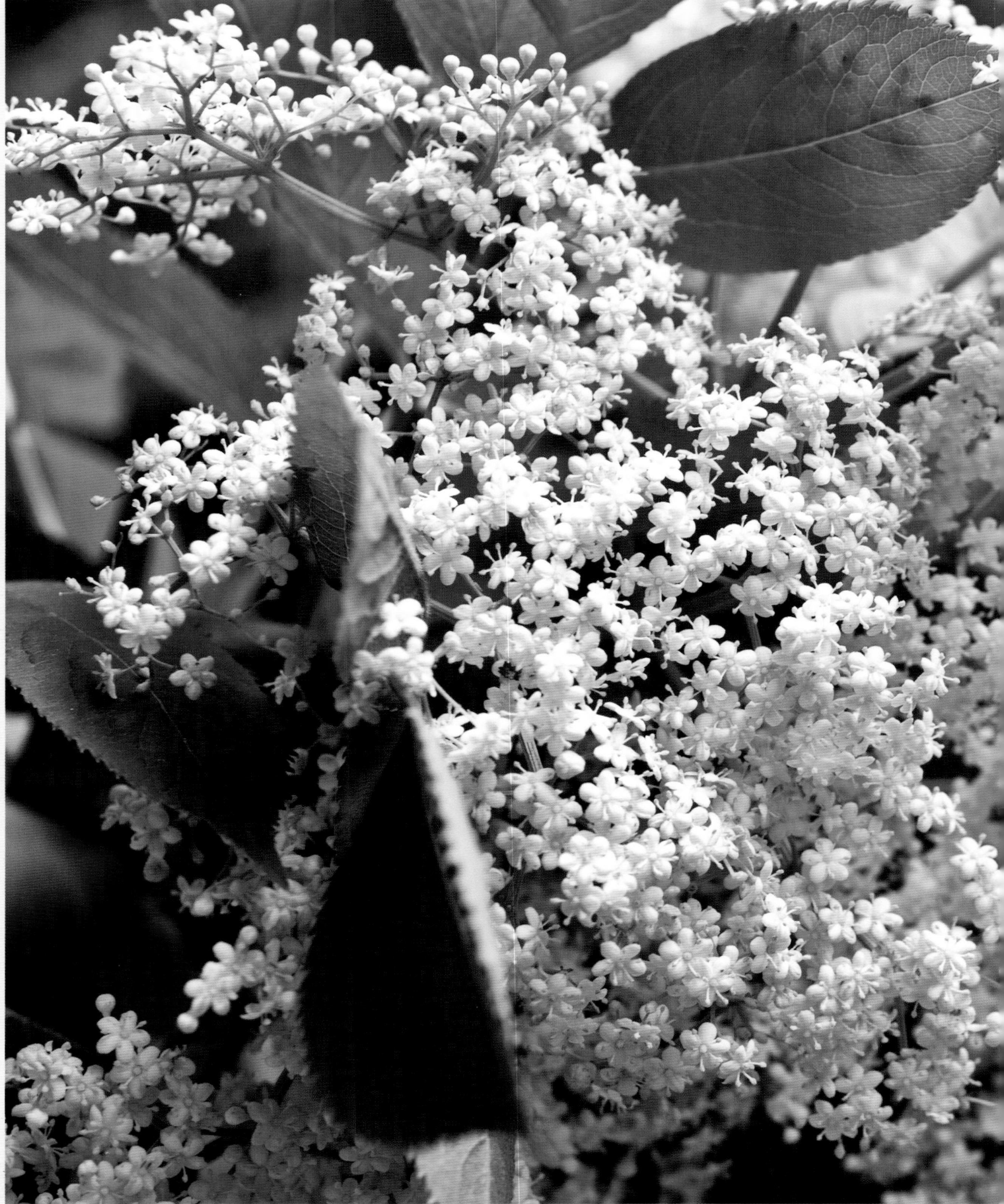

THE WILD

CHAPTER
№ 4

LIVING OFF THE (URBAN, SUBURBAN, OR RURAL) LAND

THE BOY SCOUTS DON'T OWN THE PHRASE "always be prepared"; in fact, these days it is not so uncommon for a woman to walk into the woods to see what she is made of. If you want to go camping for the first time, or have an adventure in the wilderness, these are some basic things to know to empower yourself.

Here you will learn about a few of the most common edible plants that are found growing in the woods, the garden, and even the sidewalk cracks of a city street. You will learn about their nutritional benefits should you need supplemental nutrition in an emergency, and you will also learn how to incorporate them into recipes for everyday life if you find them while weeding your garden or walking to work. You will also learn the various ways to clean water and make it drinkable . . . just in case. A range of wilderness and life lessons in the chapter, like how to use a compass, and how to find your way without one, will make you even better prepared for your adventures. You'll learn how to put together a small emergency kit for yourself, how to use cayenne pepper to stop bleeding, and how to change a tire if you find yourself broken down alone on the side of a road.

COMMON EDIBLE PLANTS

IN THE WILDERNESS, GARDEN, OR SIDEWALK CRACKS

THERE ARE MANY EDIBLE PLANTS right outside our doorstep. Knowing about these resources is of course useful in an emergency situation if you need extra nutrition, but it is also useful if you simply want to be more self-sufficient and find more meals in your backyard rather than the grocery store. Our ancestors often did this, but subsequent generations seem to have left it behind. Included in this section are a few wild foods that are common and easily identifiable. Next time you are on a hike or an evening stroll, wear extra-large pockets and see what kind of ingredients you can harvest for supper.

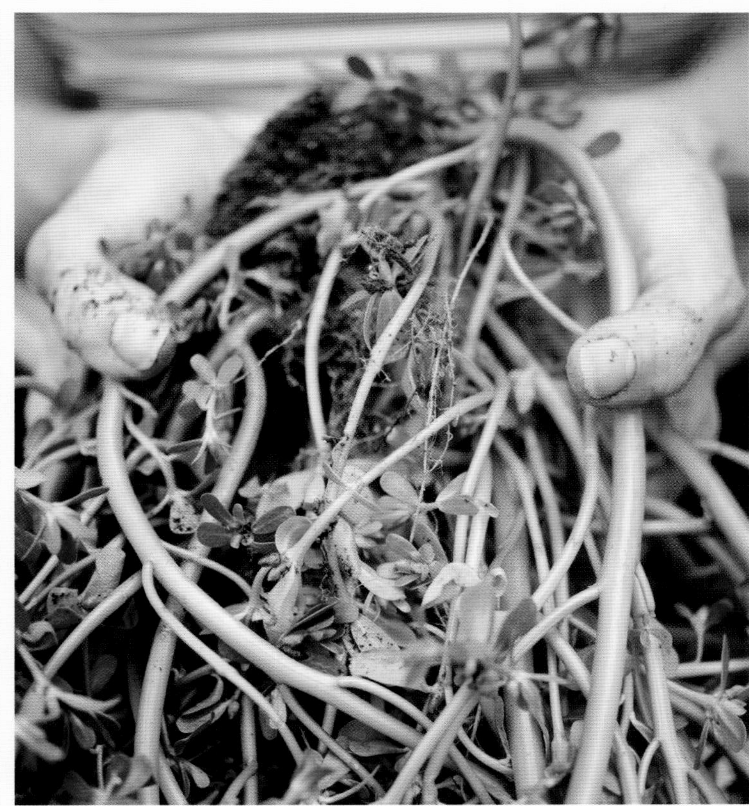

PURSLANE → PURSLANE SALAD

SERVES 4

Purslane is such an intriguing plant. For one, you'll find it everywhere in many countries, from the cracks in city sidewalks to your vegetable garden, likely where you don't want it to be. Hardy and able to withstand most weather conditions, purslane appears in the summer months, with leaves that are fleshy, plump, and oval, almost cactus-like. The flavor is a little salty, a little sour, a kind of built-in vinaigrette flavor, requiring little else to make it into a salad.

Whenever I visited my grandmother she asked if I had seen any purslane in her garden. What she liked about it most was its nutritional attributes: an extraordinary amount of omega-3 fatty acid, which is normally found in fish and flaxseeds; vitamins A, B, and C, as well as magnesium, calcium, potassium, and iron; and something called alkaloid pigments, which cause its reddish stems and yellow flowers. These are potent antioxidants. You can call this dish your new "sidewalk salad."

PREP TIME: 10 minutes
COOK TIME: None
TOTAL TIME: 10 minutes

- 1 large heirloom or beefsteak tomato
- 2 cups purslane leaves, washed well, picked from the stem
- ½ cup fresh corn kernels, raw or cooked
- ¼ cup thinly sliced red onion
- 2 large eggs, hard-boiled and roughly chopped (see pages 152 and 153)
- ¼ teaspoon sea salt
- ½ teaspoon freshly ground black pepper
- 1 tablespoon hazelnut oil (or another favorite finishing oil)

1. Cut the tomato in half and squeeze the juice into a medium bowl. Dice the remaining flesh and add it to the bowl. Add the purslane, corn, onion, and egg. Sprinkle with the salt and pepper and toss to mix.
2. Drizzle in the hazelnut oil and toss again to distribute. Serve immediately.

DANDELION GREENS AND DAYLILIES → WILTED DANDELION GREEN AND DAYLILY SALAD

SERVES 4

Dandelion greens are incredibly nutritious, with more protein than spinach and a high calcium and iron content. You will find them in early spring and summer in fields, in gardens, and wherever you see bright yellow dandelions. The leaves have sharp triangular points and the stem excretes a milky sap when torn. If you come upon dandelion greens but no daylilies, feel free to substitute any other edible flowers (see page 53) or leave them out altogether. Daylilies add a wonderful color and crunch, but the dish isn't lost without them.

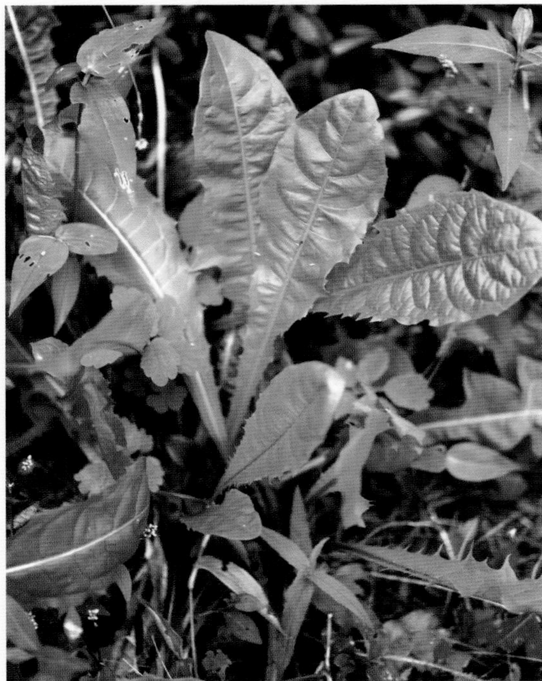

PREP TIME: 10 minutes
COOK TIME: 12 minutes
TOTAL TIME: 22 minutes

- ¼ cup diced guanciale or pancetta
- 4 tablespoons unsalted pistachios
- 2 cups chopped dandelion greens
- 10 to 15 daylily buds and petals
- ¼ medium red onion, very thinly sliced or shaved

1. In a medium sauté pan, render the guanciale over low heat until it becomes crispy, stirring regularly, about 10 minutes. Add the pistachios and stir for about 2 minutes more.

2. Add the dandelion greens, daylilies, and onions and remove from the heat. Toss the contents of the pan in the guanciale fat until it wilts slightly, then transfer to a large bowl or platter and serve warm.

DANDELION FLOWERS → DANDELION WINE

MAKES ABOUT THREE 750 ML BOTTLES

Dandelions bloom for only a few weeks in early spring, with a few stragglers throughout the summer. They look like bright yellow suns and have a particularly good supply of vitamins A and C, calcium, and phosphorus, some of which will remain even when you dry the flowers. Pick them from an open field far from any insecticide spraying, and if you can, pick early in the season when the leaves of the plant are still tender. Newly bloomed flowers are ideal.

Dandelion wine is traditionally sipped from very small glasses. I have also combined it with seltzer water for a spritzer, or you could do as my godfather does and pour it over a roasting chicken for a caramelized skin.

Some people prefer to make dandelion wine with just the petals, but I use the whole flower bud. The reason is that fermentation can sometimes get stuck before it is complete. This can happen when there aren't enough micronutrients for the yeast. You increase the chance of success by using whole buds because they contain more micronutrients, but you will have a slightly more bitter wine.

PREP TIME: 15 minutes
COOK TIME: 5 minutes
INACTIVE TIME: 2 months
TOTAL TIME: 2 months, 20 minutes

- 8 cups whole dandelion blossoms, washed well, stems removed
- Juice of 1 orange
- Juice of 1 lemon
- Peel of 1 large orange, coarsely chopped
- Peel of 1 lemon, coarsely chopped
- 2¼ teaspoons brewer's yeast
- 6 cups sugar
- 8 whole cloves
- 1-inch piece of fresh ginger, peeled and diced

1. Wash the dandelion blossoms well in a colander. Place them in a large pot with the orange juice, lemon juice, the orange and lemon peels, and 16 cups of water. Bring to a boil over high heat, and allow to boil for 2 to 3 minutes. Remove from the heat and let it cool. Let it sit, covered, for 24 hours.

2. Dissolve the yeast in the ¼ cup of warm water and let it sit for 10 minutes.

3. Add the sugar to the dandelion liquid and stir. Next, add the yeast mixture and stir to combine.

4. Fit a large jug with a funnel and set a small fine-mesh strainer in the funnel. Ladle in the liquid one spoonful at a time, pressing down onto the dandelions to ensure all of the liquid is extracted. Dump the dandelions and peels into an empty bowl to allow each new batch of liquid to strain easily.

5. Add the cloves and ginger to the jug.

6. Place an airlock on the jug, so that the CO_2 can leave the jug but bad yeast doesn't enter. This can be done with a deflated balloon—poke holes into the latex, then fasten the balloon around the neck of the jug. Alternatively, you could use plastic wrap. The airlock is used instead of the lid; if you screw the lid on tightly, you run the risk of having the bottle explode. Shake well and let it rest for 1 week in a cool, dark place as the fermentation begins.

7. Using a funnel and fine-mesh strainer, strain the liquid into bottles. Add an airlock over each of the bottles and allow the uncorked bottles to sit in a dark, cool place for 3 to 6 weeks. Then cork the bottles, or use bottles with screw-on tops, and store them in a cool, dark place for at least 2 months and up to a year. This kind of wine is best consumed while it is young, about 6 months after you cork it.

WILD GARLIC → WILD GARLIC SOUP

MAKES 6 CUPS

Wild garlic is considered one of the most versatile plants on earth. For thousands of years it has been used to maintain and improve health. It has four and a half times more sulfurous compounds than common garlic, which means it is immensely good for you, offering all kinds of antibacterial and antiviral properties. Wild garlic appears in late winter and early spring, and is best harvested young, since the plant becomes difficult to pull up as it matures and it develops more woody fibers. You can spot wild garlic because it looks vaguely like a bunch of chives, but with hollow stems and a more woody base. It will smell faintly like garlic if you get your nose very close. This soup is also wonderful served at room temperature or chilled and is even better the next day.

PREP TIME: 10 minutes
COOK TIME: 1 hour, 15 minutes
TOTAL TIME: 1 hour, 25 minutes

- ¾ cup wild garlic bulbs, cleaned, with green stalk and root removed and outer bulb layer peeled
- ¼ cup plus 2 tablespoons extra virgin olive oil
- 2 cups diced fennel
- Salt and freshly ground black pepper to taste
- 2 cups diced red potato
- 8 cups vegetable stock
- Pinch of ground cardamom
- Pinch of ground cinnamon
- Pinch of cayenne
- 2 tablespoons dry sherry
- 2 tablespoons fresh chervil, thyme, or chives

1. Bring a large, heavy-bottomed pot filled with water to a boil. Blanch the garlic for 3 minutes, then drain it and run it under cold water. Set it aside.

2. Heat 2 tablespoons olive oil in the same pot over low heat and sweat the fennel and garlic until browned, soft, and translucent, stirring occasionally, about 10 minutes. Sprinkle with salt along the way to help release the juices.

3. Add the potatoes and vegetable stock and simmer, covered, for about 1 hour, until the potatoes are fork-tender.

4. Transfer all the contents of the pot to a blender and puree on high for 2 to 3 minutes. In the last 30 seconds of pureeing, pour the ¼ cup olive oil in a thin steady stream to emulsify the soup.

5. Pour all the contents of the blender through a fine-mesh strainer back into the pot to remove the woody fibers from the garlic. Mix in the cardamom, cinnamon, cayenne, and sherry. Add salt and pepper to taste. Serve in bowls with a sprinkling of fresh herbs, such as chervil, thyme, and chives.

RAMPS → RAMP AND WALNUT PESTO

MAKES 2 CUPS

Very high in vitamins A and C, ramps appear in early spring, in patches along hillsides and especially in shady forested areas near water. They look like small, wild leeks, with broad, green leaves and burgundy coloring on the lower stem. The bulb looks similar to a scallion or wild garlic. In addition to using them for pesto, you can grill them, pickle the white bulb, and sauté the green leaves. Harvest only what you need of the bulbs and clip off more of the green leaves to use instead. The bulbs are important for plant regeneration. Incorporate this pesto into your favorite pasta or steamed vegetables.

PREP TIME: 5 minutes
COOK TIME: 1 minute
TOTAL TIME: 6 minutes

- 2½ cups coarsely chopped ramps, well rinsed
- 1 cup walnuts
- Juice and zest of 2 lemons
- 1 teaspoon freshly ground black pepper
- 1 cup extra virgin olive oil
- ½ cup grated Pecorino Romano

1. Bring a large pot of salted water to a rolling boil and prepare a bowl of ice water on the side. Drop the ramps into the boiling water for 1 minute, then remove them with a slotted spoon to the ice-water bath. Let them sit about 1 minute, then remove, shake them dry, and add them to the bowl of a food processor.
2. Add the walnuts, lemon juice and zest, and pepper to the food processor. Slowly drizzle in the olive oil as it spins on high, then add in the cheese. You may need to scrape down the sides of the bowl with a spatula and spin again until the mixture is as smooth as you'd like. If you plan to freeze this mixture, simply blend it without the olive oil and cheese and add those two ingredients once you have defrosted it and are ready to use it. Store in the refrigerator for 2 weeks and freeze for up to 12 months.

WILD MUSTARD → WILD MUSTARD DRESSING

MAKES 1 CUP

There are many kinds of mustard, including yellow rocket, field mustard, and garlic mustard. The plant is part of the Brassicaceae family, related to broccoli, cabbage, kale, and turnips, and is said to have cancer-fighting agents, along with a whole host of vitamins from A, C, and D to K, as well as folate, potassium, calcium, iron, fiber, and phosphorus. Delicious when sautéed on its own, wild mustard can also give other dishes, like this dressing, a little kick. Use this dressing on salads or as a dip for crudités.

PREP TIME: 5 minutes
COOK TIME: 30 seconds
INACTIVE TIME: 1 hour
TOTAL TIME: 1 hour, 5½ minutes

- 1 large bunch (about ¼ pound) wild mustard greens, soaked in water several times to remove any grit
- ½ cup plain yogurt
- 1 tablespoon fresh dill sprigs
- ½ cup fresh basil leaves
- 1 clove garlic
- 2 tablespoons fresh lemon juice
- ½ teaspoon sea salt

1. Bring a large pot of salted water to a rolling boil and prepare a bowl of ice water on the side. Drop the mustard greens into the boiling water for 30 seconds and remove with a slotted spoon to the ice-water bath. Let them cool, then squeeze the water from them and lay them on a cutting board.
2. Chop the greens roughly and transfer them to a food processor. Add the yogurt, dill, basil, garlic, lemon juice, and salt, and puree until smooth, scraping down the sides of the food processor once if necessary. Spoon the dressing into a mason jar or small bowl and let it sit in the refrigerator, covered, for 1 hour so that it becomes full-flavored before serving.

ELDERFLOWER → ELDERFLOWER FRITTERS

SERVES 4 TO 6

Elderflowers are like a fine lace that bloom in spring and summer—soft and delicate, nutty and earthy-smelling. They are found primarily in sunny, moist areas. Elderflower and its berries are known to have medicinal qualities; a few drops of their extract under the tongue is said to boost the immune system. This recipe, though, is more decadent than healthy, a delicious sweet treat in summer.

PREP TIME: 25 minutes
COOK TIME: 10 minutes
INACTIVE TIME: 30 minutes
TOTAL TIME: 1 hour, 5 minutes

- 1½ to 2 cups amaretto, brandy, sambuca or your other favorite liquor or liqueur
- ½ teaspoon vanilla extract
- 6 cups elderflowers, short stems intact
- 2 cups all-purpose flour
- Zest of 1 lemon
- 1 pinch of salt
- ½ teaspoon ground cinnamon
- 2 large eggs, separated
- ¾ cup Almond Milk (page 262)
- 1 cup grape-seed or vegetable oil, plus more as needed
- ¼ cup powdered sugar

1. Combine the amaretto and vanilla in a large mixing bowl, and soak the flowers in the mixture for at least 30 minutes.
2. In a separate large bowl, combine the flour, lemon zest, salt, and cinnamon.
3. In a small bowl, whisk the egg yolks, then add the almond milk. Stir the egg mixture into the dry ingredients.
4. In a medium bowl, beat the egg whites into stiff peaks with a hand mixer, and fold them into the rest of the batter.
5. Heat the oil in a large, heavy-bottomed skillet over medium-high heat. Line a large plate with paper towels.
6. Dip a flower into the batter, holding it by the stems and shaking it gently to remove excess batter. Place it into the hot oil and cook until it is golden brown on one side, about 1 minute. Turn the flower over and cook for about 1 minute more, then transfer the flower to the serving plate. Repeat with the rest of the flowers.
7. Sprinkle with powdered sugar and serve immediately.

PINE NEEDLES → PINE TREE TEA

SERVES 2

Best harvested in winter and early spring when the aroma is strongest, needles from the white pine tree have about five times the amount of vitamin C of a lemon, and they make a delicious tea, slightly pink and sweet. The white pine grows in all but the hottest climates in the United States; it has slender cones and flexible needles that are in bundles of five per stem. It is a fun tea to make while camping, or collect some needles on your walk and bring them home for an exciting brew.

PREP TIME: 1 minute
COOK TIME: 5 minutes
INACTIVE TIME: 10 minutes
TOTAL TIME: 16 minutes

- 1 cup white pine needles
- Honey to taste (optional)

1. Cut the needles into 1-inch pieces and place them in a small sauce pot with 4 cups of water. Cover the pot, place over medium-high heat, and bring to a boil.
2. Turn off the heat and let the needles infuse for 10 minutes.
3. Strain the liquid through a fine-mesh strainer into cups. Stir in honey, if desired.

WILD MINT → WILD MINT AND DARK CHOCOLATE MILKSHAKE

SERVES 1

Wild mint contains several bioactive compounds, including menthol, an antibacterial. It is also known to aid digestion, while the aroma serves as a mood booster. Wild mint flourishes in open fields, sunny gardens, and moist woods. Plants in the mint family have square stalks, which make them easy to identify. Their leaves will also smell strongly like mint when pressed together in your hands. Every mint variety will taste different, so chew on a leaf and see if it suits your fancy. Then blend it into this delicious chocolate milkshake.

PREP TIME: 5 minutes
COOK TIME: None
TOTAL TIME: 5 minutes

- ½ cup fresh wild mint leaves, plus additional for garnish
- ½ cup milk (whichever type you prefer)
- Pinch of cayenne
- 1 tablespoon brandy (optional)
- 1 cup chocolate ice cream
- Dark chocolate shavings for garnish (optional)

1. Combine the mint leaves, milk, cayenne, and brandy, if desired, in a blender and mix on high for about 30 seconds, or until smooth.
2. Add the ice cream and blend for 10 seconds.
3. Pour into a tall glass, garnish with mint and chocolate shavings, if desired, and serve.

WILD MINT AND DARK CHOCOLATE MILKSHAKE

HOW TO CREATE A
POCKET-SIZE 48-HOUR SURVIVAL TOOL KIT

A TRAVEL-SIZE KIT THAT FITS IN A POCKET, PURSE, OR GLOVE COMPARTMENT IS TRULY USEFUL. A RECYCLED ALTOIDS OR TOBACCO TIN MAKES THE PERFECT CONTAINER; YOU WILL BE SURPRISED TO SEE HOW MUCH YOU CAN FIT IN THERE. HERE ARE THE USEFUL THINGS TO INCLUDE IN YOUR KIT, AVAILABLE IN SMALL SIZES:

» Safety pins, for mending clothing, lost buttons, and tears in a tent or a sleeping bag

» Thin wire, for many purposes, from fastening to hanging items in trees (it can be rolled into a small circle)

» Button compass, a small compass for finding your way

» Candle, the nontallow durable kind to help you light a fire (you can cut it down to short pieces to fit)

» Matches, the waterproof/windproof kind

» Magnesium fire starter

» Steel striker for starting fire

» Magnifying glass, for starting fires and getting tinder to smoke

» Two magnetized sewing needles, for sewing or making an emergency compass (floated in water on a leaf, the needle will face north) (see page 228)

» Salt packets (essential in hot conditions, salt helps keep minerals in your body as you sweat)

» Cayenne pepper in a plastic packet (it will help stop bleeding when applied to most wounds by equalizing the body's blood pressure) (see "How to Use Cayenne Pepper to Stop Bleeding," page 232)

» Antibiotic tablets and ointment, for when a cut is infected and medical help is far off

» Adhesive bandages in various sizes to cover cuts and blisters

» Water sterilizing tablets, for when you aren't able to boil water and make it safe to drink

» X-Acto knife blade or scalpel for cutting

» Pencil and small paper for making notes on directions, edible plants, etc.

» Plastic bag for transporting water from a source or collecting wild edibles

» 2 feet of aluminum foil folded over many times into a small square, for making a cup, signaling, cooking fish, etc.

» Wire saw, for cutting through most things (will roll into a small circle)

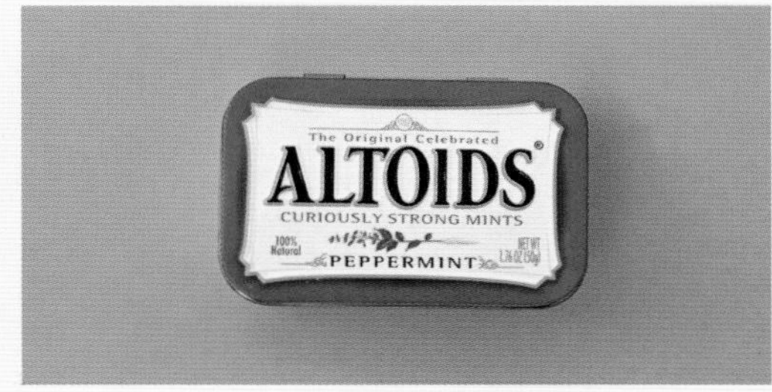

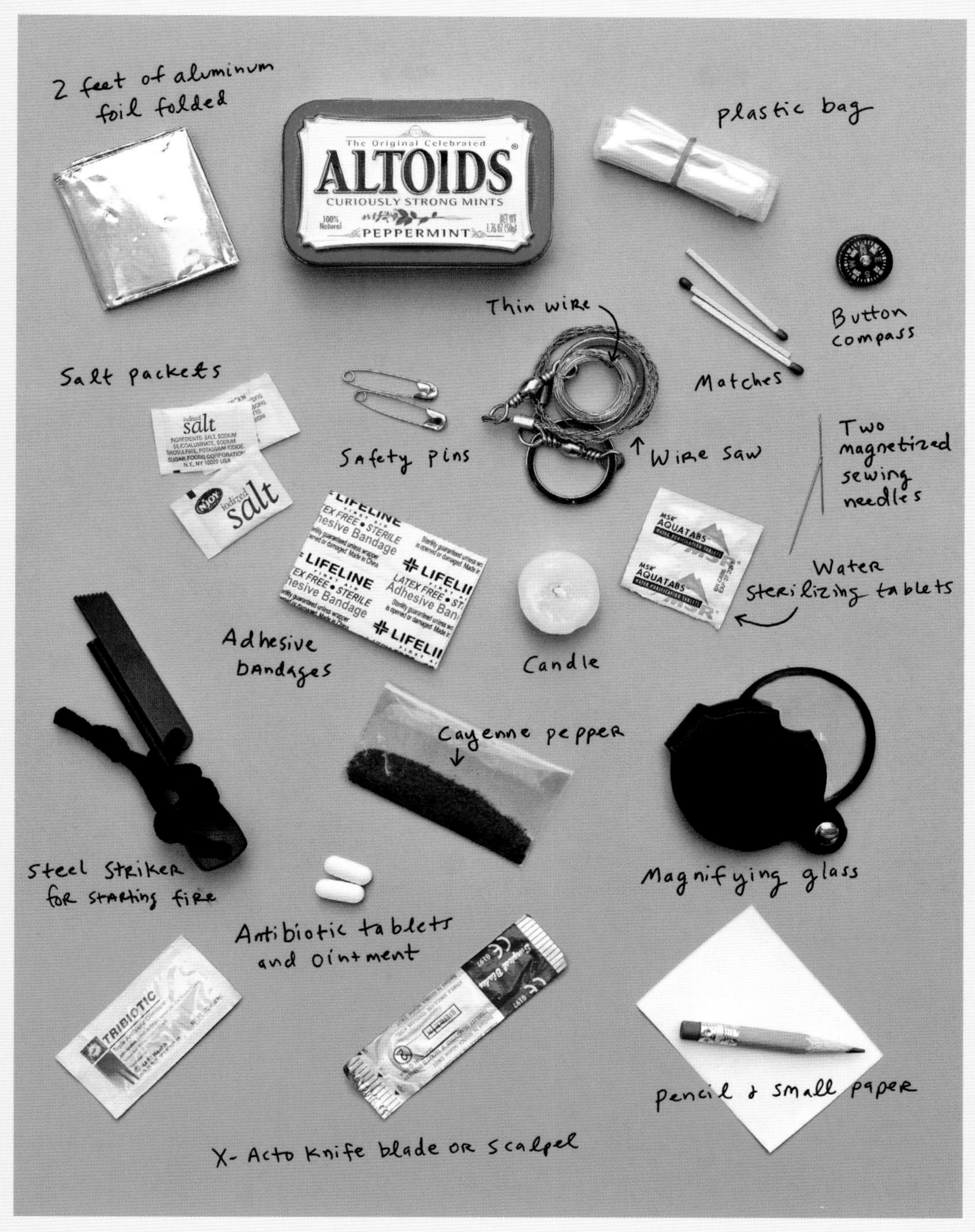
2 feet of aluminum foil folded
The Original Celebrated
ALTOIDS
CURIOUSLY STRONG MINTS
PEPPERMINT
plastic bag
Thin wire
Button compass
Matches
Salt packets
salt
salt
Safety pins
Wire saw
Two magnetized sewing needles
LIFELINE
Adhesive Bandage
AQUATABS
Water sterilizing tablets
Adhesive bandages
Candle
Cayenne pepper
Steel striker for starting fire
Magnifying glass
Antibiotic tablets and ointment
TRIBIOTIC
Pencil & small paper
X-Acto knife blade or scalpel

7 WAYS TO

CLEAN WATER

You never know where life's adventures will take you, whether you're lost in the woods or stuck in your apartment during a power outage. Empower yourself by learning the best options for accessing clean water:

BOIL IT. Heating water to a rolling boil for 1 to 10 minutes at 212°F is the best way to kill microorganisms. It won't improve the taste or filter out debris, but it will make it safe to drink. To improve the taste, pour the water back and forth between a few containers to aerate it.

DISTILL IT. This process works especially well when you are trying to obtain fresh water from salty water. Place a cloth over a pot of boiling water and let it collect the condensation. When the cloth is soaked, remove it carefully and let it cool, then squeeze out the pure water. Repeat this and use several cloths to continue to catch all of the steam. This is very effective in removing protozoa, bacteria, and viruses. The drawback is that it takes a long time.

BLEACH-TREAT IT. Use 3 drops of bleach per quart of water, unless the water is cloudy, in which case 5 drops per quart. If you don't have a dropper estimate a spoonful per gallon. Stir the water thoroughly and let it stand for 30 minutes. Use chlorine bleach and avoid bleaches that contain dyes and perfumes.

USE IODINE. Iodine will kill most waterborne contaminates. Five drops per quart works in clear water and 10 drops for cloudy. Let it sit for 30 minutes before you can drink it. There are also plenty of water-purifying tablets on the market.

FILTER IT. A handkerchief, sock, or other fine cloth will remove coarse dirt and debris. But to remove the majority of waterborne contaminates the water needs to be purified through a pore size of 1 micron or smaller. There are select water filters that are classified as true water purifiers that will eliminate all bacteria, protozoa, and viruses. But if you are in the wilderness and need a rudimentary filter, fill up a clean sock with a combination of sand, loam, rocks, and charcoal with the most coarse material at the top and pour the water through it. It will improve the smell and taste and reduce the overall bacteria .

STRAIN IT. When you don't have a sock or sufficient material to make a filter, you can dig a 1-foot-deep hole, 1 foot away from a water source like a stream. It will fill with water, which will be more purified than the main source since it has passed through sand and rocks. Transfer what you collect by placing a scarf or other cloth over a plastic water bottle or other container and dip it sideways in the hole to fill.

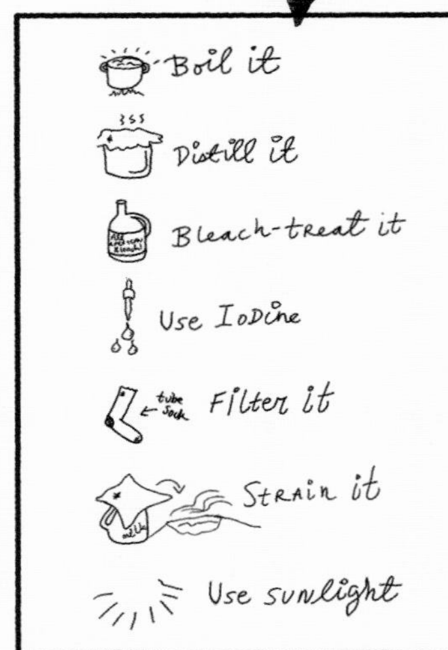

Boil it
Distill it
Bleach-treat it
Use Iodine
tube sock
Filter it
Strain it
Use sunlight

USE SUNLIGHT. The sun's natural UV rays can be used to your advantage when your other options are limited. First, the water should be filtered to remove debris. Then it should be poured into plastic bottles or a clear plastic bag and set in the sun at 86°F for a minimum of 6 hours, longer for water that is very cold. It will heat up faster if you set the water on a black, dark, or metal surface. The UV rays disrupt microbial DNA so that it can't multiply. So while it is better than nothing, it should be used only when there are no other options because it doesn't kill the microbes already in there. It also won't remove dirt and particles or improve color. Ultraviolet lights are available to purchase as a portable device.

HOW TO MAKE A

SOLAR STILL TO GET FRESH WATER

WHEN THERE IS NO OBVIOUS WATER SOURCE AT ALL, YOU CAN MAKE A SOLAR STILL. IN THIS PROCESS, THE HEAT FROM THE SUN WILL DRAW THE MOISTURE FROM THE MATERIALS UNDERNEATH THE TARP ONTO THE UNDERSIDE OF THE TARP, WHILE THE WEIGHT OF THE ROCK WILL DIRECT THE MOISTURE TO DRIP TOWARD THE CENTER, ABOVE WHERE THE CONTAINER IS SET. WATER WILL COLLECT IN THE CONTAINER. THE AMOUNT YOU GATHER WILL VARY GREATLY DEPENDING ON YOUR ENVIRONMENT, THE HUMIDITY, AND THE MOISTURE IN YOUR VEGETATION.

- Shovel
- Large bowl
- Vegetation
- Poncho, tarp, or some sort of plastic
- Rocks

1. Dig a cone-shaped hole 1 to 3 feet deep and as wide as your tarp.
2. Place a large bowl or similar container in the center of the hole and surround it with green vegetation that you have picked, such as cacti, leaves, and any other moisture-retaining plants.
3. Cover the hole with the tarp and secure the edges of the tarp with rocks so that it doesn't fall into the hole. Place a rock in the center of the tarp so that it dips down slightly toward the container underneath it.

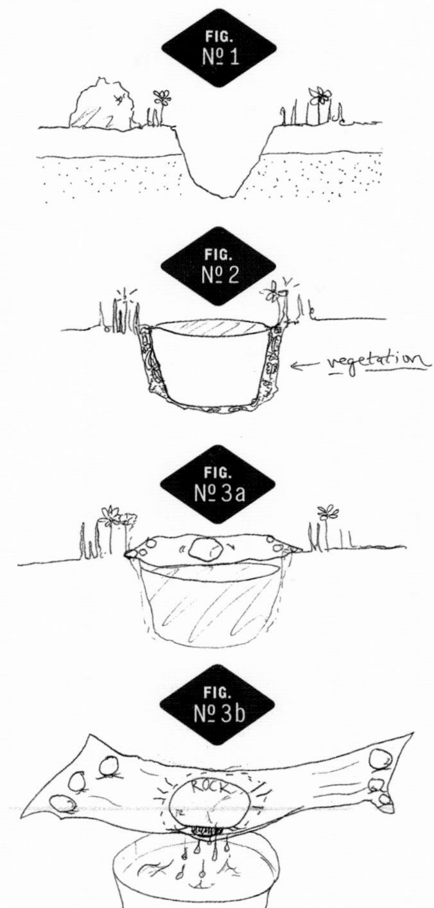

COLLECT EARLY MORNING DEW

DEW THAT COLLECTS ON PLANTS AND IN THE GRASS IS A GREAT SOURCE OF WATER IN THE EARLY MORNING. USE A CLOTH AND WIPE IT OVER THE GRASS AND PLANTS UNTIL THE CLOTH IS SOAKED. YOU CAN EVEN TIE CLOTHS AROUND YOUR ANKLES AND WALK THROUGH THE GRASS TO SOAK IT UP EFFICIENTLY. SQUEEZE THE CLOTH INTO A CONTAINER OR YOUR MOUTH AND REPEAT.

HOW TO USE A

COMPASS

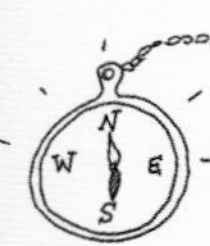

In a camping or outdoor adventure, do you want to follow the leader and watch someone else set up the tent, or do you want to be the girl who knows how to use the compass? If it is the latter, then the first thing you should know is that the needle on a compass contains iron, which naturally gravitates toward the north and south poles of the earth's magnetic field. Based on that you should:

1. Keep the compass away from metal objects like jewelry and watches.
2. Hold the compass parallel to the ground so that the needle spins freely.
3. Let the needle spin until it stops and points in one direction. This is north.
4. Move your body so that it is facing the same direction as the needle. Raise your right arm and that is east, raise your left arm and that is west. Your rear end is facing south.

parallel to ground

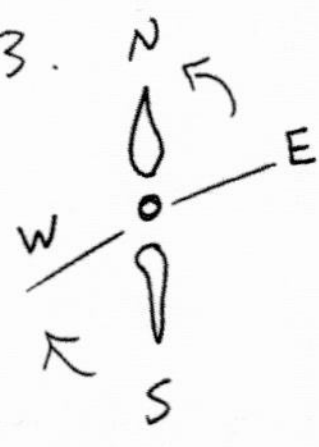

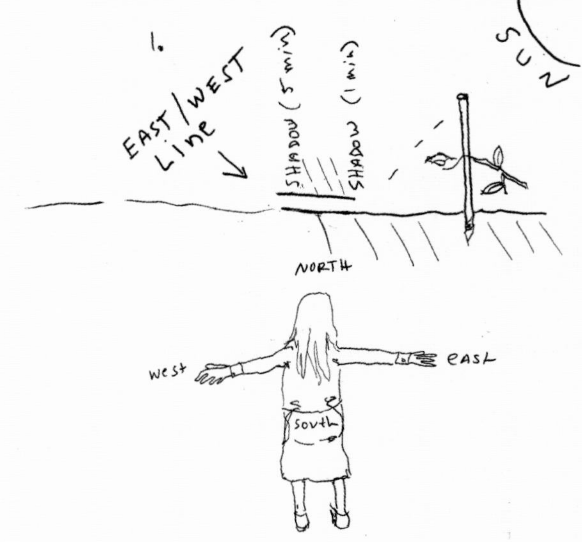

HOW TO FIND YOUR WAY WITHOUT A

COMPASS

If you don't have a compass available to you, here are some other options.

Plants will often indicate the direction of the sun as they reach for light. Look for plants that are growing at odd angles or that are lopsided, with more vegetation on one side than the other. In the Northern Hemisphere, the favored side will be directing north. In the Southern Hemisphere, the favored side will be directing south.

1. Find an open area with full sunlight and secure the end of a 1-foot stick into the ground. Note where the tip of the shadow falls by marking the dirt clearly or using an object as a signpost. Wait about 5 minutes as the shadow moves and then mark where the tip of the shadow falls again. Draw a straight line between the two points: This is your direct east-to-west line. Put your feet on the markers, placing your left foot at the first marker and your right foot at the second marker. You are now facing north. This method will work whether you are in the Northern or Southern Hemisphere.
2. Float a magnetized sewing needle in water on a leaf; the needle will point north and south. You can temporarily magnetize a needle or anything else that contains iron by rubbing a straight bar or refrigerator magnet against it in one direction about ten or more times. This will create a current that runs from one end of the needle to the other.

HOW TO START A

FIRE WITHOUT MATCHES

1 Pick a good location for your fire before you attempt to make one. Make sure there is enough space around the area for you to settle.

2 Gather tinder, kindling, and fuel. Tinder is light material that can be crumbled into powder or formed into a jumbled ball. Lint, hair, pine needles, fine strips of bark, cattail, tree fungus, milkweed, and moss are all good options. Kindling is small delicate twigs and sticks that are not much larger than a match or pencil. Fuel is the larger sticks and logs.

3 Make a teepee formation by laying down a bed of kindling and a small pile of dry leaves to elevate your fire from the ground and allow oxygen to flow underneath it. Lean the small sticks against one another around the pile so there is a cone shape, and space in the center.

4 Create a nest-like ball with the tinder and soft materials you have collected and set it next to the teepee where there is an opening through which to fit the tinder.

5 Locate two dry, dead sticks made of soft wood. You can give it the soft wood test by pressing your fingernail into the wood to see if it leaves a dent. The best place to collect this wood is not on the ground where there is moisture, but caught in bushes or hanging from the dead branch of a tree. Rub the soft wood sticks together vigorously to create friction. It will take some work, but if your sticks are dry and soft, they will give way to friction and will produce a spark or ember.

6 Light your tinder with the small ember and gently blow on it until it goes from smoldering to flaming.

7 Place the flaming tinder into the opening at the base of the teepee and lay it on top of the elevated twigs and leaves. Continue to gently blow on it to encourage the flame.

8 As the teepee twigs begin to catch fire, slowly add more kindling to the outside of the teepee to fortify the walls. Continue to strengthen the fire with sticks until it is large and active, then add larger wood one piece at a time. Patience will pay off and ensure you don't snuff out your fire with too much wood.

Fire-enhancing elements are all around you. Anything with alcohol as the primary ingredient will help boost your fire, things like hand sanitizers, perfumes, and astringents. Vaseline, steel wool, pinesap, rubber, and high-fat foods are other good fire enhancers.

9 Gather a circle of rocks or logs to set around the fire to contain it.

OTHER METHODS TO GET A SPARK

A magnifying glass, shard of glass, flashlight lens, or glass bottle held above tinder in very strong sunlight will create a fire. The bigger the magnifying glass, the more easily the fire starts. Use the same steps as at left, substituting the magnifying glass in place of the soft wood in step 5.

Striking together flint and other rocks will cause a spark if you have the right type of rocks. The best way to know is to just try several times. If you have a steel knife, striking it against the flint will be even more effective.

HOW TO COOL YOURSELF DOWN

- **Lie down in a cool, shaded area and elevate your feet.**
- **Spray water on your face and body.**
- **Soak your feet in cold water.**
- **Add cold towels to your head and neck.**
- **Wear a wet bandanna.**
- **Drink cold water and eat salty snacks.** Eating salt while drinking water will slow down the rate at which your body releases important minerals and water as you sweat.
- **Avoid all caffeine and alcohol, which promote dehydration.**
- **Avoid dense protein like jerky, which increases the metabolic rate and heats up the body in the process.**

HOW TO USE CAYENNE PEPPER TO STOP BLEEDING

Cayenne pepper equalizes the body's blood pressure, which also helpfully reduces excess pressure where a wound is. This factor, mixed with the spice's coagulating properties, helps blood clot quickly. You can stop the bleeding from most wounds in under 60 seconds by using a cotton swab or gauze pad and rubbing the bleeding area with a liberal amount of cayenne pepper. It may sting temporarily but the pain will pass. You can also take cayenne pepper internally in capsule form or mixed with food, which will stimulate the circulatory system and aid any internal bleeding.

HOW TO TIE A VERSATILE AND STRONG KNOT FOR MANY USES

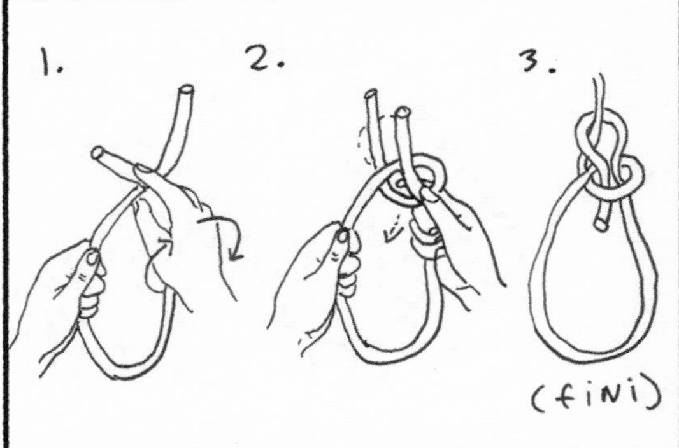

A bowline is a great go-to knot because it won't tighten or loosen on its own. Here is how to make one:

1. Make a small loop and bring the end up through it from behind.
2. Take the end around the main rope and bring it back to the top, then back down through the loop.
3. Pull the end and main rope to tighten.

If your lace broke and it is too short, skip the eyelets near the toes and lace up the ankle (and cuff if it is a boot) to get a tight fit. If you lose an entire shoelace, cut the other one in half and use the tight-ankle method for both shoes.

HOW TO
PICK A LOCK

YOU NEVER KNOW WHERE AND WHEN YOU MAY NEED TO PICK A LOCK. YOU MAY JUST NEED TO GET INTO YOUR APARTMENT, OR A ROOM FULL OF TREASURE. WITH A LITTLE PRACTICE, YOU CAN LEARN HOW TO MACGYVER YOUR WAY THROUGH THESE SITUATIONS.

First, it is important to understand how locks work—that way, you will know what exactly you are feeling for. Most are basic pin-and-tumbler locks, which consist of a cylinder kept in place by several pairs of pins. When you insert a key into the lock, the unique cut of the key's ridges matches the unique levels of the pins, pushing each pin a specific distance to the shear line—the point where the pins are outside of the cylinder, and the cylinder can turn freely (and so can the lock).

Now you're ready to begin picking the lock itself. The idea with picking a lock is to get all of the pins to bind, or rest on something called a drive pin, above the shear line. To do this, you will need to guide your pick around to find pins that bind in a unique order. The tools to accomplish this, a tension wrench and a hook pick, can be found online or at large retail and hardware stores.

1. Start by putting the tension wrench in the bottom of the keyhole, and apply a slight amount of turning pressure to the lock.

2. Take your pick and slowly lead it (hook side up, toward the pins) into the keyhole. Start feeling your way through the lock, testing each pin as you come to it. When you apply pressure, does the pin spring back, without any change? If so, that pin is not the binding pin—the pin you will need to find to begin moving each pin to the shear line.

3. The binding pin is the pin that, due to imperfections in the lock (maybe from size issues, maybe from drilling imperfections), binds before all the other pins. When you find a pin that doesn't spring back, but resists you, you have found your binding pin. Carefully move that pin upward with your pick until you feel the pin stop—that means it has reached the shear line. When this happens, the cylinder of the keyhole should turn (very, very little—so little that it will be nearly imperceptible).

4. Repeat this process for every pin in the lock, feeling each pin until you find the next binding pin. The order will be unique for each lock, so you will need to feel each pin until you find the one that binds. The binding pin will stay up at the shear line when you go on to find the others each time. Moving the first binding pin will allow a new one to become a binding pin and so forth.

5. Once the last binding pin has been pushed above the shear level, the cylinder of the lock will turn freely, and you will have successfully picked the lock.

HOW TO BUILD A

BASIC LEAN-TO SHELTER

THE EASIEST AND QUICKEST TYPE OF SHELTER IS A LEAN-TO. THE ROOF SHOULD BE BUILT LEANING AWAY FROM THE WIND AND IT SHOULD BE CONSTRUCTED ON A LEVEL, SAFE SITE. SHOULD YOU FIND YOURSELF LOST IN THE WILD AND IN NEED OF SHELTER AGAINST THE ELEMENTS, THIS IS WHAT TO BUILD.

Beam pole, a sturdy and relatively light, straight branch or pole trimmed of any protruding twigs (reach your arm straight above you and the distance from the ground to about 2 feet higher than your fingertips is an ideal length)

2 support poles, at least 4 to 6 feet tall, with Y-shaped ends—tree branches, for example

Various dead branches or other poles for the ribs

Debris, like leaves and grass, for roofing

Heavy rocks

1. Search for a place to build your lean-to shelter. An immovable support, such as two sturdy trees or a large rock, is the best place against which to build. Avoid creating a freestanding lean-to, which can easily fall down in wind, creating a hazardous trap for anyone inside.
2. Lean the support poles against the immovable support and using a heavy rock, hammer the support poles into the ground. Since they are on a diagonal you will be able to reach the top. The distance between them should be 2 feet less than the length of the beam pole.
3. Place the beam pole within the forked ends of the support poles. The beam and support poles should now be leaning against the immovable support, with the open side of the shelter facing away from the wind. Gently shake them to make sure they are all sturdy.
4. Add the ribs, that is strong branches, along the windward side of the beam by leaning them against the beam. Make sure to place the ribs close together so that your roofing material, which will most likely be dead leaves or grass, doesn't fall through any gaps.
5. Weave saplings over and under the ribs to create a lattice roof. Use branches with foliage for added insulation. Tuck in more leaves and pine needles on top of the ribs. Make sure to layer heavier materials, like twigs, on top of the leaves and lighter material, to keep the lighter things from blowing away. Continue to do this until you have a densely thatched roof. For even better water resistance, place a plastic tarp on top of the roofing material.
6. Place heavy rocks at the base of the rib branches to keep them in place during high winds.
7. Over the next several days, replace any foliage that has withered for maximum insulation.

NOTE: Build your campfire near the opening of the shelter, and away from any of the thatching.

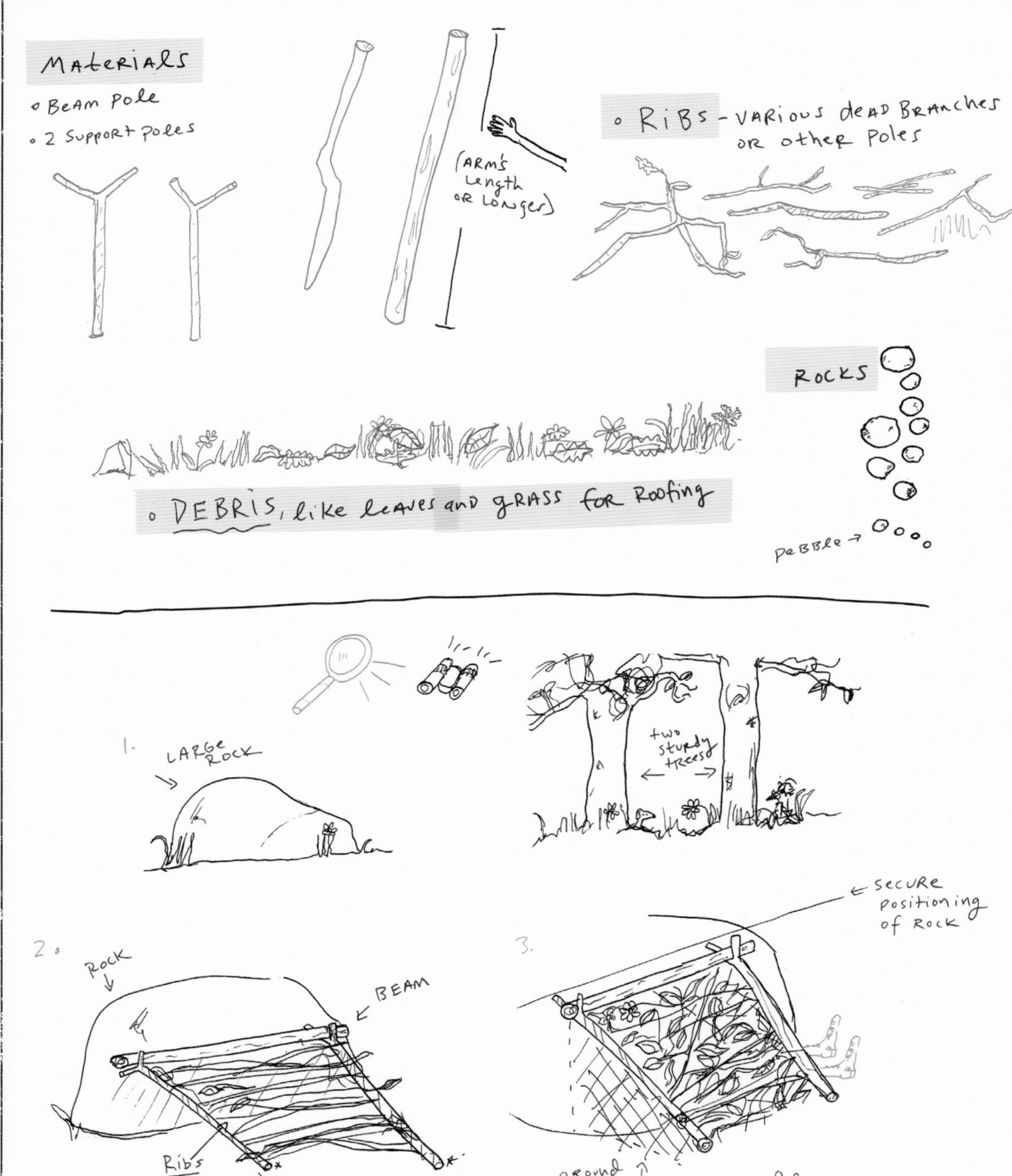
Materials
◦ Beam Pole
◦ 2 Support Poles
(ARM'S Length OR Longer)
◦ RiBs - VARIOUS dead Branches or other Poles
Rocks
pebble →
◦ DEBRIS, like leaves and grass for Roofing
1.
LARGE ROCK
two sturdy trees
2.
ROCK
BEAM
Ribs
support* poles
3.
← SECURE positioning of Rock
ground
position yourself in here

HOW TO

CHANGE A TIRE

EVERYONE SHOULD KNOW HOW TO CHANGE A TIRE IN A PINCH. CHECK YOUR CAR'S SPARE TIRE PERIODICALLY TO MAKE SURE IT HAS ENOUGH AIR IN IT, AND LOOK AT YOUR CAR'S MANUAL TO FAMILIARIZE YOURSELF WITH ANY UNIQUE FEATURES. THEN LEARN THESE BASIC STEPS. YOU WILL BE BACK ON THE ROAD IN NO TIME.

Wood, brick, or metal wheel chocks
Scissor jack or hydraulic jack
Screwdriver
Wrench
Soft rag

1 Choose a safe spot to change your tire—someplace well lit, out of the flow of traffic, and with no inclination (it is unsafe to jack up a car on an incline). Turn on your hazard lights so your vehicle is visible to others, and use some kind of block (wood, brick, or metal wheel chocks) on the opposite end of the car that is going to be raised to make sure the wheels don't move. Remove the spare tire from the car.

2 Using a jack, start to raise the car up. If you are using a scissor jack, insert the rod over the knob and crank. If you are using a hydraulic jack, place the handle in the appropriate location and pump up and down using even strokes.

3 Using a screwdriver, pry the wheel cover off by applying a bit of pressure where the cover meets the wheel. You may have to do this in several places, but the cover should eventually pop off (think of it almost as if you were opening a can of paint).

4 Take the lug nuts off, using the end of the lug wrench that fits your particular vehicle's lug nut size. Apply pressure to the left, which loosens the lug nuts.

5 Take the lug nuts completely off and remove the flat tire. Using both your hands, pull the flat tire toward you until you feel yourself supporting its full weight (instead of the bolts supporting the weight). Roll it on the ground to a spot away from you.

6 Once the flat is removed, lift the spare onto the bolts. Then replace the lug nuts and tighten them, first by hand as much as you can and then using the wrench. Tighten them enough to keep them in place, but don't tighten them fully until you lower the car.

7 Lower the car (by reversing step 2) and then finish tightening the lug nuts all the way. Replace the wheel cover, using the heel of your hand (not a hammer or wrench, which might dent the cover). Place a soft rag against the wheel cover before you bang on it with your hand to cushion the blow. Place the flat tire in the car. Remove and stow the wheel block and you're on your way!

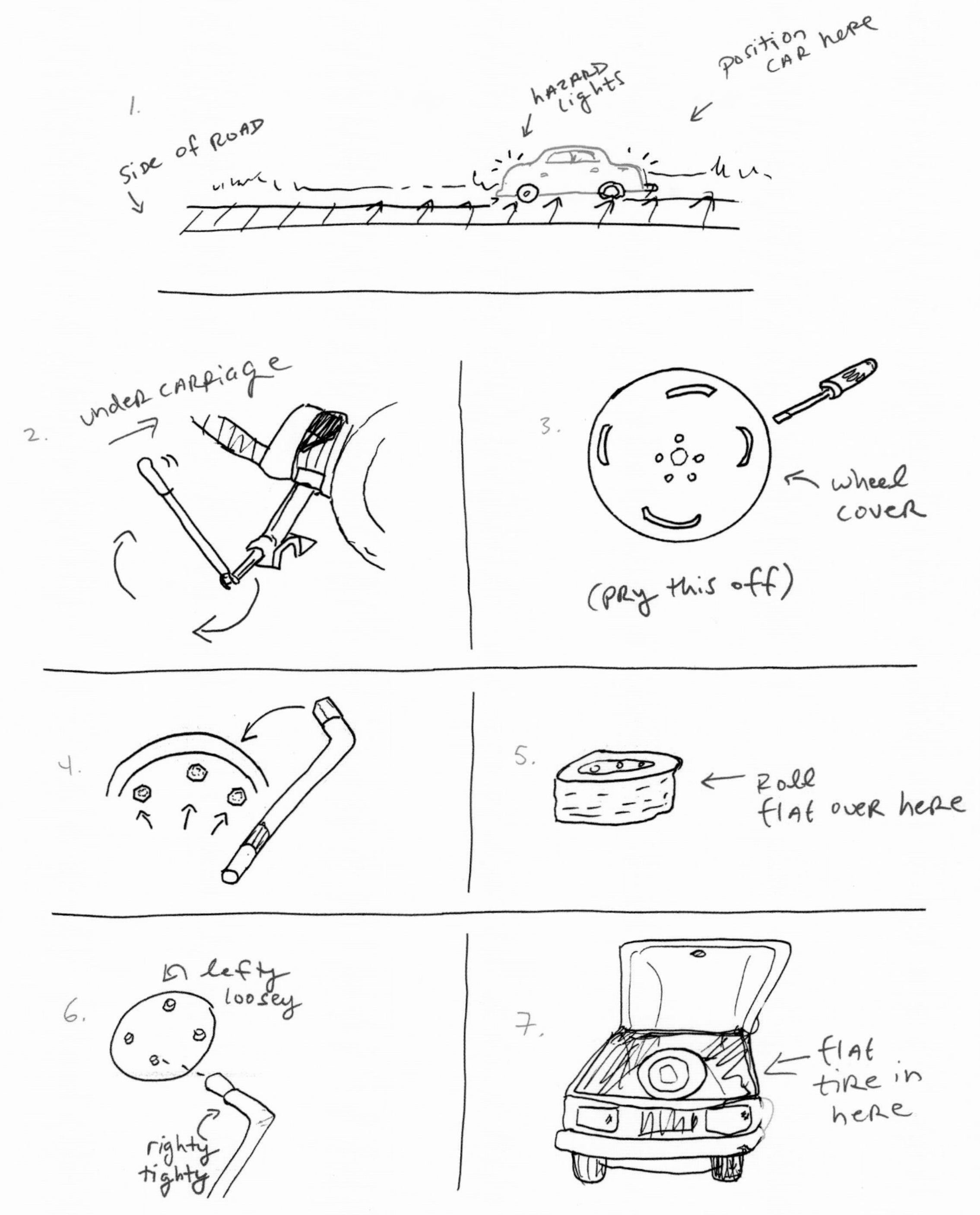
1.
side of ROAD
hazard lights
position CAR here
2.
under carriage
3.
wheel cover
(pry this off)
4.
5.
Roll flat over here
6.
lefty loosey
righty tighty
7.
flat tire in here

A bone has
A bone has
A bone has
A bone has
A bone has
A bone has
A bone has

THE REST
Spurs
SINCE 1973
and nerves.

CHAPTER
Nº 5

WEEKEND WARRIOR PROJECTS

SOMETIMES A GIRL DOESN'T NEED TO CHANGE A TIRE or pick a lock but still wants to be adventurous in her own way, to do something unique and exceptional with a couple of free hours on the weekend.

In this section you will learn to do just that, from how to make fresh mozzarella from scratch in 30 minutes to fresh butter in 15 minutes. You will learn to bake bread with only three ingredients in a quantity that you can eat yourself without worrying that it will go stale before you can enjoy it all.

You will also get to meet my friend Frank Fortress, an Austin-based architect and my partner in DIY crime. We will take you step-by-step through some of our favorite quick, easy, and economical projects to repurpose and upcycle things you already have. You will learn how to impress your friends with the smells emanating from your kitchen, your upcycled crafts, and your ability to be a more self-sufficient negotiator in your daily adventures.

30-MINUTE
MOZZARELLA

MAKES 12 OUNCES

Silky, stringy fresh mozzarella really can be made in only 30 minutes, so long as you have the right kind of milk. In general, the key to cheese making is to find the purest form of milk possible, one that has not been ultra-pasteurized, since the high-heat treatment of the milk will prevent curds from forming. Raw milk is the best option if your state allows it; otherwise, search at farmers' markets and health food stores for whole milk that is as unadulterated as possible. Even organic milks can be ultra-pasteurized, so read the labels.

Cheese-making kits are available with everything you will need other than milk, but you can also buy citric acid tablets and rennet online. If you want to make the curds in advance, store them in an airtight container for two weeks, or freeze the curds and reheat them. Save the whey, which you can freeze and use for baking high-protein bread or even scones.

PREP TIME: 5 minutes
COOK TIME: 10 minutes
INACTIVE TIME: 15 minutes
TOTAL TIME: 30 minutes

- 1½ teaspoons citric acid powder, either tablet form or powder form
- ¼ cup nonchlorinated water, such as spring water, distilled water, or filtered water from a Brita or other filtration system
- 1 gallon whole milk (not ultra-pasteurized; raw milk works best)
- ¼ rennet tablet (vegetable or animal) combined with ¼ cup of cool nonchlorinated water (also comes in a liquid form, and the proportions remain the same)
- 1 teaspoon kosher salt
- Fresh herbs, olive oil, balsamic vinegar, red pepper flakes, chopped garlic, or other seasonings (optional)

1. Sprinkle the citric acid into a large, nonreactive stockpot. Pour in the nonchlorinated water and stir to dissolve the powder, with the heat off.

2. Pour the milk into the citric acid solution and stir it vigorously to combine. Turn the burner to medium heat and let the milk's temperature rise to 88°F if it is raw/unpasteurized and 90°F if it is pasteurized (use an instant-read digital thermometer). You may see the milk begin to curdle, which is what you want. Remove the pot from the heat and pour in the rennet solution. Give the mixture a gentle, circular stir for about 30 seconds. Then use the spoon to stop the motion of the milk so it will be still. Place the lid on the pot and walk away for 5 minutes if the milk is pasteurized, 10 minutes if the milk is raw or unpasteurized. When you return, the mixture will resemble a very soft custard, with a clear separation between the curds and whey (the liquid that separates from the curd). If this hasn't happened let it set for a few more minutes.

3. With a long knife or offset spatula that reaches to the bottom of your pot, cut the curd into a 1-inch checkerboard pattern. This will separate the curds, making them easier to stir.

(continued on following page)

4 Return the pot to the burner and stir it gently over medium heat until the temperature of the whey reaches no more than 90°F for raw or unpasteurized milk and 105°F for pasteurized milk. Remove from the heat and continue to stir for about 5 minutes.

5 Use a slotted spoon to transfer the curd to a colander set over a large bowl. It will look stringy. Slowly spin around the colander once the curds are in it to allow the whey to drain from the curd, which will now have a soft-cheese consistency.

6 Remove the curds from the colander and gently squeeze them a few times to drain off more excess whey. Then transfer the curds to a microwave-safe bowl and microwave on high for 30 seconds.

7 Remove the bowl from the microwave and pour off as much whey as you can into another container, pressing the curd together with your hands to get more whey out. Add salt to the curds at this point, if you wish.

8 Return the curds to the bowl and microwave them again on high for 30 seconds, then remove the bowl from the microwave and drain the whey, pressing the curds together. The more whey you can get out, the more dense the cheese will be and the longer it will store in the refrigerator.

9 Stretch and knead the curds like taffy to drain more whey, then microwave them one last time for 30 seconds. The cheese should be at an internal temperature of 135°F at this point in order to stretch properly. If at any point it feels too hot or too liquid to stretch, run it under cold water to help it cool slightly before working with it.

10 Roll the cheese into a neat ball, or into smaller balls for bocconcini. You could even braid it or turn it into string cheese–sized pieces.

11 Fill a medium bowl with tap water that is at a temperature of about 50°F. Set the cheese ball(s) into a water bath for 5 minutes to cool.

12 Fill another medium bowl with water and ice, then transfer the cheese into it and let it rest until totally cool, about 15 minutes. This step will ensure that the texture stays silky rather than grainy.

13 Remove the mozzarella, pat it dry with paper towels, plate it, and top it with your favorite seasonings, if desired, like chopped garlic, fresh herbs, or red pepper flakes, along with a drizzle of olive oil. It is best to eat the mozzarella within a day, or it can be kept in water in the refrigerator for up to 3 days.

SAVE THE WHEY

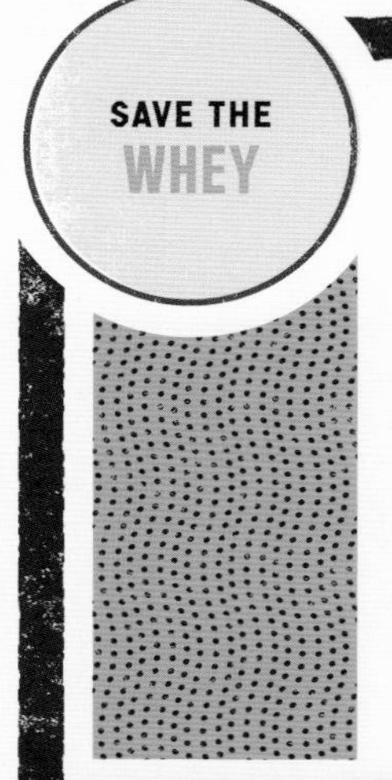

Save the whey by freezing it in an airtight container and using it later to make high-protein bread. It will store for 6 months. Alternatively, add it to a bath for softer skin or pour it into your garden soil to lower the pH for plants that enjoy acidity (like tomatoes).

SPREADABLE

FARMER'S CHEESE

MAKES 1 CUP

What I love about this cheese is that you can let it form while you go about your day. Raw milk works best, but it is illegal in some states, so at the very least, choose milk that has not been ultra-pasteurized, because it forms better curds. You will need cheesecloth, kitchen twine, and a fine-mesh strainer to form the curds and gather them up to hang. Then you can leave and when you return you will have a delicious, spreadable cheese.

PREP TIME: 1 minute
COOK TIME: 5 minutes
INACTIVE TIME: 1 hour, 10 minutes
TOTAL TIME: 1 hour, 16 minutes

- 1 quart whole milk (not ultra-pasteurized; preferably raw)
- ½ teaspoon salt, plus additional to taste
- Juice of ½ lemon, strained, plus more as needed
- Freshly ground black pepper to taste
- Chopped fresh herbs, minced garlic, spices, and/or hot sauce (optional)

1. In a medium saucepan over medium heat, combine the milk and ½ teaspoon salt and heat until the sides begin to bubble, about 5 minutes. Stir frequently so the milk doesn't scorch.

2. Remove from the heat and add the lemon juice. Stir and let sit for 10 minutes so the curds form. If curds do not form, juice and strain another ½ lemon and add the lemon juice to the pan.

3. Rinse a piece of cheesecloth and squeeze it dry. Place the damp cheesecloth into a fine-mesh strainer and set it over a large bowl, then pour the curds and whey through the strainer and let the whey drain into the bowl.

4. Gather the four corners of the cheesecloth and tie them at the top with a length of kitchen twine. Hang the bundle of cheese over the bowl and let it drip slowly for at least 1 hour and up to 8 hours, until the cheese is firm and at room temperature. The less whey in the cheese, the longer it will keep.

5. Untie the cheesecloth, put the cheese into a bowl, and mix in salt and pepper to taste. Add chopped fresh herbs, minced garlic, spices, or hot sauce, if desired, for a variation. Store the whey in the refrigerator for up to 1 week or in the freezer for 3 months to use in baked goods.

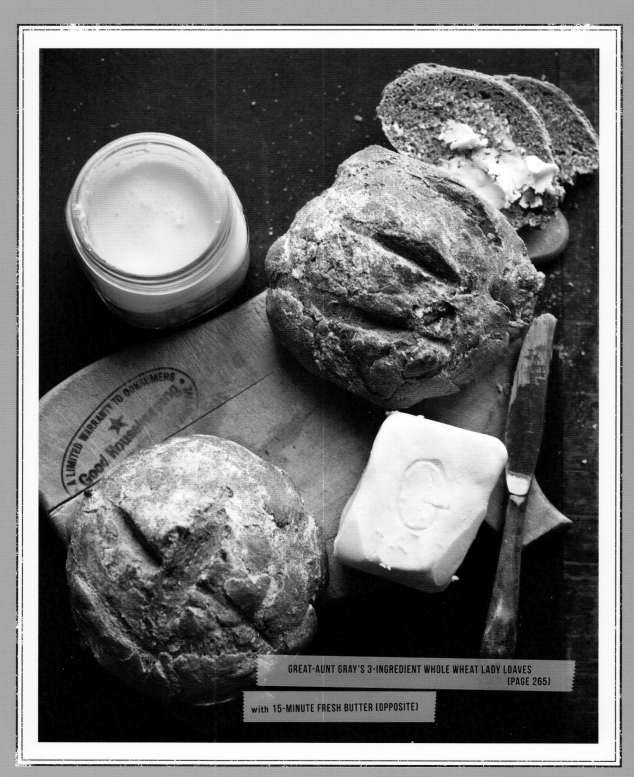

GREAT-AUNT GRAY'S 3-INGREDIENT WHOLE WHEAT LADY LOAVES (PAGE 265)

with 15-MINUTE FRESH BUTTER (OPPOSITE)

15-MINUTE

FRESH BUTTER

MAKES ⅓ TO ½ POUND BUTTER PLUS 1 CUP BUTTERMILK

Making butter from scratch is something you can do while getting ready in the morning, checking your e-mail, or watching your favorite evening TV show. You just need heavy cream and an electric stand mixer. It is especially worth making when you have access to high-quality cream from a local farm.

For a really special butter, find a farmer who will sell you cream from grass-fed cows. In the summertime, when the cows have been snacking on green grass, the butter will be an especially bright-yellow color. You don't need a farmers' market or a stand mixer to make your own butter, though. Heavy cream from the store will work, and you can separate the cream by adding it to a mason jar with a tight-fitting lid and shaking it well for a little while. This is a fun activity for kids to do, since they can watch the cream change right before their eyes. This butter would also make a wonderful hostess gift along with an armload of croissants. And save the leftover buttermilk to use for baking scones or lightening your coffee. Fresh buttermilk is not thick and sour like store-bought but rather is very sweet and thin.

PREP TIME: 1 minute
COOK TIME: None
INACTIVE TIME: 14 minutes
TOTAL TIME: 15 minutes

- 2 cups (1 pint) heavy cream
- ¼ teaspoon fine-grain sea salt (optional)
- Minced garlic, chopped fresh herbs, cinnamon, and/or honey (optional)

1. Pour the cream into the bowl of a stand mixer, and stir it with the paddle attachment on medium-low speed. Churn the cream until it separates into butterfat and buttermilk, scraping down the sides of the bowl once about halfway through. The time will vary depending on the temperature (colder cream will turn more quickly), but it will take approximately 15 minutes, and will sound like water sloshing when it is done.

2. Once the buttermilk has separated from the butterfat, place the chunks of solidified butterfat into a colander and rinse it thoroughly with very cold water, squeezing it gently with your hands to release any excess buttermilk. The less buttermilk it has in it, the longer it will store.

3. Separate the butterfat into desired portions. Add salt, if you wish, and knead it into butter. You can also create a compound butter by mixing in minced garlic, chopped herbs, cinnamon, honey, or any other flavorings, if desired.

4. Use a piece of parchment paper to roll the butter into a log, shape it into blocks with your hands, or press it into a ramekin with a spoon. Once you have formed it into your desired shape, carve a decoration into the top with the tip of a paring knife. To help the butter last longer, you can also wrap it tightly in several layers of plastic and store it in the freezer for up to 3 months or in the refrigerator for up to 2 weeks.

QUICK HOMEMADE

TEA BLENDS

There is something so satisfying about picking the fresh leaves from your garden for your morning brew. It doesn't take long, and even if it is not snipped from your windowsill, a mixture you devise from your spice cabinet will be satisfying, too. All of the spices and herbs in the following recipes can be found in the bulk herb section of natural food stores and some large grocery stores. Feel free to use the same basic technique and experiment with the ingredients that you already have.

As a rule of thumb for experimenting, 1 tablespoon of dried herbs or 2 tablespoons of fresh herbs per cup of water is about right. Very dry herbs float to the top so you'll need a strainer.

TO STEEP

OR TO BOIL?

If you are using leaves, petals, or flowers, it is better to steep them in boiling water, letting them brew for as long as your tastes like.

If you are using seed, bark, or peel, which have oils that are harder to release, you should simmer them, even crushing them first before you do. The ratio should be about 1 tablespoon of seeds to every 2 cups of water. Taste the liquid as you simmer and turn it off when it is as strong as you desire.

HOMEMADE CHAI

SERVES 2

Really good chai doesn't have to come from a box of concentrate at the coffee shop. This tea recipe relies on strong spices that, when brewed, make a potent and delicious chai. Or, if you want to go café style, the second option here is to make a concentrate and combine it with hot, foamy milk. Here are the two methods.

PREP TIME: 2 minutes
COOK TIME: 15 minutes
INACTIVE TIME: 3 minutes
TOTAL TIME: 20 minutes

- 5 cardamom pods
- 5 whole cloves
- 1 teaspoon dried lavender
- ½ teaspoon pink or black peppercorns
- 1 tablespoon dried ginger flakes
- 2 tablespoons kukicha twigs (also known as twig tea)
- ½-inch piece of vanilla bean, cut lengthwise (optional)
- 1 cinnamon stick
- Milk and honey (optional)

METHOD 1: POTENT CHAI

1. Combine the cardamom, cloves, lavender, peppercorns, ginger, and kukicha twigs in a small bowl. Using the back of a spoon, press on the herbs to increase the surface area and release the oils. Alternatively, you can use a mortar and pestle.

2. Pour the mixture into a medium French press or teapot. Add the vanilla bean, if desired, cinnamon stick, and 2 cups of hot water. Let steep for 5 to 7 minutes and serve in a teacup or mug. Add milk and honey, if desired.

METHOD 2: CHAI CONCENTRATE

1. To make a strong chai concentrate, combine all of the ingredients but the milk and honey with 2 cups of water and bring to a boil in a small saucepan. Lower the heat to a simmer and let the liquid reduce until dark and aromatic, about 15 minutes.

2. Remove from the heat and let the chai steep for 3 minutes. Strain the concentrate through a fine-mesh strainer into a jar.

3. To serve, heat 1 cup of milk in a small saucepan over medium heat until just simmering. Whisk until foamy and add 1 cup of chai mixture, stirring well to combine. Fill the mug and add honey or sugar, if desired. Store any extra chai concentrate in an airtight container in the refrigerator for up to 6 months.

HOMEMADE CHAI (PAGE 248)

ENERGIZING TEA

SERVES 2

This mixture improves mental clarity without caffeine, thanks to the gotu kola, a plant commonly used in Eastern medicine and easily found in the bulk herb section of natural food stores. Burdock root, also popular in Eastern cultures, adds a natural, mild sweetness and is known to flush toxins from the body. The dried spearmint, dried sage, and fennel seed give the tea a fresh, bright flavor. You can even dry your own fresh herbs for this tea by tying them in a bundle and hanging them upside down from your cabinet or windowsill (see page 50).

PREP TIME: 2 minutes
COOK TIME: 5 minutes
TOTAL TIME: 7 minutes

- 1 teaspoon fennel seed
- 2 teaspoons dried spearmint
- ½ teaspoon dried sage
- 1 teaspoon gotu kola
- 1 teaspoon burdock

1. Combine the fennel seed, spearmint, sage, gotu kola, and burdock in a small bowl. Using the back of a spoon, press on the herbs to increase their surface area and release their oils. Alternatively, you can use a mortar and pestle.
2. Spoon about 1 tablespoon of the mixture into a tea ball strainer. Place the strainer in a teacup, and fill the cup with hot water. Alternatively, pour the entire mixture into a medium French press or teapot and add 2 cups of hot water.
3. Brew for 3 to 5 minutes, or longer for a stronger tea.

POTION Nº 6

CHAMOMILE HAIR LIGHTENER

Use ½ cup dried chamomile flowers boiled with 4 cups of water to lighten your hair naturally. Once the mixture cools, and after you've shampooed, conditioned, and rinsed as usual, pour the mixture all over your hair and let it soak in for 20 minutes, preferably while sitting outdoors in the sun. Follow with a vinegar rinse at a ratio of 2¾ cups water and ¼ cup distilled white vinegar. Do not rinse with water after the vinegar rinse, instead dry with a towel gently and continue with your regular drying routine.

This vinegar rinse is an important way to balance the alkalinity of your shampoo, which opens the pores in your hair and leaves them vulnerable. The acid balance can be used after every shampoo and condition to shine and soften hair. Keep it in a plastic bottle in your shower and use it regularly. It will contract your hair imbrications, which will trap moisture inside each strand, giving your hair a more buoyant, full look, and reducing any tangles.

LEMON THYME

FRESH TEA

SERVES 2

Most people think of tea as a blend of dried ingredients, but it doesn't have to be. Fresh teas use a variety of raw ingredients for a more vibrant flavor. This tea marries the simple aromatic tastes of Meyer lemon and fresh thyme, but you could include a whole host of other herbs depending on what is in season, from lemon verbena to pomegranate seeds. Honey offers a mild sweetness. If you are using honeycomb instead of honey, the wax, which is perfectly edible, will melt into the tea.

PREP TIME: 2 minutes
COOK TIME: 5 minutes
INACTIVE TIME: 5 minutes
TOTAL TIME: 12 minutes

- 1 lemon (a Meyer lemon, preferably, if they are in season), cut into wedges
- 10 sprigs fresh thyme
- 1 tablespoon honey or 1-inch square of honeycomb

1. In a small saucepan over medium-high heat, bring the lemon wedges, thyme, and honey to a simmer for 2 minutes, then remove from the heat.
2. Let the tea steep for 5 minutes, then strain it into a cup.

SPICY CHOCOLATE CHIP
SKILLET COOKIE

MAKES ONE 10-INCH COOKIE

The secret to this cookie batter is the raw sugar, which gives it a crunchy texture. Because there is far less sugar than most normal cookies, you can taste the other flavors. The cayenne spice adds a warmth to the aftertaste—just a little intrigue. When the batter is cooked all together in a skillet, it forms one large cookie that can be cut into wedges and served à la mode. If you keep this dough on hand in the freezer, you will always have a quick, crowd-pleasing dessert that can be made at the last minute.

PREP TIME: 10 minutes
COOK TIME: 35 minutes
TOTAL TIME: 45 minutes

- 1¾ cups (3½ sticks) unsalted butter, room temperature, plus more for greasing the skillet
- 1½ cups raw sugar
- ½ teaspoon salt
- ½ teaspoon cayenne
- 3½ cups all-purpose flour
- 2 large eggs
- 1 cup roughly chopped walnuts or pecans
- 1½ cups roughly chopped dark chocolate pieces

FREEZE A COOKIE DOUGH LOG

IF YOU HAVE A SKILLET THAT IS SMALLER THAN 10 INCHES IN DIAMETER, ROLL ANY LEFTOVER COOKIE DOUGH INTO A LONG LOG. WRAP THE LOG IN PLASTIC WRAP AND THEN IN ALUMINUM FOIL AND FREEZE IT. WHEN YOU ARE READY FOR A WARM COOKIE, LET THE LOG THAW SLIGHTLY, SLICE 1-INCH PIECES FROM THE LOG, AND BAKE THEM AS NEEDED, FOR ABOUT 10 MINUTES, AT 400°F OR UNTIL GOLDEN BROWN.

1. Preheat the oven to 400°F. In a mixer fitted with a paddle attachment, beat the butter, sugar, salt, and cayenne on high speed until creamed and incorporated.
2. Turn off the mixer and add the flour and eggs. Wrap a towel around the mixer bowl to prevent flour from flying out when you turn the mixer back on. Turn the mixer on at low speed and combine the eggs and flour.
3. Turn off the mixer, add the nuts and chocolate and mix again until just combined. If there are still nuts and chocolate at the bottom of the mixer, simply incorporate them with your hands.
4. Grease a 10-inch cast-iron or oven-safe skillet and place the cookie dough in the center. Press it down so that it becomes flat and even, meeting the sides of the pan.
5. Bake in the oven for 35 minutes, until the edges are golden brown. Remove and let cool. The cookie will be chunky and chewy, with lots of texture. Slice it into pie wedges and serve.

HOW TO SEASON AND CLEAN CAST IRON

CAST IRON IS MY FAVORITE COOKWARE MATERIAL BECAUSE WHEN IT IS WELL SEASONED, YOU CAN BAKE, FRY, SAUTÉ, AND STEW ALL IN ONE PAN. THE FACT THAT IT CONDUCTS HEAT UNIFORMLY MEANS IT IS ESPECIALLY GREAT FOR OUTDOOR COOKING. AND THE BEST PART? YOU DON'T HAVE TO WASH IT. IN FACT YOU SHOULDN'T. READ BELOW FOR INSTRUCTIONS ON HOW TO SEASON NEW CAST IRON AND CLEAN IT PROPERLY TIME AFTER TIME.

If the Pan Is New

1. Preheat the oven to 500°F.
2. Rinse the skillet with warm water and soap and dry it well.
3. Apply several tablespoons of grape-seed or vegetable oil and rub it around the pan inside and out with a paper towel.
4. Place the pan in the oven and bake for 30 minutes. Turn off the heat and let the pan cool in the oven for several hours.
5. Remove the pan from the oven and wipe it down with a paper towel. The skillet is now seasoned and ready to use. It will continue to season as you cook with it. To build up a good seasoning, never wash it with water (but if you must, repeat steps 1 through 5).

To Clean It Properly

1. Heat the pan until it is smoking hot.
2. Add a lot of salt to the pan and shake it so it distributes evenly.
3. After about 5 minutes, remove the pan from the heat and scrub it with a bamboo scrubber or wire brush.
4. Empty the salt into the trash and wipe out the pan with a paper towel.
5. Add a teaspoon of oil and rub it around with the towel to season the pan and remove any excess residue.

SPICY CHOCOLATE CHIP SKILLET COOKIE (PAGE 254)
with ALMOND MILK (PAGE 262)

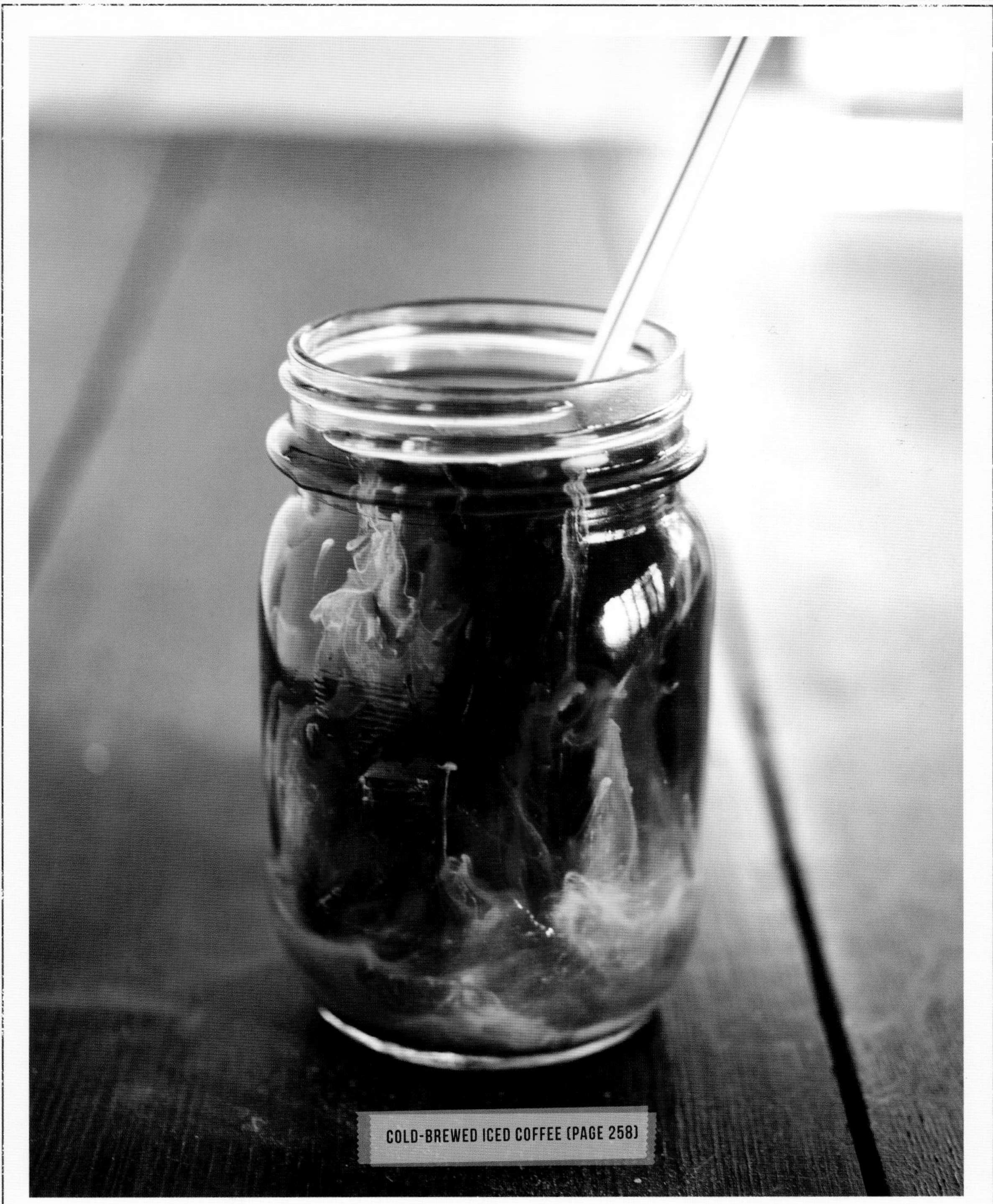

COLD-BREWED ICED COFFEE (PAGE 258)

COLD-BREWED

ICED COFFEE

MAKES 2 QUARTS OF COLD-BREWED CONCENTRATE, ABOUT 24 CUPS OF COFFEE

This concentrate is especially useful to have on hand in the hot summer months. You can store it in the refrigerator for at least a week, saving money on those ubiquitous $5 coffees. Cold-brewed coffee tastes a bit different from regular coffee because the absence of heat greatly reduces the amount of oil, acid, and bite in the brew. Instead, cold brewing will strongly concentrate the other flavors of the coffee, bringing out the more volatile and subtle flavoring elements that make each variety of coffee bean unique.

You will need to plan ahead to brew this up; it is a great idea, for example, to start in the morning before work so it is ready by the time you get home. The resulting coffee is considered a concentrate, which you can then dilute with more water or milk to your liking, depending on how strong you take your coffee.

The ratio to cold brew the coffee is 1 cup of grounds to 4½ to 5 cups water. To dilute it for drinking, the best ratio is 3 parts water to 1 part coffee. Each type of bean will respond differently to this method, so experiment a bit to see which works best for you. For the finest flavor, use beans that you grind yourself.

PREP TIME: 2 minutes
COOK TIME: None
INACTIVE TIME: 8 to 12 hours
TOTAL TIME: 8 hours, 2 minutes

2 cups freshly ground coffee
9 or 10 cups cold, filtered water

1. In a large plastic or glass container, stir together the coffee and water. Cover and let it sit at room temperature for 8 to 12 hours.
2. Rinse a piece of cheesecloth and wring it dry. Set a fine-mesh strainer over a quart mason jar and line it with the cheesecloth.
3. Pour the coffee through the strainer into mason jars, allowing all the liquid to run through and pressing with the back of a spoon. Discard the grounds or use them for compost (see page 110). The coffee concentrate will store in the refrigerator for about 1 week.
4. To serve, dilute the concentrate at a ratio of 3 parts water to 1 part concentrate. For stronger coffee, a 1:1 ratio is about right.

POTION Nº 7

COFFEE ANTI-CELLULITE BODY SCRUB

The caffeine in coffee helps temporarily reduce cellulite when applied to the skin. Save 1 cup of the coffee grounds from coffee making and mix them well with ½ cup of brown sugar; 1 cup of olive, almond, or avocado oil; and ½ cup of sea salt. When ready to use, spoon it out and rub it all over your body and let it sit for about 10 minutes. Rinse thoroughly and moisturize. Store it in a mason jar in the refrigerator for 3 months.

HOMEMADE

YOGURT

MAKES 3 TO 4 CUPS

Like the drinkable yogurt Kefir (page 191), regular yogurt is easy to make at home because it will develop as you go about your day. You can use a freeze-dried yogurt starter culture, but it is easiest to get your hands on high-quality yogurt in the store and use that as your starter.

If you use yogurt as a starter, make sure it is plain whole milk yogurt with no added pectin or preservatives, preferably organic. Raw milk is best if it is legal in your state, just be sure to avoid anything that is ultra-pasteurized, UHT, or shelf-stable. The yogurt container should also list live active cultures. The more bacterial diversity it has on the label, the better. Look for: *L. acidophilus*, *S. thermophilus*, *L. bulgaricus*, *L. bifidus*, *L. casei*, *L. reuteri*, and *L. rhamnosus*. This process works with all types of animal milks as well as soy and coconut milk; however, if you use one of the latter, you will need to add sugar or maple syrup to encourage bacteria.

PREP TIME: 5 minutes
COOK TIME: 10 minutes
INACTIVE TIME: 12 hours
TOTAL TIME: 12 hours, 15 minutes

- 3 cups whole milk at room temperature (not ultra-pasteurized; raw milk is preferable)
- ½ cup high-quality plain whole milk yogurt, organic if possible (not ultra-pasteurized; made from raw milk is preferable), or a freeze-dried starter culture used in the amount according to package instructions

1. In a small saucepan over medium-low heat, bring the milk to 170°F for pasteurized milk and 110°F for raw milk, then remove it from the heat and allow it to come to 100°F to 112°F. This will help create a thicker yogurt. If a skin develops on the surface during this cooling time, skim it off and discard it.

2. In a quart mason jar or other nonmetallic container, combine the milk and yogurt and stir gently with a spoon. Or if you use a freeze-dried starter culture, follow the ratio according to package instructions.

3. For a thinner, almost drinkable yogurt, let the jar sit at room temperature for 3 to 4 hours. For a thicker yogurt, heat the sealed jar with a heating pad, in a hot-water bath, or by setting it close to a fireplace or furnace, making sure that the temperature doesn't rise above 112°F, which will kill the bacteria. Other methods include using a cooler or a Yogotherm. A good temperature range is 70°F to 108°F, not much hotter than lukewarm. For a denser yogurt the process will take 8 to 24 hours. This will vary depending on the room temperature and strength of the starter culture. When it is as thick as you would like it, it is ready to eat, or you can store the yogurt in the refrigerator for up to 1 week. You can strain out any excess liquid to use for baking, or simply stir it back into the yogurt.

4. Make sure to save a few ounces from this batch of yogurt in your refrigerator for your next starter culture.

VARIATION

To make a Greek yogurt, strain the yogurt through cheesecloth, letting it drip for several hours into a bowl until the contents of the cheesecloth are thick and dense. You can save the liquid to bake with. Combine the yogurt with jam or crushed berries for a sweeter finish. Or freeze it for a healthy frozen dessert.

HOMEMADE YOGURT (PAGE 259)

ALMOND MILK

MAKES 6 CUPS

For the freshest, purest flavor, buy almonds in bulk and make your own almond milk. It requires soaking the almonds overnight or while you are at work, after which you can have almond milk in just minutes. Cashews are another delicious nut to use in this recipe if you want to branch out. To flavor the milk you have a whole host of options, of course, from vanilla to honey to cinnamon to cocoa powder to maple syrup.

PREP TIME: 15 minutes
COOK TIME: None
INACTIVE TIME: 6 hours
TOTAL TIME: 6 hours, 15 minutes

1½ cups raw unsalted almonds
5 cups cold filtered water

1. In a medium bowl, soak the almonds, covered in water, for at least 6 hours, preferably overnight, then drain them.
2. Pour the almonds into a blender and add the water.
3. Blend well for 1½ to 2 minutes until the mixture is white and frothy and nearly smooth.
4. Rinse a piece of cheesecloth, then squeeze out the excess water. Fold it to ensure it is several layers thick and set it in a fine-mesh strainer.
5. Set the strainer over a large bowl and pour the almond mixture through the cheesecloth a little at a time, pressing on the solids with the back of a ladle. If the cloth becomes too full of almond meal, gather the cheesecloth together at the edges to form a ball and gently squeeze the excess liquid out of the meal through the cheesecloth and strainer until no more can be extracted. Set the almond meal aside, rinse the cheesecloth and start again with more meal. You can save the meal and dry it in the oven for homemade almond flour, or use it to make Almond Exfoliating Body Scrub (below).
6. The milk will store in an airtight container in the refrigerator for 3 to 5 days.

ALMOND EXFOLIATING BODY SCRUB

Combine 1 cup of almond meal flour with ¼ cup of loosely packed light brown sugar, ⅛ cup of olive oil, and 2 tablespoons of honey and mix them together in a mason jar. When ready to use, rub it in circular motions on your skin, then rinse. The texture will exfoliate dead skin cells while the olive oil will moisturize your skin. Store it in the refrigerator for up to 3 months.

TURN LEFTOVER ALMOND MEAL INTO ALMOND FLOUR

To make almond flour out of the meal, spread it into a glass baking pan and pop it into the oven at 200°F for about 4 hours or until dry and sandy. It will yield a scant 1½ cups of almond meal flour and can be stored in an airtight container refrigerated for up to 6 months. Let it come to room temperature before using.

GINGER ALE

MAKES 6 TO 7 CUPS

This beverage celebrates the potency and vibrancy of fresh ginger, which you can't experience with store-bought ginger ale. Save your empty plastic water and seltzer bottles as containers for your homemade brew. Glass bottles with swing tops look more charming of course, especially as a gift, but you will want to have at least one small plastic bottle as a tester to feel the pressure harden against the plastic as the bubbles form. It is also a useful way to recycle empty plastic bottles. Champagne yeast is the purist way to brew, but I use active dry yeast most often because that is what is usually on hand.

PREP TIME: 15 minutes
COOK TIME: None
INACTIVE TIME: 24 hours
TOTAL TIME: 24 hours, 15 minutes

- ¼ pound fresh ginger, peeled and cut into 1-inch pieces
- 6 cups filtered water
- 1¼ cups sugar
- 2 tablespoons fresh lemon juice
- ¼ teaspoon active dry yeast

1. In a blender add the ginger along with ½ cup of the filtered water and blend until smooth.
2. Set a fine-mesh strainer over a 1-cup liquid measuring cup and pour the ginger pulp through the strainer, pressing the pulp with the back of a spoon to extract as much liquid as possible until there is about ½ to ¾ cup juice in the measuring cup.
3. Rinse out the blender and add the ginger juice, sugar, lemon juice, yeast, and the remaining filtered water and blend until incorporated.
4. Using the spout of your blender or a funnel, immediately transfer the mixture to four 12-ounce plastic bottles and seal, leaving 1 to 2 inches of headspace.
5. Let the bottles sit at room temperature until they can't be easily dented when squeezed. You will also see bubbles when you gently shake the bottles. This will take 24 to 36 hours, depending on the temperature of the room. The warmer it is, the faster the mixture will ferment.
6. Transfer to the refrigerator and chill well before serving. It will last for 1 week.

SPARKLING CIDER

MAKES ½ GALLON

What I love about this technique is that it shows you how to transform any fruit juice into something refreshing and festive with the simple addition of a bit of yeast. Plus it gives you something to do with your empty plastic seltzer or still water bottles. If apple cider is out of season when you want to try this recipe, feel free to use apple juice. Champagne yeast is what purists use, but as with Ginger Ale (at left), I typically use active dry yeast, which will create a slightly more yeasty flavor, but is much easier to find.

PREP TIME: 10 minutes
COOK TIME: None
INACTIVE TIME: 24 hours
TOTAL TIME: 24 hours, 10 minutes

- ½ gallon apple cider or juice at room temperature
- ¼ teaspoon active dry yeast

1. In a microwave-safe volume measuring cup, pour ¼ cup of cider. Microwave it on high for about 12 seconds or until it is lukewarm to the touch.
2. Sprinkle in the yeast and stir. Let it sit for 10 minutes until tiny bubbles start to form.

3 Pour the yeast mixture back into the plastic container of cider or juice, screw the lid back on, and shake well to distribute the yeast.

4 Using extra care or a funnel, immediately pour the cider into five 12-ounce plastic bottles. If you have cider left over that won't fill another bottle completely, leave it in the original plastic jug with the lid securely fastened and use that to test when your cider is done.

5 Seal the bottles with the caps and let them sit at room temperature in a dark place for 24 hours or until the bottles are stiff with air and there are plenty of visible bubbles when the liquid is gently shaken. After 24 hours, take a sip from one to see if it has enough bubbles to suit your tastes. The warmer the temperature, the faster it will carbonate.

6 Once it is fully carbonated, transfer the bottles to the refrigerator and chill for several hours before serving, otherwise they will explode when you open them. Sparkling cider will keep for 1 week in the refrigerator.

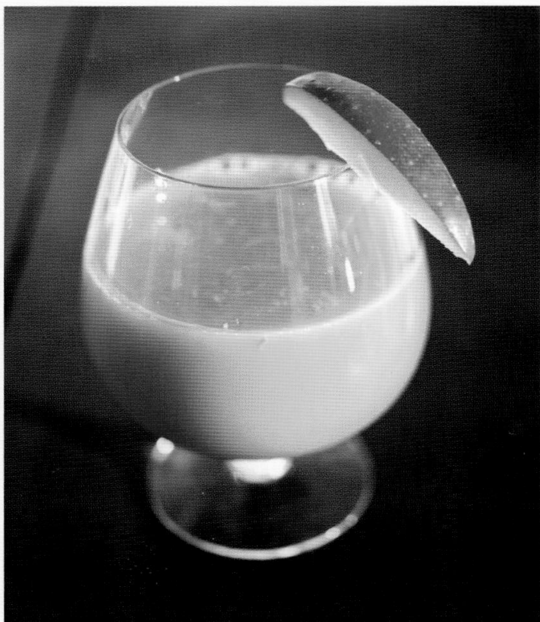

GREAT-AUNT GRAY'S 3-INGREDIENT

WHOLE WHEAT LADY LOAVES

MAKES 2 LADY LOAVES

What is so great about fresh homemade bread? That it is fresh and homemade. On the other hand, it doesn't have a long shelf life, so it is a use-it-or-lose-it type of situation. Sometimes, we can't eat a whole loaf by ourselves in the allotted time before it gets stale. This recipe allows you to make smaller loaves as you need them. And you can let the rising happen while you run errands for a few hours. This slightly denser bread is excellent toasted. If one of the little loaves does go stale, no biggie. See my suggestions on how to upcycle stale bread (page 204).

PREP TIME: 5 minutes
INACTIVE TIME: 2 to 3 hours
COOK TIME: 40 minutes
TOTAL TIME: 2 hours, 45 minutes

- 1 tablespoon fast-acting dry yeast
- 1 tablespoon kosher salt
- 3 cups whole wheat flour, plus more for dusting

1 In a large bowl stir the yeast and salt into 1½ cups of lukewarm water (about 90°F) and let it sit for 5 minutes.

2 Stir in the flour, mixing with a wooden spoon and then with your hands until the dough is uniform.

3 Cover the bowl with a kitchen towel or plastic wrap and let the dough rise at room temperature for 2 to 3 hours. You now have three options: Refrigerate the dough for up to 2 weeks, bake just one loaf and refrigerate the dough for the other, or bake both since they are small and will both fit on a pizza stone together. Note: If you refrigerate the dough and bake it at another date, be sure to let it come completely to room temperature before baking.

(continued on following page)

4 To bake both loaves, cut the dough in half and form a rounded shape with each, about 6 inches in diameter. If the dough feels wet, sprinkle it with flour so the rounds form more easily. Set two racks in the lower half of the oven, with a pizza stone on the top rack (or if you don't have one, set the loaves on a baking sheet and wait to add it to the oven). Preheat the oven to 450°F for 30 minutes to create an even, radiant heat. Cut three slashes into the top surface of the dough and sprinkle each with flour.

5 Pour 1 cup of very hot tap water into a baking dish or sheet tray with sides. Set the dough on the pizza stone on the top rack and set the tray of water underneath on the bottom rack. Immediately close the oven door to keep in the steam.

6 Bake for 40 minutes until well browned, then remove from the oven and cool completely before cutting.

HOW TO MAKE YOUR FLOOR THE BEST-SMELLING FLOOR ON THE ELEVATOR RIDE

Have you ever noticed that in some apartment buildings there are different aromas on every floor and sometimes at every door? From curry to pot roast to rosemary and lamb, good smells are the surest way to make a home feel cozy. Those smells sometimes make taking the stairs worthwhile for others. This trick is one of my favorite lessons from Grandma Pellegrini. She liked to have dinner parties but was also obsessive about the details, so she would avail herself of one of several ways to make the house smell good when she had company coming over at the end of a busy day. It would seem like she had been cooking for hours! Here are five quick ways to make the house smell good in under five minutes:

FRY ONIONS with a pat of butter in a skillet, then add a dash of sea salt. Let them sweat over medium heat until soft.

MAKE A FISH FUMET with shallots, white wine, bay leaf, celery, and fish bones or shellfish shells. Cover with water and let it simmer. It will start smelling good right away but can simmer for up to 2 hours to get full flavor. If you want, you can skim the foam from the surface, strain it, and store it in the freezer for a rainy day.

SAUTÉ GARLIC in oil or butter over low heat (don't burn it, though!)

SEAR BACON by letting it render very slowly in a skillet.

HEAT UP A STORE-BOUGHT PIE. The store-bought variety will work just fine when finished in the home oven.

COCOA AND CAYENNE PECANS

MAKES ABOUT 3 CUPS

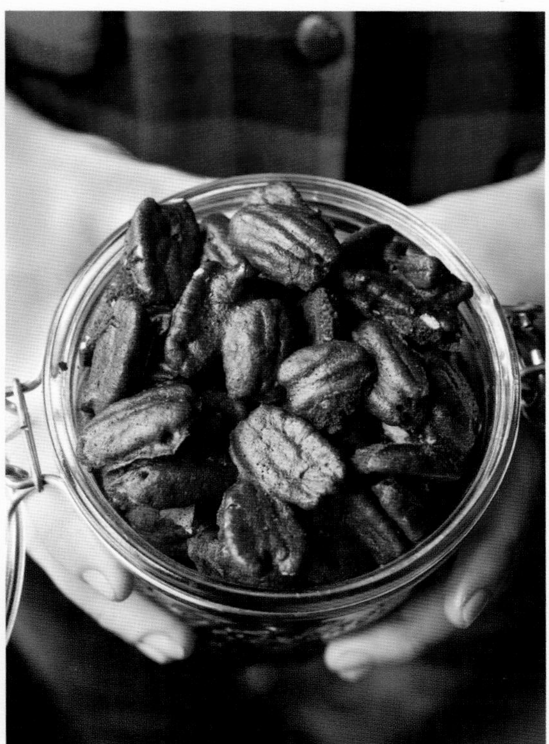

This is another pantry staple that can be made with bulk ingredients. I especially enjoy whipping this up around the holidays for a gift or party snack with a little sweetness, heat, and spice. Instead of maple syrup you could use honey or agave, and you could mix up the spices in a variety of ways, making them more savory or sweet to your liking.

PREP TIME: 15 minutes
COOK TIME: 1 hour
TOTAL TIME: 1 hour, 15 minutes

Vegetable oil or butter for greasing the baking sheet
1 large egg white
3 cups unsalted raw pecans
¼ cup unsweetened cocoa powder
½ teaspoon ground ginger
Pinch of cayenne pepper
1 teaspoon ground nutmeg
½ teaspoon ground cinnamon
¼ cup maple syrup

1. Preheat the oven to 250°F and grease a large baking sheet.
2. In a medium mixing bowl, beat the egg white until it forms soft peaks. Fold in the pecans, stirring until they are all coated.
3. Combine the cocoa powder and spices in a small bowl and stir until the mixture is uniform. Sprinkle and stir into the nuts until they are evenly coated.
4. Fold in the maple syrup until evenly distributed.
5. Spread the pecans onto the baking sheet and bake for one hour, stirring every 15 to 20 minutes, until the pecans are dry.
6. Remove the pan from the oven and let the nuts cool completely before serving or storing. Store in an airtight container for up to 1 month.

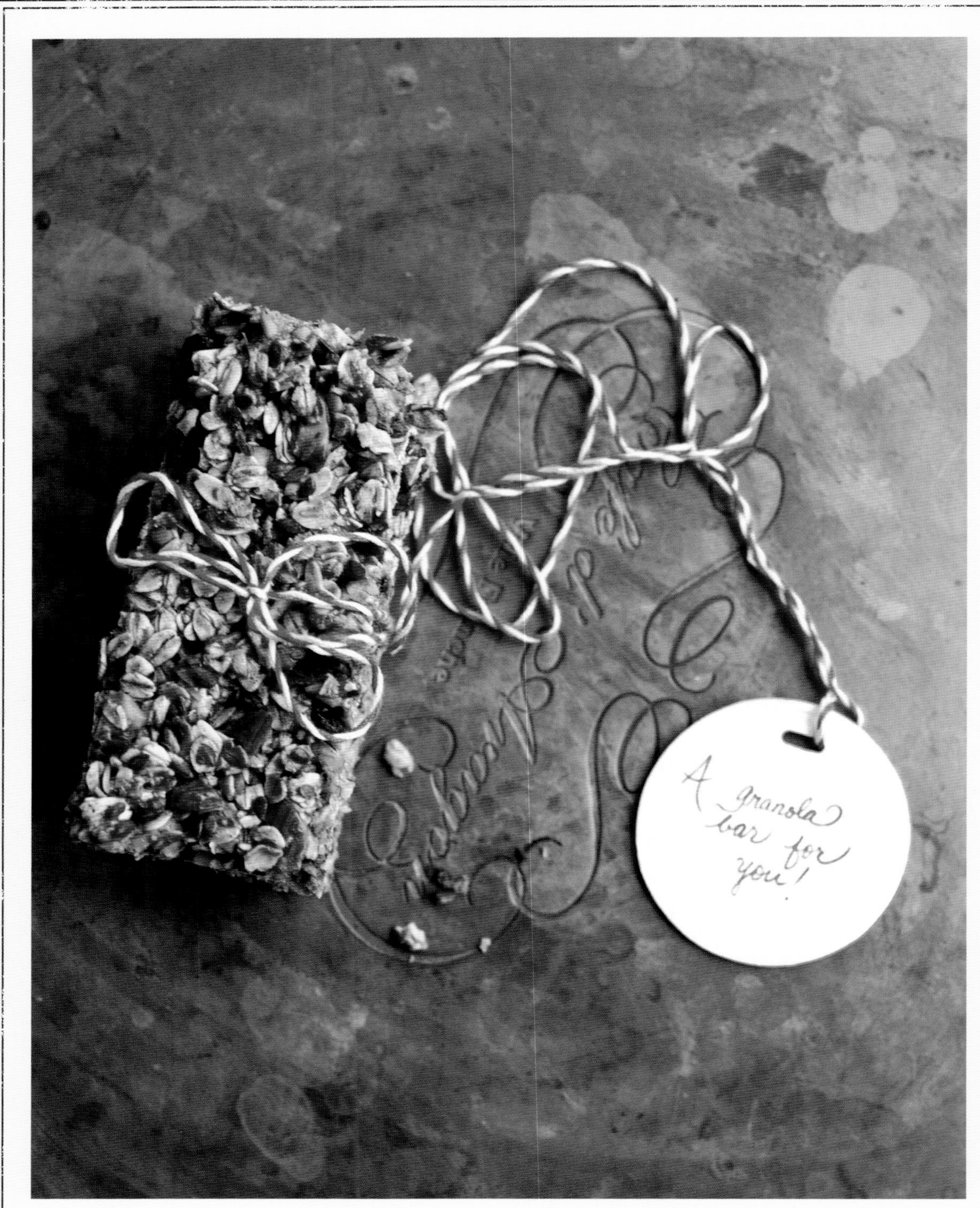
A granola bar for you!

BANANA-ALMOND

GRANOLA BARS

MAKES 12 BARS

When making granola bars, I prefer to start with whole oats rather than premade granola. It is more natural and you have more control over the flavor. If you like this combination of ingredients but don't want to spend the time making it into granola bars, you can leave it loose. Buy these ingredients in bulk, which is less expensive, and you'll always have an easy-to-prepare snack in your pantry.

PREP TIME: 30 minutes
COOK TIME: 20 minutes
INACTIVE TIME: 24 hours
TOTAL TIME: 24 hours, 50 minutes

- ¼ cup (½ stick) unsalted butter, plus more for greasing the pan
- 3 cups whole oats
- ¼ cup flaxseeds
- ½ cup unsalted almonds, chopped
- ½ cup dried cranberries, roughly chopped
- 1 teaspoon ground cinnamon
- ¼ teaspoon sea salt
- ½ cup honey
- 1 teaspoon vanilla extract
- 1 ripe banana
- 2 tablespoons Almond Butter (page 184)
- 1 tablespoon fresh lemon juice
- 2 large egg whites

1. Preheat the oven to 350°F and grease a 9 × 13-inch baking pan with butter. Combine the oats, flaxseeds, almonds, cranberries, cinnamon, and salt in a large bowl. Mix well.
2. In a small saucepan, melt the butter with the honey and vanilla and stir. Remove from the heat and let cool slightly.
3. Add the banana and almond butter to a blender or food processor and puree, pouring the honey-butter mixture in as it spins. Add the lemon juice and egg whites and puree for about 1 minute, until incorporated and foamy.
4. Pour the banana liquid over the oat mixture and combine thoroughly until all ingredients are well coated.
5. Spread the mixture into the baking pan, using the back of a large spoon to press it firmly and evenly. Bake for 20 minutes, until lightly browned. Remove the pan from the oven and let it cool completely. Cut it into bars, about 2 × 4 inches. Let the pan sit out for 24 hours to become firm, then transfer the bars to an airtight container. Store for up to 1 month.

HARD APPLE CIDER
DOUGHNUTS

MAKES 12 DOUGHNUTS AND 12 HOLES (USING 3½- AND 1½-INCH CUTTERS)

I like to make these in the fall months, when the leaves are turning and apple-picking season is in its prime. There is nothing better than coming in from the cold, sitting by the fire, and sinking your teeth into the crunchy outside and warm pillowy inside of a fresh doughnut. Make the dough in advance, place it in the fridge, and fry it up when everyone is ready to settle in and eat it fresh.

PREP TIME: 20 minutes
COOK TIME: 20 minutes
INACTIVE TIME: 50 minutes
TOTAL TIME: 1 hour, 30 minutes

- 4 cups all-purpose flour, plus additional for the work surface and the baking sheet
- 2 teaspoons baking powder
- 1 teaspoon baking soda
- 2 tablespoons plus 1 teaspoon ground cinnamon
- ¼ teaspoon ground cardamom
- ⅛ teaspoon cayenne
- ½ teaspoon salt
- 4 tablespoons unsalted butter, at room temperature
- 1¼ cups sugar
- 2 large eggs
- ¼ cup hard apple cider
- ½ cup buttermilk
- Vegetable oil for frying

1. Line two baking sheets with parchment or wax paper, dust with flour, and set aside.
2. In a large bowl, combine the 4 cups flour, baking powder, baking soda, 1 teaspoon of the cinnamon, the cardamom, cayenne, and salt and set aside.
3. In an electric mixer, using the paddle attachment, cream the butter and ¾ cup of the sugar together until fluffy. Then add the eggs one at a time until they are incorporated. Slowly add the cider, then the buttermilk. Stop the mixer, scrape down the sides, then turn it back on and incorporate the flour mixture in three parts and combine until uniform.
4. Transfer the dough to the baking sheet. Using your hands, roll or flatten the dough to ½-inch thickness. Place both baking sheets in the freezer for 30 minutes.
5. Remove the baking sheets from the freezer. Use a 3½-inch ring cutter to make the outer doughnut circle, and a 1½-inch ring cutter to remove the doughnut hole. Place your doughnuts on one baking sheet and your holes on the other. Do this until all of the dough has been cut. Feel free to reroll any scraps to cut them into doughnuts or holes. Place the baking sheets in the refrigerator for 20 minutes.
6. Meanwhile, fill a Dutch oven or deep-sided pan with about 3 inches of vegetable oil and let it heat to 350°F. Set a platter or third baking sheet next to the Dutch oven and line it with paper towels. In a small bowl, combine the remaining cinnamon and sugar.
7. When the oil is ready, remove the baking sheet of doughnuts from the refrigerator. Using a spatula to lift the dough rings, fry the doughnuts in batches, about three at a time. Cook for about 2 minutes on each side (1 minute on each side for the doughnut holes), or until dark golden brown. If the raw dough on the baking sheet gets warm while you are frying, place the sheet back in the fridge for 10 minutes.
8. With a slotted spoon, transfer the fried doughnuts or holes to the platter and sprinkle them with the cinnamon and sugar mixture on all sides. Serve them as soon as possible, since these are best eaten when still warm.

HOW TO TURN

MASON JARS INTO LANTERNS

I HAVE A FRIEND NAMED FRANK FORTRESS. WELL, HE WOULD SAY HIS NAME IS FRANK CASTLE, BUT I CALL HIM FRANK FORTRESS. NEITHER OF THOSE NAMES IS ACTUALLY HIS NAME. HIS REAL, TRUE, BIRTH NAME IS FRANCISCO ARREDONDO. HE IS ORIGINALLY FROM MEXICO BUT HE RESIDES IN AUSTIN, TEXAS, NOW AND IS A WORLD-CLASS ARCHITECT. THE NAME CHANGE OCCURRED AT MY BIRTHDAY DINNER WHEN HE JOKINGLY SAID HE WAS THINKING OF MAKING HIS NAME MORE MAINSTREAM FOR THE PURPOSES OF HIS WORK . . . LIKE "FRANK CASTLE." I SAID IT SOUNDED TOO MUCH LIKE A SPY NOVEL DETECTIVE AND IT SHOULD BE SOMETHING STRONGER THAN "CASTLE . . ." "FORTRESS!" I BLURTED OUT OVER MY PLATE OF MEATBALLS. "FRANK FORTRESS!" AND SO FROM THEN ON, HE WAS FRANK FORTRESS TO ME.

We dream up a lot of DIY projects together and execute them in his garage. This one and others in this chapter are some of our favorites. These lanterns are an inexpensive way of personalizing and styling your home, and can also be given to friends as gifts. Hang them from tree branches or set them on tables for a romantic evening light.

- 22-gauge (or thicker) nontarnish silver wire
- Quart mason jar
- Wire cutters
- Fine pea pebbles, available at garden supply stores
- Votive candles
- Long lighter

1. Wrap the wire around the neck of the jar, leaving an inch of slack. Cut the wire and twist the ends together.
2. Cut another piece of wire to make the wire handle, about 8 inches, or a piece that's long enough to attach to both ends of the wire around the neck in a loop.
3. Tuck the second wire under the first one and twist together. Repeat this on the other side, combining the wire twist from the first wire so that they connect.
4. Pour in the pebbles and secure a votive candle inside. Light it with a long lighter and hang the lantern wherever you please.

FIG. № 1a
FIG. № 1b
FIG. № 3a
FIG. № 3b
FIG. № 3c
FIG. № 4a
FIG. № 4b
Ball
MASON
FIG. № 4c
FIG. № 4d

HOW TO USE

CHALK PAINT FOR MANY PURPOSES

CHALK PAINT IS AN ECONOMICAL WAY TO PERSONALIZE MATERIALS AND SURFACES, AND TO GET CREATIVE WITH PARTIES AND PLANNING. YOU CAN EVEN MAKE THE STORAGE BINS IN YOUR SELF-SUFFICIENT PANTRY GLAMOROUS! HERE ARE SOME FUN WAYS TO USE CHALK PAINT AND THE STEPS TO TAKE.

- Newspaper to work on
- Object of your choice such as a flowerpot, serving dish, wineglasses, or small porcelain jars
- Primer spray or brush-on paint (like Rustoleum)
- Pourable chalkboard paint
- Paint container to pour your paint into
- Paintbrush that suits the size of what you are painting
- Cotton swab or rag to wipe away any mistakes

1. Lay down some newspaper and place your object on top. Apply the primer evenly and let it dry for an hour.
2. Pour your chalk paint into a container and dip in your brush.
3. Use very light pressure to apply the paint, making your strokes in one direction. Any mistakes or imperfect paint lines can be wiped away with a rag or cotton swab, unless it is a porous surface like a clay pot, in which case you can just say it is the human touch.
4. Let the object air-dry for 1 hour, and wash the brushes between coats so they don't harden. Apply a second coat in the opposite direction and let the paint set for 24 hours before using.

Brie [FRANCE]
Chimay [BELGIUM]
Bufala [ITALY]
RUFFINO
LUMINA
PINOT GRIGIO
DELLE VENEZIE
FRANK
GEORGIA
Thyme

HOW TO MAKE A

STYLISH VASE WITH RUBBER BANDS AND SPRAY PAINT

TRY THIS TECHNIQUE WITH PITCHERS, JARS, AND OTHER GLASS STORAGE CONTAINERS IN ADDITION TO VASES. EVEN THE MOST BORING OLD CONTAINER CAN BE REPURPOSED AND MADE INSTANTLY MODERN AND UNIQUE.

- Glass vase
- Rubber bands of varying thickness
- Newspaper
- Spray paint
- Utility or pocket knife

1. Cover the vase with rubber bands of various thicknesses, creating a random pattern and making sure none of them are twisted. The objective is to cover the glass with enough rubber bands to create a pattern, not to cover the whole vase.
2. When your pattern is complete, lay some newspaper on a flat surface.
3. Turn the vase upside down on the paper and spray with a light coating of spray paint about 6 inches from the vase. Spraying a light coating in three stages will prevent dripping.
4. Let the vase dry for about 15 minutes and then apply another coat. Let dry for 15 minutes more and apply a third coat. Let dry completely before removing the rubber bands, about 1 hour.
5. Carefully cut into the rubber bands with the knife and let them pop off. You will be left with a painted vase with see-through stripes where the bands were.

FIG. №1a

FIG. №1b

FIG. №3

FIG. №5a

FIG. №5b

FINISH

HOW TO DECORATE WITH
COLORED MASON JARS

SPRAY-PAINTED MASON JARS ARE A GREAT ACCESSORY FOR DECORATING, ESPECIALLY AROUND THE HOLIDAYS. BECAUSE SPRAY PAINT COMES IN ALL KINDS OF FINISHES, FROM METALLIC TO MATTE, IT ALLOWS YOU TO PLAY WITH COLORS AND STYLES. TRY METALLIC GOLD AND SILVER FOR CHRISTMAS, OR A MATTE WHITE, BLACK, AND ORANGE FOR HALLOWEEN. FILL THEM WITH SMALL ROCKS OR MARBLES, THEN ADD FLOWERS, BRANCHES, OR WHATEVER ELSE YOU WOULD LIKE.

Fast-drying glue pen (optional)
Quart mason jars
Newspaper
Spray paint

1. If desired, use the glue to draw any design on your jars and let them dry completely. You may want to practice first on a piece of paper to make sure you're familiar with how the glue writes and how much space you have to write on. If you choose to write in glue, note that it will take some time to dry and you may need to touch up parts of your letters so that they stay in high relief.
2. Lay the mason jars upside down on the newspaper and spray them with paint from 6 inches away. Depending on the color you may need more than one coat.
3. Let them dry completely.

Kerr
"SELF SEALING"
MASON
Kerr
"SELF SEALING"
MASON

COLORED MASON JARS (PAGE 280)

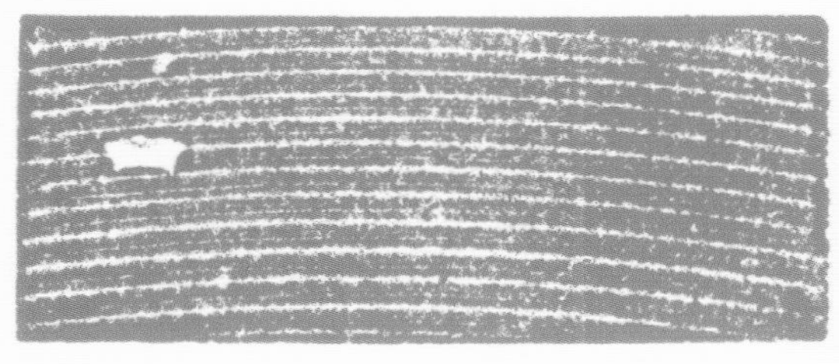

HOW TO MAKE

GLASS BOTTLES INTO GLASSWARE

FRANK FORTRESS GAVE ME THESE FOR A HOUSEWARMING GIFT AND WHEN HE TOLD ME HE MADE THEM, MY JAW DROPPED AND I ASKED IF HE WOULD TEACH ME. WE BECAME CRAFT BUDDIES AFTER THAT, WORKING ON ALL KINDS OF HOME DESIGN PROJECTS IN HIS GARAGE. HE WOULD "ARCHITECT" THINGS IN AN ORDERLY FASHION WHILE I APPROACHED THINGS WITH THE FLY-BY-THE-SEAT-OF-YOUR-PANTS METHOD.

START

Rather than recycle your glass bottles, upcycle them and enjoy them as glassware. Bonus points if you have bottles with screen printing on them rather than a sticker; the former makes for an edgy-looking glass. There will be some casualties in this process, so have extra bottles on hand.

FINISH

- Large pot
- Pitcher
- Glass bottle of any size that you would like to drink out of, from wine bottles to beer bottles
- Glass bottle cutter
- Pliers
- Sandpaper or electric drill with a drum sand bit (sand bit makes the job easier)

1. In a large pot, bring 2 quarts of water to a boil over high heat. Remove from the heat to cool slightly.
2. Prepare a pitcher of ice water.
3. Determine the desired height of your glasses and lock in the bottle cutter by tightening the screws so that each glass is the same height.
4. Fit the bottle to the bottle cutter and apply pressure to the blade, rotating the bottle in as few motions as possible so it makes one continuous mark around the glass. Repeat for each bottle you are cutting.
5. Over a bucket or the sink, hold a bottle that you've already scored and pour hot water over the circular crack while rotating the bottle so that the water touches all sides.
6. Repeat with the cold water.
7. Do this three times with each temperature of water, and you will hear a crack. Gently break the bottle neck apart from the lower half of the bottle.
8. If there are any jagged edges, you can often snap them off with pliers.
9. Use the electric drill with a drum sand bit or sandpaper to smooth out the edges of the glass.

FIG. № 3

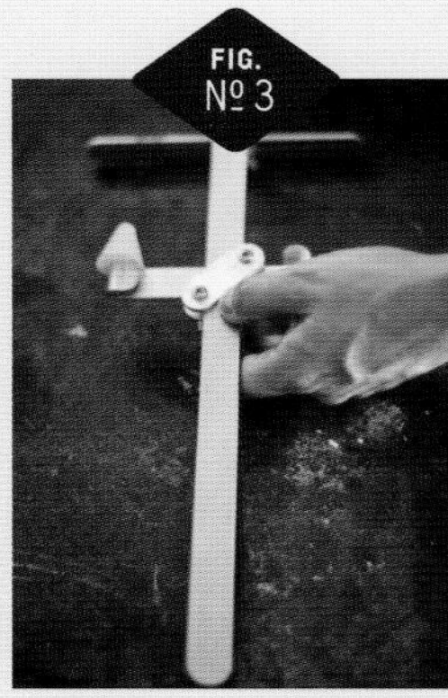

FIG. № 7a

FIG. № 9a

FIG. № 9b

FIG. Nº 4a
FIG. Nº 4b
FIG. Nº 5
FIG. Nº 6
FIG. Nº 7b
FIG. Nº 8
FIG. Nº 9c
FINISH
ROLLING ROCK
Extra Pale
©1939

HOW TO MAKE

QUICK AND EASY BEESWAX CANDLES

PURE BEESWAX IS THE ONLY FUEL THAT CAN EMIT NEGATIVE IONS INTO THE AIR, IN THE PROCESS PURIFYING THE AIR BY BURNING POSITIVELY CHARGED IONS LIKE DUST AND POLLEN. NEGATIVE IONS ARE MOTHER NATURE'S NATURAL CLEANING TOOL AND THEY ALSO PROMOTE HARMONY IN A SPACE. BURN A BEESWAX CANDLE WHILE YOU ARE WORKING, MEDITATING, OR BEFORE YOU DRIFT OFF TO SLEEP AND SEE IF YOU DON'T NOTICE A DIFFERENCE.

Beeswax candles burn slowly and at a higher temperature than other candles, so you need a thicker wick to allow the wax to burn evenly, at least a #2 cotton wick, square and braided if possible. These are available from candle suppliers and online.

Scissors
Cotton or hemp wick, at least a #2
1-cup mason jars
Wick tabs
Pliers
Superglue
Beeswax pellets

1. Preheat the oven to 200°F.
2. Cut a length of wick that is 1 inch longer than the distance from the base of your jar to the opening.
3. Run one end of the wick through a wick tab and use the pliers to close the open end of the wick tab.
4. Place a drop of superglue at the bottom center of the jar and press the tab into the glue.
5. Fill the jar with beeswax pellets so that the pellets rise about 1 inch higher than where you want the melted wax to settle. Make sure the other end of the wick is well above the wax; drape it over the lip of the jar if possible.
6. Place the jar on a baking sheet and put it in the oven for 20 minutes, until the wax is completely melted. Remove it carefully and set it on a flat, heatproof surface to cool completely.
7. If the wax cracks at all, simply add more pellets and return it to the oven to melt again, then let it cool completely.
8. The candles are ready to use, or place the lids back on and give these as gifts.

HOW TO MAKE

A WREATH FROM VINES

TO GATHER THE KEY INGREDIENT FOR THIS PROJECT, HANG FROM THE VINES IN THE WOODS UNTIL THEY DROP, OR USE YOUR CLIPPERS AND GO IN SEARCH OF THE THINNER KIND. TYPES OF VINES THAT ARE GOOD FOR WREATH MAKING INCLUDE WISTERIA, HONEYSUCKLE, AND GRAPE, BUT A WALK IN THE WOODS WILL NO DOUBT REVEAL OTHERS. THIS IS A FREE WAY TO DECORATE YOUR HOME YEAR-ROUND.

Vines, about a 10-foot length total, depending on the size

Wreath decorations

1. Take a single piece of vine and wrap the ends together to form a circle. I recommend using a piece that is at least 4 feet long to start.
2. Use another piece of vine and wrap it around the frame.
3. Repeat this with vines until you have a thick frame, tucking in any ends as you go, and building on any areas that are thinner than others.
4. Use rose hips, spruce and pine, holly, dried flowers, and berries and tuck them between the vines to decorate the wreath. Hang it!

HOW TO MAKE

PAPER

WHEN GIVEN THE CHOICE BETWEEN PAPER AND PLASTIC BAGS AT A GROCERY STORE, ALWAYS OPT FOR PAPER. ALONG WITH ALL OF YOUR OTHER PAPER WASTE, THOSE BROWN PAPER BAGS ARE A WONDERFUL OPPORTUNITY TO MAKE HOMEMADE NOTE CARDS AND STATIONERY. ONCE YOU HAVE YOUR BASIC PAPER RECIPE DOWN, EXPERIMENT WITH DESIGNS AND COLORS. LAY IN DRIED FLOWERS, SEEDS, AND OTHER TEXTURES TO YOUR PAPER AS IT DRIES ON THE FRAME. TIE IT UP IN A BUNDLE AS A GIFT, OR REVIVE THE OLD-FASHIONED WAY OF CORRESPONDING.

You can use most types of paper waste, keeping in mind that what you choose will affect the final color of the homemade paper. Try printer paper, newspaper, magazines, egg cartons, toilet paper, paper bags, tissue paper, wax-free boxes, napkins, and construction paper. The higher-quality your paper, the longer it will need to soak. Pour in boiling water to speed up the soaking process. Make multiple frames at once to produce sheets more quickly.

- Recyclable paper products
- Metal hanger
- Pair of stockings
- Scissors
- Felt
- Wet paper
- Blender
- Plastic basin or tub large enough to immerse your metal hanger frame
- Baking sheet
- Decorating elements like leaves, grass, flowers, yarn, and feathers (optional)
- Paring knife

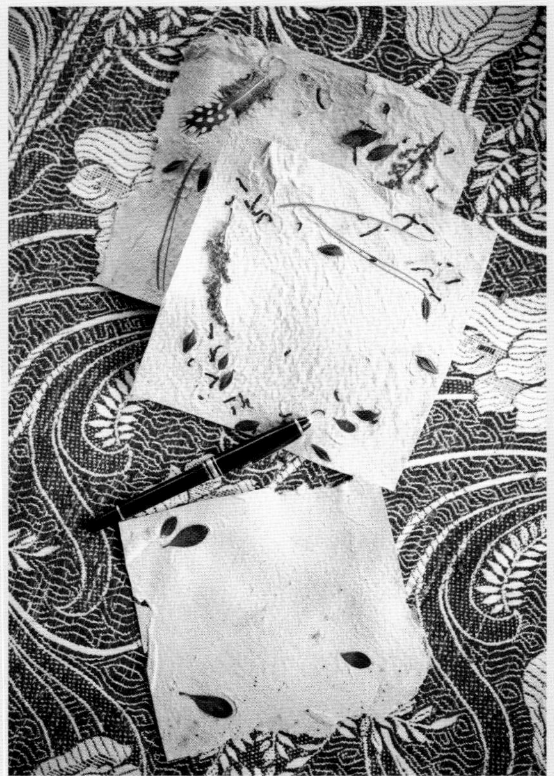

1 Tear your paper into 1-inch square pieces and soak it in water overnight.

2 Unravel a metal hanger into one long piece, then bend it into a rectangle and twist together where the corner meets.

3 Cover the wire rectangle with the leg of a stocking. Wet the stocking before you tie it to ensure it doesn't sag later. Then tie both ends so that the stocking is taut. Trim the edges with scissors. Set aside.

4 Cut the felt into squares the same size as your frame. Cut as many squares of felt as pieces of paper you would like to make and lay several of them out on a baking sheet.

5 Place two small handfuls of wet paper into a blender, followed by 4 cups of water, and blend for about 30 seconds. The mixture should look uniform with no large bits, though if there are a few it will add character to the final paper.

6 Pour the contents of the blender into a plastic basin and repeat step 5 several times, then add more cold water until your basin is about three-fourths full of paper pulp and water.

7 Mix the pulp with your hands. Immediately slide the metal hanger frame down the side of the basin so that it lies horizontally underneath some of the pulp.

8 Move it from side to side, then carefully lift the frame, keeping it level as it drains the water. Tilt it slightly in all directions to let any excess water runoff. You should have an even coating of pulp lying on the stocking frame.

9 Invert the frame onto a piece of felt and press down on the surface. Slowly and carefully lift the mesh stocking back from the paper as it sticks to the felt. Pressing on the stocking will help it release the paper. Repeat this process with more felt. You can stack the felt pieces once the surface of the baking sheet is full.

10 Decorate the paper by pressing any leaves, grass, flowers, yarn, or feathers, if desired, into the surface while it is still wet.

11 Bring the baking sheet outdoors, unstick the felt squares if possible, and leave them in the sun. A breezy day will speed up the drying process considerably. Just be sure to keep it out of the rain and bring it in at night. Alternatively, set the paper near a heat source like a fireplace or heater, or set it in the oven at 200°F for 2 hours or more, checking every 30 minutes.

12 To remove the paper from the felt, slide a paring knife under one corner and gently pry it away. For especially flat paper, you can set the sheet between two heavy books for several days after it is dry.

13 To store the extra pulp, drain it and let it hang to dry in a stocking. When you want to make paper again, break up the dried lump and soak it in water for an hour and blend again.

HOW TO TURN
A TREE STUMP INTO A TABLE

PART OF MY GRANDMOTHER'S ARTISTIC TALENT WAS TO FIND BEAUTIFUL TREE BRANCHES OR STUMPS ON THE SIDE OF THE ROAD, PUT THEM IN HER TRUNK, AND BRING THEM HOME TO MAKE INTO A DRAMATIC DISPLAY FOR HANGING OR SETTING THINGS ON.

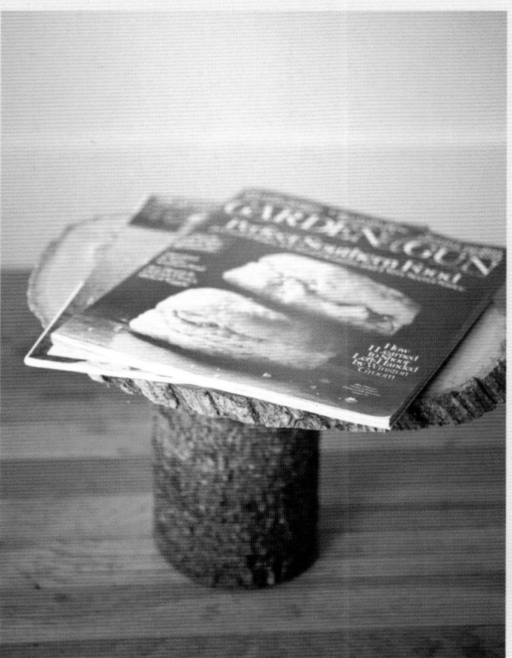

Handsaw or chain saw
Drill (optional)
Wood screws (optional)

1. To make a simple table to set in your garden or at your bedside, find yourself a nice round tree stump. Then find yourself a second tree stump that is slightly wider and equally round. You will need a chain saw or a handsaw and some good arm muscle.
2. Cut the top and bottom of the smaller stump so the surfaces are level.
3. Cut a slice of wood 3 inches thick from the wider stump, and set your round slice on top of the smaller stump.
4. You can then secure it with a drill and some heavy-duty long wood screws, or you can leave it loose so that it can be taken apart at will.
5. Make thinner 1-inch-thick slices from a fallen tree branch about 4 inches in diameter for some beautiful wooden coasters—a perfect homemade gift!

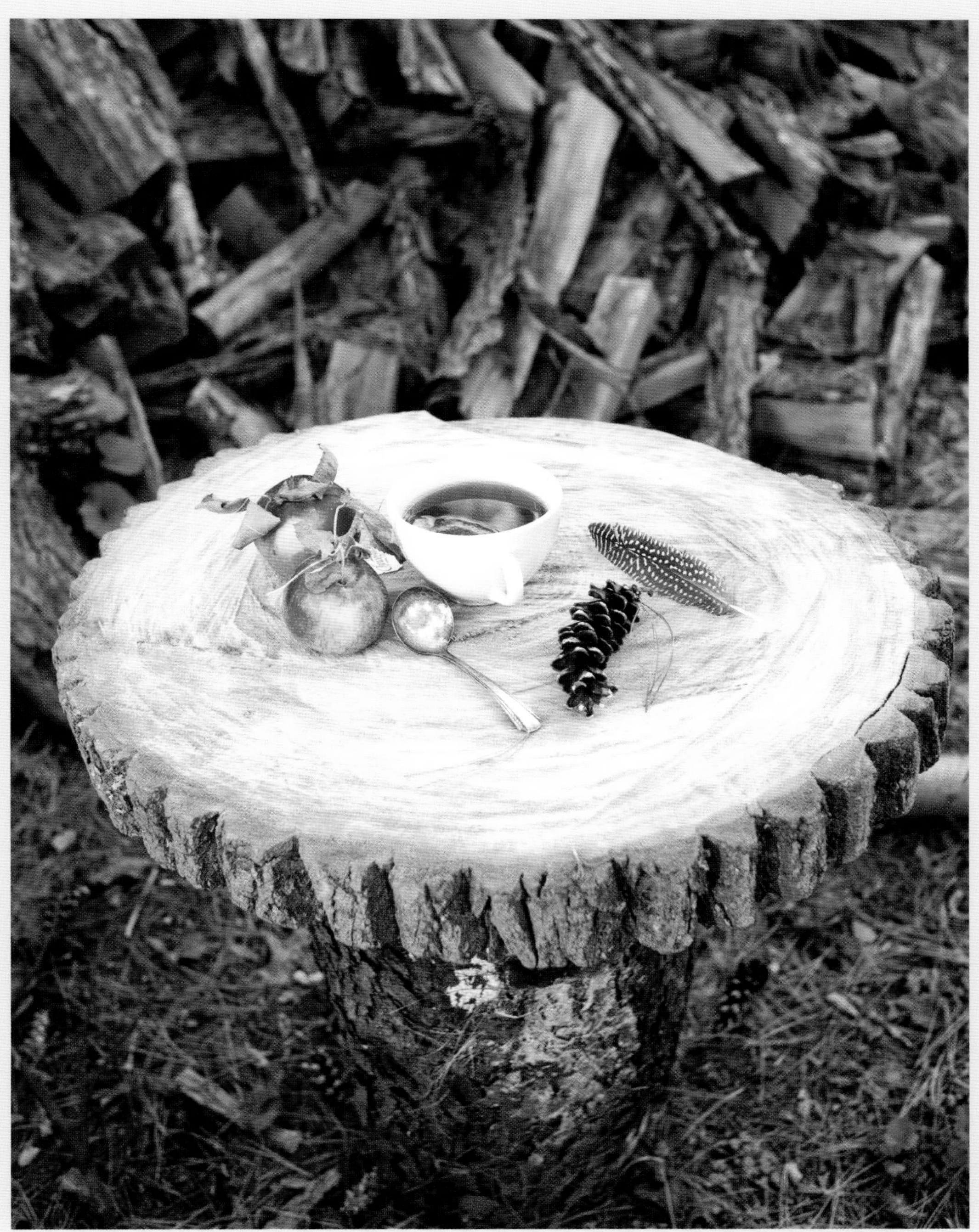

HOW TO MAKE

GOURD BIRDHOUSES

GOURDS ARE A BEAUTIFUL SQUASH TO GROW IN THE GARDEN, BECAUSE THEY COME IN ALL COLORS, SHAPES, AND SIZES, AND CAN GROW VERTICALLY UP SIMPLE FENCES. THEY CAN BE USED AS TABLE CENTERPIECES AND THEN DRIED TO MAKE NATURAL GOURD BIRDHOUSES, WHICH PROVIDE MORE FAVORABLE CONDITIONS FOR BIRDS THAN COMMERCIAL BIRDHOUSES BECAUSE THEY ARE NATURAL. HANG THIS OUTSIDE OF YOUR WINDOW AND LOOK FOR THE PURPLE MARTIN, TREE SWALLOW, AND RED-HEADED WOODPECKER, AMONG OTHERS. IT WILL TAKE AT LEAST TWO MONTHS FOR THE GOURD TO DRY OUT INSIDE, SO PLAN TO BUY THEM IN THE LATE SUMMER AND FALL AND MAKE THEM IN THE WINTER AS HOLIDAY GIFTS.

Gourd, at least 4 × 4 inches on the interior
Bleach
Sandpaper or wire brush
Pencil
Power drill
5/32-inch drill bit
2-inch hole saw with a mandrel
Knife
Single 12-inch strand of 16-gauge coated wire
Wire cutters
Tung oil or clear polyurethane
Disposable sponge brush or paintbrush

1. Select a gourd with a large round base and a tapered neck.
2. Allow the gourd to dry out over the course of several months. The outer color will become tan and it will weigh much less than it did when it was fresh.
3. Soak the gourd for 15 minutes in hot water with a ratio of 1 tablespoon bleach to 1 gallon water. This will disinfect it and prevent rot and mold.
4. Scrub the gourd thoroughly with sandpaper or a wire brush. Rinse and let it dry.
5. Draw an X with a pencil in the round base, slightly above the center of the area. Using a 5/32-inch drill bit, drill a pilot hole into the center of the X.
6. Cut a hole around the mark with a hole saw.
7. Smooth out the edges of the hole with a small knife.
8. Using a 5/32-inch drill bit, drill three holes into the bottom surface of the gourd for drainage.
9. With the same drill bit, drill two opposite holes at the top of the neck so that you can run a wire through and form a hanging loop.

10 Shake out any excess dried inner pulp, but don't spend too much time trying to pry it out; whatever you don't get the birds will.

11 Bend the wire in a slight U shape and run it through the two holes at the top of the neck and tie the ends together in a 3-inch loop. This will allow you to hang your birdhouse from a tree.

12 Paint the outer gourd with tung oil or clear polyurethane and let it dry, then hang your new birdhouse!

FIG. № 1

FIGS. № 5, 6

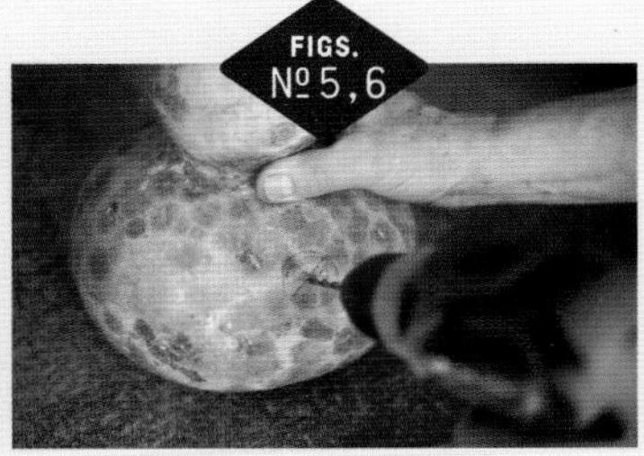

FIG. № 7

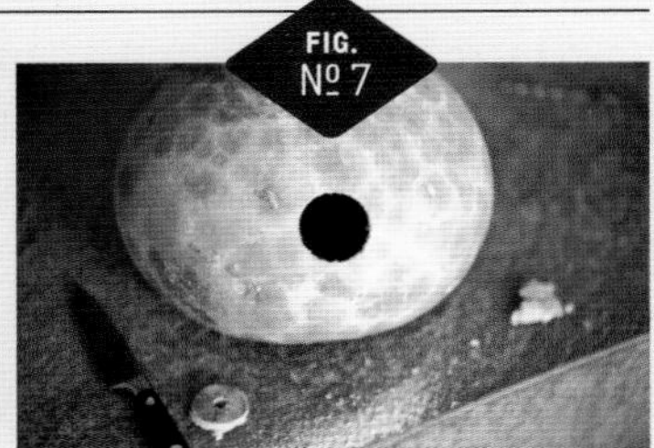

FIG. № 8

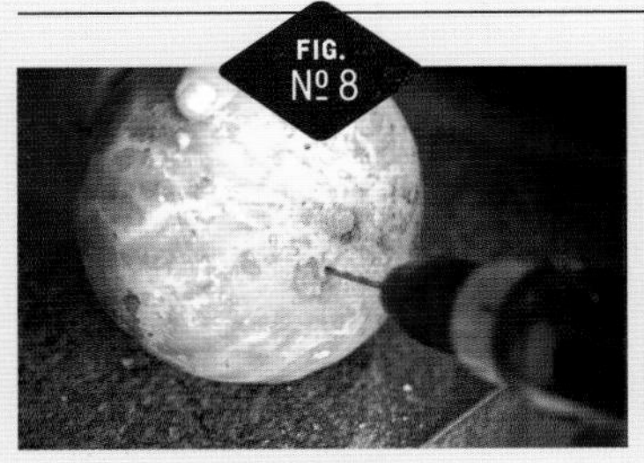

FIG. № 9

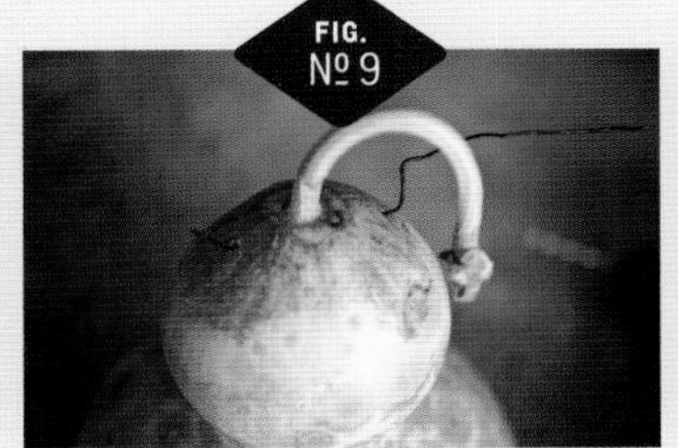

FIG. № 11

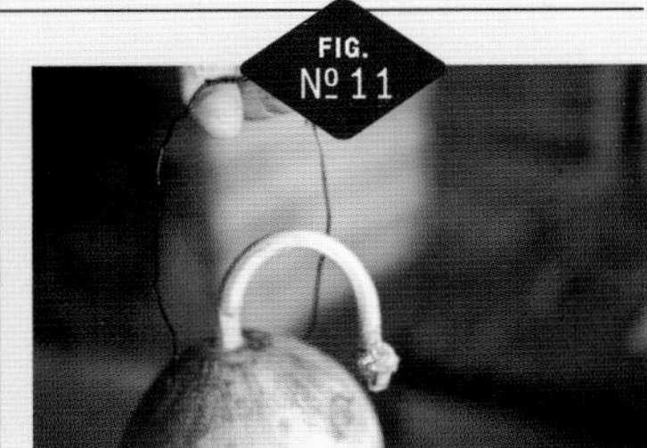

FIG. № 12a

FIG. № 12b

FIG. № 12c

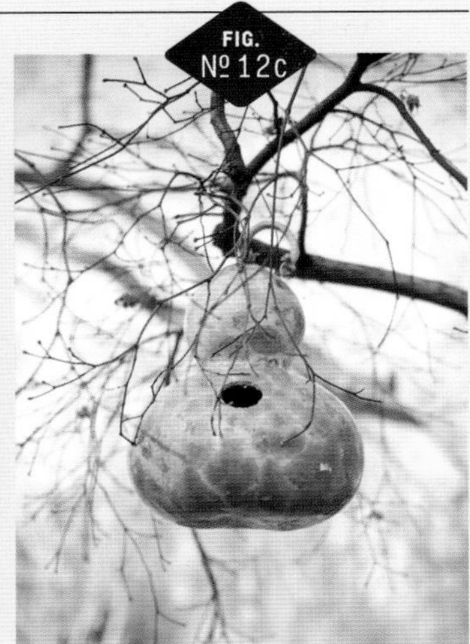

HOW TO NEGOTIATE

AT AN ANTIQUE MARKET

WE COULD ALL USE A LITTLE PRACTICE NEGOTIATING ON OUR OWN BEHALF FROM TIME TO TIME. HERE ARE SOME TIPS TO TAKE WITH YOU NEXT TIME YOU EMBARK ON AN ANTIQUING OR FLEA MARKET ADVENTURE. MANY OF THESE SAME PRINCIPLES, WHEN PRACTICED, WILL GIVE YOU A SENSE OF SELF-RELIANCE AND CONFIDENCE, WHICH WE NEED IN ALL OF OUR DAILY ADVENTURES.

1. Dress down and leave your fancy shoes, purse, and jewelry at home.

2. Be observant about who you are negotiating with and try to get a sense of whether this is the seller's livelihood or if he or she is doing this on the side. Watch the seller work and talk with others and get a sense of how anxious he or she is to make a deal. Be patient.

3. Smile and make eye contact. You can even introduce yourself and shake hands. As you get to know vendors over time, you will develop a rapport, which will make it easier to negotiate. Vendors are much more willing to give a deal to someone they like being around.

4. If you are also a vendor or are planning to resell the item within your business, let the vendor know so he or she realizes that you are a wholesale customer who has to sell items at retail. This will make a difference in negotiating price because they understand you are also running a business.

5. Ask for what you want. You won't be given a discount if you don't ask for it, so make sure to be clear and up-front.

6. It helps to have some idea of the value of the item in which you are interested. If it is worth it to you, offer slightly more than half of the asking price. Always offer less than what you are willing to spend with the expectation that you will have to negotiate up.

7. Keep a poker face. If you spend more time examining an item it will lead the seller to doubt the value of what he is offering.

8. If you make an offer on an item and the counteroffer is rejected or very high, put the item back on the table. This psychologically distances you from it in the seller's mind.

9. A valuable phrase next is "Is that the best you can do?"

10. If the seller won't budge and he or she is close to your price, the next best thing is to sweeten the deal by suggesting you will pay that price if he or she also includes X.

11. When possible, offer to buy items in bulk. Sellers might be more inclined to cut you deals if you are buying multiple items.

12. If you still can't reach an agreement, try subtly suggesting that it is a mighty fine item and would be worth that price if it weren't for . . . and point out the wear and tear.

13. Another tip is to learn the art of silence. Count to 20 after receiving a counteroffer. That will cause most people to want to fill the silence and they will often take themselves to your price without your having to say anything.

14. As a last resort, you can thank the seller for his or her time and walk away. That will be a gauge of how anxious the vendor is to sell it. Keep

in mind that you should have reached your indifference point here, where you are willing to walk away at the price he or she is asking. If the seller calls you back it means there is more wiggle room, but if you have to return later, you will be boxed in to the seller's price.

15 One of the best times to get a good deal is at the end of a market or antique show when the vendors are cash-rich and want to unload inventory rather than load it back into the truck and haul it home. Sometimes you can wait until right before their teardown. You may miss out on some of the best items, but you will get some of the best deals.

16 Bring cash and offer to pay it. Vendors who don't have to worry about credit card fees are much more likely to cut you deals on the merchandise. Cash translates to easy profits for vendors, which makes it a valuable asset to bargain seekers.

HOW TO CLEAN A GRILL OR CUTTING BOARD
WITH CITRUS AND SALT

A little bit of lemon can work miracles on your recently used grill or cutting board, especially one on which you have recently cut fish or meat. To clean a stained plastic or wooden cutting board, slice a lemon in half, dip it into a plate of salt, rub it all over the surface of the board, then let the juice and salt sit for 20 to 30 minutes. Give it a rinse and the cutting board will be fresh-smelling and much cleaner. To clean a grill, rub salted lemon halves all over the grate, then let the juice and residue burn off or use a scraper or towel to wipe down the grill.

HOW TO PICK
THE BEST FISH AT THE MARKET

WHEN WALKING THE STALLS OF A FISH MARKET OR THE AISLES OF A GROCERY STORE, THE SAVVY, SELF-RELIANT WOMAN WITH DISCERNING TASTE BUDS SHOULDN'T SETTLE FOR ANY PIECE OF FISH THAT IS HANDED TO HER. A FISH CAN BE TOO FRESH. IT SHOULD GO THROUGH RIGOR MORTIS BEFORE YOU BUY IT AND HAVE THE ASPIC SLIME ON ITS SKIN, WHICH FORMS DURING RIGOR MORTIS. IF IT IS TOO FRESH, IT WILL CONTRACT WHEN IT HITS THE PAN, AND THE CELL WALLS WILL TEAR, CAUSING THAT WHITE GOO THAT YOU OFTEN SEE ON COOKED SALMON. THAT WHITE SUBSTANCE IS ALBUMEN FROM A TISSUE BREAKDOWN, AND CAN ALSO INDICATE THAT THE FISH WASN'T HANDLED PROPERLY OR IT WAS PREPARED POORLY. WHEN BUYING A PIECE OF FISH, YOU WANT THE FLESH TO HAVE A LIMPID QUALITY, A VIVID TRANSPARENCY. WHEN BUYING A WHOLE FISH, THE SCALES SHOULD BE INTACT AND THE BODY FIRM. SEE IF THE FISHMONGER WILL LET YOU PRESS THE BODIES TO FEEL FOR THE FIRMEST ONE.

OREGANO
Fresh Herbs
TARRAGON
THYME
ROSEMARY

FIND IT

BEES

Betterbee.com
Brushymountainbeefarm.com
Mannlakeltd.com

CANNING EQUIPMENT

Ace Hardware
Amazon.com
Canningpantry.com
Crate & Barrel (for Weck Jars)
Home Depot
Lowe's
Target
Wal-Mart
Weckjars.com

DIY KITS

My latest finds can be found in my online shop at: https://opensky.com/georgiapellegrini
Bttrventures.com
Fieldforest.net
Fungi.com
GMushrooms.com
MushroomAdventures.com
MushroomPeople.com

CHICKENS

Backyard-chickens.net
McMurrayhatchery.com

FREE MATERIALS

City streets
Craigslist.org
Dumpster diving
Freecycle.org
Garage sales

GARDENING SUPPLIES AND FORUMS

Biodynamic.net
Gardenweb.com
Harmonyfarm.com
Forums.organicgardening.com
Helpfulgardener.com

HIGH-QUALITY GARDEN TOOLS

Claringtonforge.com
Gardentoolcompany.com
Redpigtools.com

ORGANIC, HEIRLOOM, OPEN-POLLINATED SEEDS, AND SEED EXCHANGES

Bountifulgardens.org
Gardenweb.com
Genesisseeds.com
Growitalian.com
Heirlooms.org
Seedsavers.org
Southernexposure.com

SEEDS AND SUPPLIES FOR GROWING SPROUTS

Sproutpeople.org

VERTICAL GARDENS

Windowfarms.com
Woollypocket.com

WORM COMPOSTING

Wormwoman.com

BIC#280
30 yd
BW
30 yd
BESTWAY
(718)-423-6473
BW
30 yd
NO PARKING

ACKNOWLEDGMENTS

A BIG HELPING OF THANK-YOUS TO MY EDITOR, Aliza Fogelson, and the entire team at Clarkson Potter for championing my ambitious vision for this book and entrusting me with such creative freedom in the process. It was a true dream team that ensured this book would be the best it could be: Doris Cooper, Pam Krauss, Sally Franklin, Sigi Nacson, Derek Gullino, Keonaona Peterson, and Emma Brodie. An extra thank-you to the book's design hero, Danielle Deschenes, who meticulously customized this book with the most imaginative and beautiful attention to detail. Thank you as well to my wonderful publicity and marketing team, particularly Sean Boyles and Carly Gorga.

Rebecca Oliver, there aren't enough ways to express my gratitude for your friendship, wisdom, and handholding. In managing my career you have also had to manage my life and you have done it all with such brilliance and grace. I am so lucky we are in "constant contact."

Natasha Geiling, you are the research assistant to end all research assistants. I wouldn't have survived without you!

Francisco "Frank Fortress" Arredondo, thank you for being my partner in DIY-crime and indulging my sometimes-crazy ideas for this book. I have so much fun being your friend and learning to "architect" with you.

Cookbook recipes need extra-special testing, and I couldn't have asked for a better recipe tester than Chef Jamie Levine. You worked miracles and moved mountains for me, and the recipes within these pages are more delicious for it.

Also, thank you to my recipe-testing queens—my girlfriends who tried these recipes in their home kitchens and gave me feedback: Marissa Reibstein, Abigail Murthy, Christine Carroll, Molly Keller, Tricia Brennan, Breanne Vandermeer, Courtney McLeod, and Nate Brahms.

Thank you to my brother, Gordon for lending me your photography skills when I was on the brink, and for keeping it cool in the process. I love you tons and tons. Thank you also to my dad, Roger, for lending your photography talent when I couldn't have my hands in two places at once. Not surprisingly, you produced some of the best photos in this book.

Also, thank you to my mom, Maureen, and to my second family, the Leporis, for their love, prayers, and lifelong nourishment.

Thank you to Miriam Wexler, my great-aunt Gray's lovely friend from the Nyack Garden Club, who took a call from a random girl and generously read the gardening pages of this book for me. Your meticulous feedback was invaluable and I have no doubt my great-aunt Gray was smiling over us.

And to my grandmother Frances Pellegrini, thank you for reading this manuscript and adding your creative genius. You have taught me more than you know and I am grateful that we are cut from the same cloth.

INDEX

NOTE: Page numbers in *italics* indicate recipes.

T

V

W

Y